Contents

Teachers note: For a full description of the contents, see the introduction to the Teacher's Book

6840401096 1 944

PRE[illegible]
Student's Book

WITHDRAWN FROM STOCK

in English

PETER VINEY
KAREN VINEY

OXFORD
UNIVERSITY PRESS

OXFORD
UNIVERSITY PRESS

Great Clarendon Street, Oxford OX2 6DP

Oxford University Press is a department of the University of Oxford.
It furthers the University's objective of excellence in research, scholarship,
and education by publishing worldwide in

Oxford New York

Auckland Cape Town Dar es Salaam Hong Kong Karachi
Kuala Lumpur Madrid Melbourne Mexico City Nairobi
New Delhi Shanghai Taipei Toronto

With offices in

Argentina Austria Brazil Chile Czech Republic France Greece
Guatemala Hungary Italy Japan Poland Portugal Singapore
South Korea Switzerland Thailand Turkey Ukraine Vietnam

OXFORD and OXFORD ENGLISH are registered trade marks of
Oxford University Press in the UK and in certain other countries

© Oxford University Press/Three Vee Limited 2005

The moral rights of the author have been asserted

Database right Oxford University Press (maker)

First published 2005
Fourth impression 2007
2009 2008 2007
10 9 8 7 6 5 4

No unauthorized photocopying

All rights reserved. No part of this publication may be reproduced,
stored in a retrieval system, or transmitted, in any form or by any means,
without the prior permission in writing of Oxford University Press,
or as expressly permitted by law, or under terms agreed with the appropriate
reprographics rights organization. Enquiries concerning reproduction
outside the scope of the above should be sent to the ELT Rights Department,
Oxford University Press, at the address above

You must not circulate this book in any other binding or cover
and you must impose this same condition on any acquirer

Any websites referred to in this publication are in the public domain and
their addresses are provided by Oxford University Press for information only.
Oxford University Press disclaims any responsibility for the content

ISBN: 978 0 19 434062 5

Typeset by Oxford University Press in Meta

Printed in China

LEICESTER CITY LIBRARIES	
944	
Bertrams	14/11/2008
428.24 :L	£9.50
FC	

Know your book

Student's Book

1 Where do these sections of the Student's Book begin? Match the page numbers to the correct sections.

SECTION	PAGE
Extensions	6
Transcripts	190
Know your book	210
Grammar index	55
Communication Activities	3
Student Book, Unit 9	221
Contents	192

2 If you have the 3-in-1 Practice Pack, find these pages in the Practice Books.

Grammar Practice Book

Circle the correct page numbers.

Unit 8, Responses	23	24	29
Unit 19, sounds exercise	46	64	47
The answer key for unit 3	69	71	78
The transcript for the audio exercises, unit 23	91	92	93
The transcript for the audio exercises, track 17	83	85	89

Vocabulary Practice Book

Underline the correct page numbers.

Picture dictionary 21 *Internet*	40	42	56
Everyday English 4, *People you've met before*	58	61	72
Self Test 1	78	79	83
Reading for pleasure, *True stories*	84	92	86
Word games, *Sports*	4	17	10

3 If you have the 3-in-1 Practice Pack, first find the red plastic square, then go to Everyday English 1, *In Class* and practise the classroom language.

Your class

Complete the spaces:

1 What's your teacher's name? ....
2 Where's your teacher from? ....
3 How many students are there in your class? ....
4 Which room does your class meet in? ....

Timetable

1 Which days does your class meet? Highlight them.
Monday Tuesday Wednesday Thursday Friday
Saturday Sunday

2 How long are your lessons? Tick (✔) the correct box.
☐ 30 minutes ☐ 45 minutes ☐ one hour ☐ 90 minutes
☐ two hours ☐ two and a half hours ☐ longer

3 What times do your lessons begin? ~~Delete~~ the wrong times.
hour 1 2 3 4 5 6 7 8 9 10 11 12 am pm
minutes o'clock 05 10 15 20 25 30 35 40 45 50 55

1 Personal information

A What do you think?

1 **You don't know anything about these people. Guess the information for 1) him 2) her:**

What does he / she do?
Is he / she married?
How old is he / she?
Has he / she got any children?

2 **Listen to two people discussing him. Are any of their guesses the same as your guesses?** (✻ 1.02)

3 **Discuss your guesses about her with a partner. Use the language box.**

Guesses	**Responses**
I think she's a secretary / she works in an office.	Me too. / Yes, I agree. / I think so too.
She **looks** about thirty.	No, I don't agree. / I don't think so.
I think she's married.	I think she ... / I don't think she ...
I don't think she's got any children.	Maybe. / I don't know. / I've got no idea.

4 **Listen to her. She's talking about herself. What extra information does she give?** (✻ 1.03)

B About your class

1 Choose a student in your class. Choose someone you don't know at all, or don't know very well. Guess these things about them:

Job? Any children? Hobbies? Favourite kind of music?

2 Interview the student and check your guesses. Note the answers.

1 What do you do?
2 Have you got any children?
3 What do you like doing in your free time?
4 What's your favourite kind of music?

3 Change partners. Ask and answer about the previous partner.

4 Emphasis. Listen and practise the emphasis in these sentences. (✻ 1.04)

contraction / normal spoken English	formal written English / emphatic English
She isn't a teacher.	She is not a teacher.
They aren't English.	They are not English.
He doesn't work in a bank.	He does not work in a bank.
They don't live there.	They do not live there.

5 Imagine. Make guesses about the people below. Discuss your guesses with the class. Which one would you like to sit next to?

C At home ...

CELEB *The celebrity magazine*

At home with ... Sheri & Leo

It was love at first sight for 29-year-old Sheri Casey and 24-year-old Leo Jordan when they met at the 'Sports Person of the Year' TV Awards last year. She's a popular TV newsreader and he's an international football star. They're an unusual couple. Sheri was born in Dublin, Ireland and has got a first class degree in politics from Oxford University. Leo plays football for England, and he left school at sixteen. Leo lives in a penthouse flat in Manchester, and Sheri lives in an 18th century house in London. They're both very busy, and they only meet two days a week. 'It's difficult,' says Sheri, 'because I work in the evenings in London, and Leo trains in the mornings in Manchester. I fly to Manchester, or Leo drives to London in his Ferrari on Saturday night, and then we both go back to work on Tuesday morning.'

In the kitchen ...

Leo's hobby is cooking. 'My father's a chef,' he says, 'And my mother's a great cook too.' Sheri likes reading biographies of famous people, and she is a keen chess player, but she doesn't like cooking. She watches every news programme on TV, but Leo only watches sports programmes. They eat at home on Sundays and Mondays. 'I'm in restaurants and hotels every day of the week,' she says, 'I go to a lot of charity dinners. Leo cooks a romantic dinner with wine and candles on Sundays, but I'm happy with a sandwich and a nice hot cup of tea in front of the telly.'

1 Find the information and complete the table. (✳ 1.05 – 1.06)

	Him	Her
Full name		
Age		
Job		
Hobbies		

2 Are these sentences true or false?

1 Sheri is Irish.
2 Leo plays tennis for England.
3 Sheri lives in Manchester.
4 Leo doesn't train in the evenings.
5 Leo has got an expensive car.
6 Sheri works from Monday to Friday.
7 Leo doesn't like cooking.
8 Sheri likes playing chess.
9 Leo doesn't watch the news on TV.
10 Sheri goes to a lot of charity dinners.

3 Make questions about the texts. Use the words below.

Who When How often Where What (x 2)

1 .... was Sheri born?
2 .... does Leo do?
3 .... lives in a penthouse flat?
4 .... do they eat at home?
5 .... does she eat in restaurants?
6 .... does Sheri like doing?

Ask and answer the questions.

4 Vocabulary. Find words which mean ...

1 not the same as most people or things
2 two people in a relationship
3 a flat on the top floor
4 the story of a person's life
5 very interested (in something)
6 an organization that gives money or help to people for free
7 an informal word for television

5 Pair work. Ask your partner the questions.

1 Where do you live?
2 Who do you live with?
3 Where do you work / study?
4 What days of the week do you work / study?
5 What kind of TV programmes do you watch?

D Credit card

1 **Trisha is paying by credit card. There's a problem with the transaction. The credit card company asks to speak to her on the phone. Listen.** (✻ 1.07)

2 **Listen again, and complete the information about her.**

Family name	□□□□□□□□□□□□□□
Middle initial	□□□
First name	□□□□□□□□□□□□□□
Title	Mr □ Mrs □ Miss □ Ms □ Other □
Mother's maiden name	□□□□□□□□□□□□□□
Place of birth	□□□□□□□□□□□□□□
Date of birth	□□/□□/□□□□
Confirmation number	□□□□□□□□

3 **Role play a conversation with your partner, and complete the information.**

Family name	□□□□□□□□□□□□□□
Middle initial	□□□
First name	□□□□□□□□□□□□□□
Title	Mr □ Mrs □ Miss □ Ms □ Other □
Mother's maiden name	□□□□□□□□□□□□□□
Place of birth	□□□□□□□□□□□□□□
Next birthday	□□/□□/□□

E What do they call you?

1 **Listen and read.** (✱ 1.08)

My name's Michael Carter. My parents and sisters always call me Micky. But my wife and close friends call me Mike. My kids call me Dad. At work, most people call me Michael. People I don't know call me Mr Carter, and my friends' kids call me Mr Carter too. In expensive shops, they call me 'sir'. The one name I don't like is Mick. Please, never call me Mick.

2 **What do you call these people? What do they call you? Complete the table.**

Your parents Your children Your doctor Your boss
People you work with Close friends New acquaintances
Hotel receptionists Your next door neighbour Assistants in shops
Your partner (wife, husband, boyfriend, girlfriend)

Form of address	Who calls me this?	Who do I call this?
Family name only (*Carter*)		
First name (*Michael*)		
Diminuitive (*Mike*, *Micky*, *Mick*)		
Title + family name (*Mr Carter*)		
Sir / Madam		
Job name (*Doctor*, *Nurse*, *Waiter*)		
Others (*Dad*, *luv*, *darling*)		

See **Extension 1** p.192

2 Shopping

E

A Everyday English

1 Match the conversations with the pictures.

- ■ Are you ready to order? (✳ 1.09)
- ● Not yet. I'm waiting for someone.

- ■ Can I help you? (✳ 1.10)
- ● No, thanks. I'm just looking.

- ● Have you got one of this in extra-large? (✳ 1.11)
- ■ I don't know. I'll go and check for you.

- ● Can I try this on? (✳ 1.12)
- ■ Sure. The changing room's over there.

- ● Excuse me, I'm looking for the DVD section. (✳ 1.13)
- ■ It's upstairs on the first floor.

- ● I'd like one of those, please. (✳ 1.14)
- ■ Certainly, madam. How would you like to pay?

2 Practise the conversations. Change the words in blue.

someone	a friend my boyfriend / girlfriend some friends
Can I help you?	May I help you? Do you need any help?
extra-large	small medium large a size 14
this	these it them this skirt these trousers
upstairs/first floor	downstairs / ground floor second floor third floor
one of those/madam	one of these this one that one / sir

3 Pronunciation. Contractions. Tick the words you hear. (✱ 1.15)

1 (☐ I ☐ I'd) like tea.
2 (☐ I ☐ I'd) like this one!
3 (☐ I ☐ I'll) pay by credit card.
4 (☐ I ☐ I'll) usually pay cash.
5 (☐ I ☐ I'm) a size 12.
6 (☐ I ☐ I'm) want a size 12.

B Special offers

1 Read the signs.

50% off = half price = 50% discount =
50% reduction = Buy one, get one free

You want two T-shirts. They normally cost £10 each. How much are you going to pay in these shops?

2 Prices. Read the text.

In Britain shops have fixed prices, but you can bargain in street markets. Shops have sales in January and again in the summer, when a lot of items are cheaper. Superstores have special offers on some items every week. Shops don't usually give a discount for cash. The British usually bargain when they buy houses and cars, or anything that is second-hand.

3 Culture comparison. Discuss.

Which things can you bargain for in your country?

☐ everything ☐ clothes ☐ food ☐ cars ☐ jewellery
☐ furniture ☐ houses ☐ nothing

Where can you bargain in your country?

☐ everywhere ☐ superstores ☐ markets ☐ small shops
☐ department stores ☐ nowhere

A carpet is £200 in a market. You're going to bargain. What do you offer?

☐ £180 ☐ £150 ☐ £100 ☐ £50 ☐ less than £50

C Bargaining

1 You're going to listen to a conversation in a market. A tourist is looking at an Oriental carpet. Guess who says these things, the buyer (B) or the seller (S)?

☐ It normally costs two hundred in the shops.
☐ That's too much.
☐ I don't know.
☐ That's my best price.
☐ Make me an offer.
☐ It cost me a hundred.
☐ That's my final price.
☐ It's a bargain.
☐ It's a deal.

Listen and check. (✻ 1.16)

2 Listen again. Write down the prices you hear.

COMMUNICATION

Students A and B Look at Activity 12 on p.215.

D Shopping for clothes

1 Tanya and Dave are a couple. They're shopping. Listen and answer the questions. (✻ 1.17)

How much does the sweater cost?
Does Dave buy it?

Then complete the sentences with the correct form of these verbs.

like / likes   love / loves
want / wants   need / needs

Dave doesn't .... shopping for clothes. He .... a coffee. He .... a new sweater. He doesn't .... the first sweater. Tanya .... the second sweater, but he doesn't .... the colour.

2 Listen to Tanya and Dave. Underline the emphasis. (✻ 1.18)

Tanya Well, what about this one? / I love the colour. / I really like it. / You look good in it.

Dave I really don't like it. / I'm not paying that much.

3 Pair work. Role-play a similar conversation.

E The shopping experience

1 Label the pictures:

Shopping Mall   Retail Park   Superstore
High Street shops   Market

2 Where can you buy these items?

Furniture (tables, beds)	Fruit and vegetables	Shoes
D.I.Y (Do-it-yourself) items	CDs and DVDs	Clothes
Food	Cosmetics	Electrical items

Retail Parks are best for furniture.

3 Match these words to the shop locations in 1.

cheap   expensive   large selection   good quality   designer labels
cafés   easy to park   good public transport
self-service   personal service   friendly service
noisy   boring   better for families   better for young people

4 Match the meanings.

Easy to park		the products are reliable and well-made.
Good public transport		fashionable clothes by famous designers.
Personal service	**means**	there's a large car park near the shop.
Large selection		you can get there by bus or train.
Good quality		an assistant helps you.
Designer labels		you can choose from many different items.

5 Discuss. Where do you prefer shopping? Why?

See **Extension 2** p.192

3 The present

A Viewing habits

1 Interview a partner and complete the questionnaire.

1 Which of these programmes do you watch on TV?
Ⓐ news Ⓑ game shows Ⓒ sitcoms Ⓓ sport Ⓔ soap operas
Ⓕ documentaries Ⓖ chat shows Ⓗ reality TV

2 Do you watch the weather report on TV?
Ⓐ always Ⓑ usually Ⓒ sometimes Ⓓ hardly ever Ⓔ never

3 How often do you watch sport on TV?
Ⓐ frequently Ⓑ quite often Ⓒ sometimes
Ⓓ occasionally Ⓔ never

4 Do you watch soap operas?
Ⓐ always, I never miss my favourite soap Ⓑ regularly
Ⓒ sometimes Ⓓ occasionally Ⓔ never, I can't stand them

5 Think of a popular soap opera in your country.
How many times a week is it on TV?
Ⓐ once a week Ⓑ twice a week
Ⓒ three or more times a week Ⓓ every day

2 Compare the answers with the class. Talk about your partner's viewing habits.

Remember to use the third person:
*She do**es**n't watch ...*
*He hardly ever watch**es** ...*

soap opera (also *informal* **soap**) *noun* [C, U] a story about the lives and problems of a group of people which is broadcast every day or several times a week on television or radio

B Soaps

1 **Read the text. Can you match the photos below to the character types? Make complete sentences.**

The villain *The villain is usually charming but he is dishonest.*

Classic characters

The senior
Usually female, but occasionally male. Old. Often the head of a family. Bad-tempered, but wise.

The villain
Male. Always in trouble. Charming but usually dishonest.

The bitch
Female. Always gets her man.

The heart-throb
Male. Young. Always good-looking.

The gossip
Nearly always a middle-aged female. Often a funny character. Important to the story because she tells everyone what's happening, and what people are doing.

The victim
Male or female. Often, their partner is having an affair. This character has a tragic life with many problems.

The babe
Female. Young. Always good-looking.

The meeting place
The characters always live in a small area. They have a central meeting place. In Britain, they usually meet in the local pub. Sometimes they work in the same place, or go to the same social club.

Soaps and education
TV producers often include educational messages in the stories. They give advice and information about health questions, like AIDs, or discuss social issues like women's rights.

2 **Give examples of the classic characters from a popular soap opera in your country. Where do they usually meet? Can you remember any educational messages in soaps?**

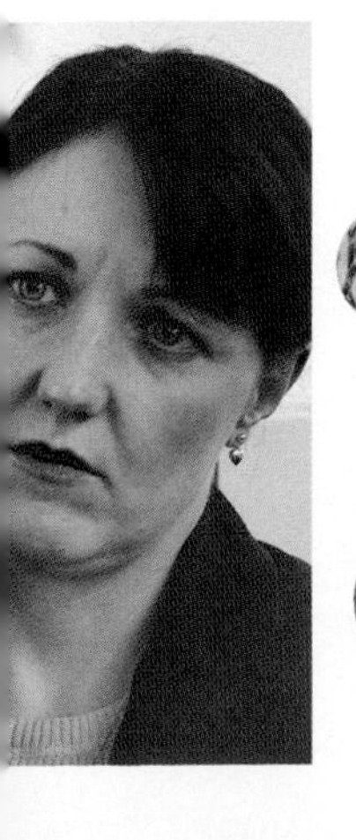

C Frequency

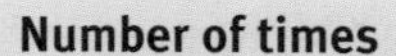

Number of times

very often frequently every (day)	often three times a (week)	quite often sometimes twice a (month)	occasionally once a (year)

Percentage of the time

  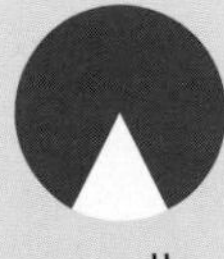  

always	nearly always	usually normally	hardly ever rarely	never

You can add negatives: *don't often / usually / always / ever*
BUT you can't add negatives with *sometimes*, *occasionally*, *hardly ever*, *never*

Word order

Frequency adverbs come before a main verb: *I usually watch the news.*
They come after the verb *to be*: *We're rarely late for class.*
They can also start or end a sentence (except for *always*, *never*, *hardly ever*, *rarely*. But, *always* and *never* can start imperative sentences however.) *Sometimes I watch the news. I watch the news occasionally.*

1 Make the sentences true for you.

I go to the hairdresser once a month.
I go to the hairdresser once a week. / I never go to the hairdresser. / I don't often go to the hairdresser – maybe once a year.

I usually remember my friends' birthdays.
I always read the morning newspaper.
I normally pay for expensive items by credit card.
I quite often watch game shows on TV.
I hardly ever use public transport.
I use the Internet every day.
I don't always buy a lottery ticket.
I occasionally read my horoscope in magazines.
I never walk on my own at night.
I sometimes have bad dreams after horror films.
I'm rarely late for work.

2 Compare your answers with a partner. Ask questions.

How often do you go to the hairdresser?
Do you ever have bad dreams after horror films?

D What's happening?

1 **This is a scene from a British soap, 'Jubilee Avenue'. What's happening? Describe the people. What are they doing? What are they wearing?**

2 **Listen. Ask and answer.** (✳ 1.19)
Who is Linda?
Where is she? What's she doing?
Why is Linda working for Max at the moment?
Why is this a problem?

3 **Listen. Ask and answer.** (✳ 1.20)
Who is Robbie?
What's his father doing?
Why doesn't Robbie see his mother very often?
What's the educational message in this conversation?

4 **Listen. Then finish Linda's sentence ...** (✳ 1.21)
A .... just good friends.
B .... not having an affair.
C .... flying to Acapulco this evening.

5 **Listen again. Can you match these people to the classic characters in Section B?** (✳ 1.19 – 1.21)

Jean Margaret Robbie Lulu Max Colin Linda

E Simple or continuous?

Anna works in a bank. It's Sunday today, and she isn't working.
She's sitting on the beach.
Q: What **does** Anna **do**? A: She **works** in a bank. (routine)
Q: What **is** Anna **doing**? A: She**'s sitting** on the beach. (now)

Look at the grammar notes. There are two examples for each point. Add a third and fourth example from the orange box below.

Routines – things you do everyday

1 I work in an office. 3 ....
2 She normally gets up at 7.30. 4 ....

Facts – general truths

1 The sun rises in the east. 3 ....
2 This book costs $15. 4 ....

Verbs which are generally in the present simple form

1 I don't like coffee. 3 ....
2 Do you feel tired? 4 ....

Things which are happening now.

1 Sorry, I'm driving at the moment. 3 ....
2 What are you doing now? 4 ....

Describing pictures and people.

1 She's lying on the sun lounger. 3 ....
2 He isn't wearing an apron. 4 ....

Things which are happening over a longer period of time.

1 She's having driving lessons. 3 ....
2 I'm reading 'Lord of the Rings'. 4 ....

When something is temporary, and different to the routine.

1 My car's off the road, so I'm travelling by bus this week. 3 ....
2 She's a student, but she's working in a café for the summer. 4 ....

Water boils at 100° Celsius.	She's wearing sunglasses.
I don't understand.	He doesn't work on Fridays.
I'm saving money for a new car.	We're studying English this year.
We usually have cereal for breakfast.	They aren't wearing uniforms.
Does he love her?	He's working in America for 3 weeks.
It's raining.	Eight million people live in London.
I haven't got a flat, so I'm living with friends.	Who are you phoning?

See **Extension 3** p.193

4 Arrangements

A A weekend away

1 Listen and practise. (✱ 1.22)

Sandra What are you doing this weekend?
Clare Simon and I are going away.
Sandra Anywhere interesting?
Clare We're going to Rome.
Sandra Just for the weekend?
Clare Yes. We're meeting at the airport on Friday. I'm going there straight after work. Our flight leaves at 7.30. Then we're coming back on Sunday on the late flight. Our plane doesn't arrive at Heathrow until 10.30.
Sandra Sounds fun! Are you going to see the Sistine Chapel?
Clare No way! Manchester United are playing in Rome on Saturday. Simon's going to watch the game, and I'm going shopping!

2 Add more examples from the conversation.

Arrangement	*We're meeting at the airport on Friday.* ....
Timetable	*Our flight leaves at 7.30.* ....
Intention	*Are you going to see the Sistine Chapel?* ....

3 Role-play a similar dialogue. Change the place and times, but choose somewhere well-known. Think of a similar surprise ending.

B Timetables

1 **Look at the web page. Find this information:**
The time difference between London and Mexico City.
The time difference between Miami and Mexico City.
The departure time of Flight AM**006**
The arrival time of the British Airways flight in Miami.
The airline with a direct flight from London to Mexico.
The airport code for Madrid.
The airline between London and Paris.

2 **Pronunciation. Say these airport codes aloud:** (✳ 1.23)
MIA MEX LHR CDG ATL MAD SOU CWL
JNB VCE YQB

Listen and check.

Which airports are they? Guess and match them.

Southampton Johannesburg London - Heathrow
Mexico City Miami Venice Madrid Quebec
Paris - Charles de Gaulle Cardiff - Wales Atlanta

3 **Listen. A travel agent is explaining one of the routes to a customer. Find the route on the web page and follow it while you listen.** (✳ 1.24)

COMMUNICATION

Student A Role-play a travel agent. Use the timetables.
Student B Look at Activity 22 on p.220.

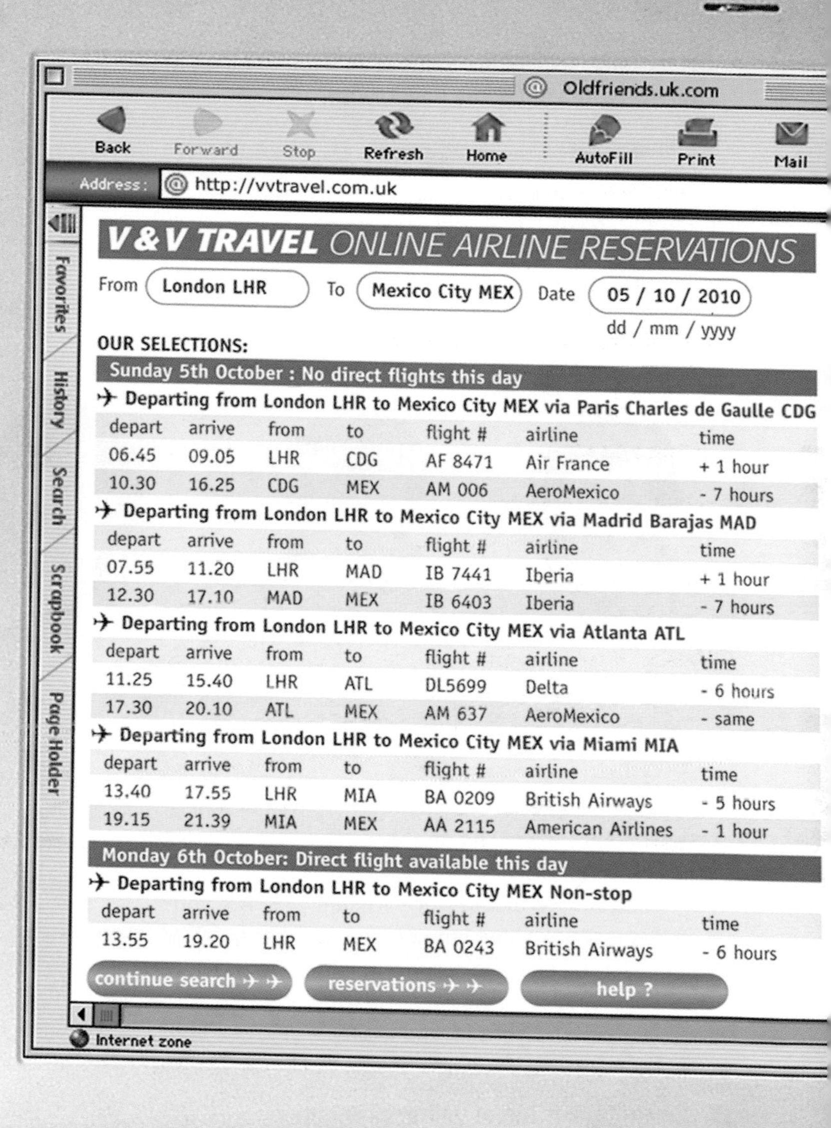

Oldfriends.uk.com

Back | Forward | Stop | Refresh | Home | AutoFill | Print | Mail

Address: http://vvtravel.com.uk

Favorites | History | Search | Scrapbook | Page Holder

V & V TRAVEL ONLINE AIRLINE RESERVATIONS

From: London LHR To: Mexico City MEX Date: 05 / 10 / 2010 (dd / mm / yyyy)

OUR SELECTIONS:

Sunday 5th October : No direct flights this day

✈ Departing from London LHR to Mexico City MEX via Paris Charles de Gaulle CDG

depart	arrive	from	to	flight #	airline	time
06.45	09.05	LHR	CDG	AF 8471	Air France	+ 1 hour
10.30	16.25	CDG	MEX	AM 006	AeroMexico	- 7 hours

✈ Departing from London LHR to Mexico City MEX via Madrid Barajas MAD

depart	arrive	from	to	flight #	airline	time
07.55	11.20	LHR	MAD	IB 7441	Iberia	+ 1 hour
12.30	17.10	MAD	MEX	IB 6403	Iberia	- 7 hours

✈ Departing from London LHR to Mexico City MEX via Atlanta ATL

depart	arrive	from	to	flight #	airline	time
11.25	15.40	LHR	ATL	DL5699	Delta	- 6 hours
17.30	20.10	ATL	MEX	AM 637	AeroMexico	- same

✈ Departing from London LHR to Mexico City MEX via Miami MIA

depart	arrive	from	to	flight #	airline	time
13.40	17.55	LHR	MIA	BA 0209	British Airways	- 5 hours
19.15	21.39	MIA	MEX	AA 2115	American Airlines	- 1 hour

Monday 6th October: Direct flight available this day

✈ Departing from London LHR to Mexico City MEX Non-stop

depart	arrive	from	to	flight #	airline	time
13.55	19.20	LHR	MEX	BA 0243	British Airways	- 6 hours

continue search ✈ ✈ | reservations ✈ ✈ | help ?

Internet zone

C Plans

1 **Listen. Tony is speaking to his grandmother about his future plans. Complete the sentences below with:** (✱ 1.25)

a place   a job   a company

I'm going to **work for** ....
I'm going to **work in** ....
I'm going to **be a** ....

2 **Intonation. *Do you? Have you?* etc. Listen again. What does she say when she's expressing interest?** (✱ 1.25)

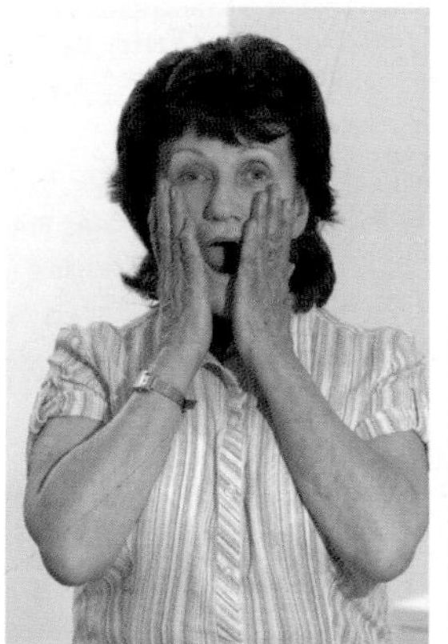
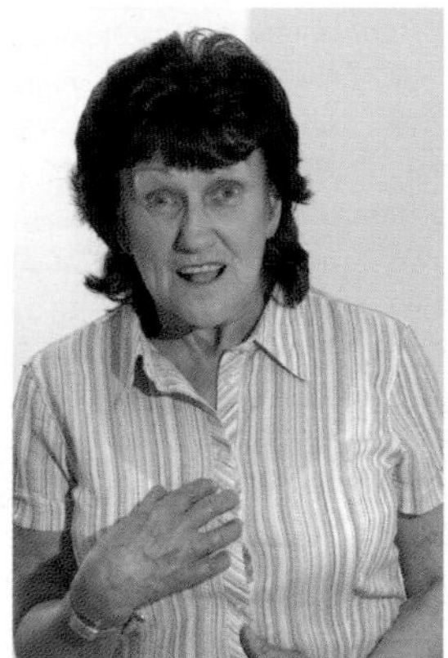
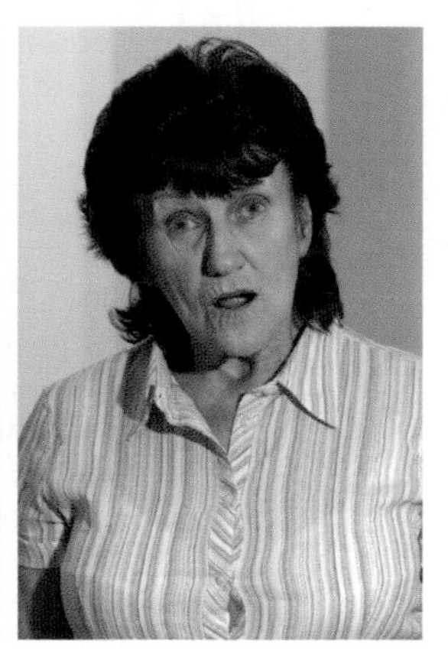

3 **Listen. Does the second speaker sound (1) surprised, (2) interested, (3) not interested?** (✱ 1.26)

1 A I'm going to meet Prince William. B Are you?
2 A I can speak three languages. B Can you?
3 A I've got a car with a 2 litre engine. B Have you?
4 A I like collecting stamps. B Do you?
5 A I've got an Olympic gold medal. B Have you?
6 A I run 5 kilometres before breakfast. B Do you?

4 **Write sentences about yourself. Begin:**

I've got ...
I can ...
I'm going to ...
I like ...

Say the sentences. Your partner chooses the correct verb form for the reaction. Then say them again. Your partner tries to sound surprised, interested or not interested.

D *doing / going to do*

1 Match the sentences in the middle column to the pictures.

	A It's going to rain.	
	B The taxi's coming in five minutes.	
	C I'm going to have an early night.	
	D He's having lunch with a client at 12.30.	
	E I'm going to be sick!	
	F England are going to lose!	

2 Add these sentences to the table.

Before

G I don't want to watch TV.
H Oh, no. Look at those clouds!
I Hurry up!
J There are only five minutes left.
K I feel terrible!
L Sorry, he can't see you then.

After

M We don't want to miss the plane.
N The score's 3-0 to France.
O How about 3 o'clock?
P I want to get off!
Q I'm really tired.
R Did you bring an umbrella?

Listen and check. (✱ 1.27)

Prediction / Fact:	*It's going to snow. She's going to have twins.*
Intention:	*I'm going to stay in this evening.*
Arrangement:	*I'm seeing the doctor on Friday.*

3 Ask and answer.

What's the weather going to be like tomorrow?
What are you going to do next Saturday? / Sunday?
Have you got any arrangements for next week? What are you doing?

E Film script

1 **Listen.** (✳ 1.28)

2 **Role-play the conversation and improvise an ending.**

TRAVELLER Can I check in here for the London flight?
CLERK WV376? I'm sorry. You're too late. The flight's closed.
TRAVELLER But I've got a ticket …
CLERK The flight always closes thirty minutes before departure. I'm very sorry.
TRAVELLER Look, it's really important …
CLERK The flight's boarding now. It's leaving in fifteen minutes. There's nothing I can do.
TRAVELLER Oh no! My brother's getting married in London tomorrow! I've only got hand-baggage … I can run to the gate!
CLERK No, you can't. It's closed.
TRAVELLER Can I speak to your supervisor?
CLERK No, I'm sorry, you can't.
TRAVELLER I don't believe it! This is really stupid! I'm going to miss my brother's wedding. Do you understand?
CLERK Please don't lose your temper, sir. There's nothing we can do.
TRAVELLER OK, OK. When's the next flight?
CLERK This is the last flight today, I'm afraid. The next flight doesn't leave until 8.30 tomorrow morning.
TRAVELLER Tomorrow? When does it get to London?
CLERK It arrives at 10.30 local time.
TRAVELLER OK, change me to that flight.
CLERK Let me check. That flight's usually quite busy …

See **Extension 4** p.193

5 Restaurants

A Something to drink?

1 Listen and practise. (✻ 1.29)

Waiter	Would you like something to drink?
Carl	Yes. Two bottles of mineral water, please.
Waiter	Still or sparkling?
Carl	Sparkling for me.
Ellie	Could I have still, please? I don't like sparkling.
Waiter	One still, one sparkling. Thank you.

2 Which responses go with the questions? Write *A* or *B* in the boxes.

A Would you like some sparkling water?
B Do you like sparkling water?

Possible responses:

☐ No, I wouldn't ☐ No, thank you. ☐ Not much. ☐ No, I prefer still.
☐ Yes, please. ☐ Not at the moment. ☐ Yes, I do. ☐ Yes, I would.
☐ No, I don't.

B Ordering a meal

1 Reading. Look at the menu. Make four lists of ingredients.

1 vegetables	2 meat	3 fish	4 other

2 Listen to Carl and Ellie discussing the menu. Look at the menu and put (✗) by the things they don't like. (✳ 1.30)

What do you know about them?

Are they married? Do they know each other well? Is this their first date?

3 Listen and practise. (✳ 1.31)

Waiter Are you ready to order?
Ellie Yes, please. I'd like a Napoletana. Can I have it without olives, please?
Waiter One Napoletana, no olives. Anything with that?
Ellie A green salad.
Waiter And for you?
Carl I'd like a Hot American, please. Could I have extra chillies on that?
Waiter Sure.
Carl And extra garlic.
Waiter OK. Hot American with extra chillies and garlic. Anything else?
Carl Yes, some garlic bread.
Waiter Would you like anything else to drink?
Ellie No, I'm fine with just the water.
Carl I'd like a beer.
Waiter Coming right up.

4 Group work. Role-play a conversation. One of you is the waiter. Order a meal from the menu.

Would you like something to drink? **an offer**. You expect a 'yes' answer.
Would you like anything to drink? **a question**. You don't know the answer.

5 Culture. In your country, who does the waiter ask first / serve first?

☐ the nearest person ☐ men ☐ women ☐ children
☐ the oldest person ☐ the host (person who is paying)
☐ the guest (person who isn't paying)

C Whose is it?

1 Listen and practise. (✻ 1.32)

Waiter Who's the Napoletana for?
Ellie That's for me.
Waiter And whose is the green salad?
Ellie That's mine, too.
Waiter Would you like some black pepper on that?
Ellie No, none for me, thank you.
Waiter What about you?
Carl Oh, yes. Some for me.
Waiter More?
Carl Yes, a bit more, please. And could you bring me another beer?
Waiter Sure. No problem.

2 Group work. Role play. One is the waiter. Everybody else writes their order for food on a piece of paper. Give the paper to the waiter. The waiter arrives with all the food.

3 Listen. The meal is over. Find the answers. (✻ 1.33)

How much is the bill?
How much does she give him?

Who says these things? Write *C* (Carl), *E* (Ellie), *W* (waiter).

☐ Could I have the bill? ☐ Was everything OK? ☐ Is service included?
☐ Let me pay half. ☐ This is on me. ☐ Let's split the bill.

4 Culture. Tipping.

How much do you tip the waiter in a restaurant in your country?
☐ nothing ☐ small change
☐ 10% ☐ 12.5% ☐ 15% ☐ more than 15%

Who else do you tip in your country?
☐ nobody ☐ taxi-drivers ☐ hairdressers ☐ hotel porters ☐ others

D Pizza (✱ 1.34)

Everybody loves pizza. Nobody 'invented' pizza, but 2000 years ago flat bread (like a pizza base) was popular in Egypt, Greece and Rome. Naples is the home of pizza. Tomatoes arrived in Italy in the 16th century from Mexico and Peru. Mozzarella cheese comes from buffalo milk, and arrived from India in the 18th century. The oldest pizzeria in Naples opened in 1830 and is still in business today.

In 1889 Queen Margherita of Italy visited Naples, and somebody made her a special pizza in the colours of the Italian flag. There was white mozzarella, red tomato sauce and green basil. Today Pizza Margherita is the classic pizza.

Italian immigrants introduced pizza to the USA. The first pizzeria opened in New York in 1895. In the 1950s and 1960s pizza restaurants opened everywhere in the USA. Pizza is a good fast food. You can buy frozen pizzas, and you can get take-away pizzas. Many companies deliver pizzas to your home.

You can find pizza nearly everywhere in the world. You can put anything on a pizza. In Britain you can find pizzas with bolognese sauce and Indian tandoori chicken. In Japan, sweetcorn is a popular topping and Idaho pizza has potatoes on it. In a modern pizza restaurant there's usually something for everybody.

1 Match the paragraphs with these titles.

Pizza to go Food for a Queen International pizzas
The origins of pizza

2 Complete the table with indefinite pronouns.

some		some*where*	
any	any*body*		
no		no*where*	
every			every*thing*

Linda Madeira
PORTUGUESE & ITALIAN CUISINE
Tel. 0238036 9666
Retro
bistro cafe
lebanese cuisine
LEBANESE RESTAURANT
مطعم لبناني
O'Briens
IRISH SANDWICH BAR
Mustang Sally's
American Diner
INDIAN
indi's
CUISINE
salsa
Latin Bar
Restaurant

Florida Cafe
CUBAN RESTAURANT
BREAKFAST-LUNCH-DINNER
385-3013
1401 S. Las Vegas BLVD.

English Food & Wines

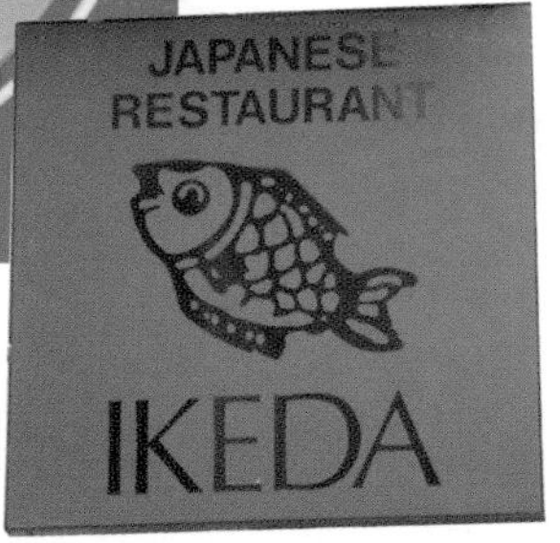

JAPANESE RESTAURANT
IKEDA

BACCHUS
GREEK TAVERNA
020 7435 1855
BACCHUS
www.donmiguel.co.uk

E Ethnic food

1 Read the signs.
Find the nationality words. Which countries are they from?

2 Pair work.
► Have you ever eaten American food?
◄ Yes, I have. / Yes, often. / No, I haven't. / No, never.

3 Discuss.
Are there any ethnic restaurants in your town?
Are they from foreign countries, or from different regions of your country?

Look at this. The coloured area = the food that you like.

I eat everything! I like all kinds of food. I like **any** foreign food.	I like **some** foreign food.	I don't like **any** foreign food.	I don't like **some** foreign food.

- *any* is 'complete'. It means *all* or *none*.
- *some* is 'incomplete'.

The pink examples are more frequent than the blue examples.
This is why grammar books often say 'Use *some* for positive. Use *any* for negatives and questions.' This is a good general rule for English, especially in exams, but it isn't always true.

4 What do you think of different kinds of ethnic food?
► Do you like *American* food?
◄ I (like / don't like) (some / any) *American* food ...
or I don't know. I've never eaten any *American* food.

See **Extension 5** p.194

6 Old friends

A Websites

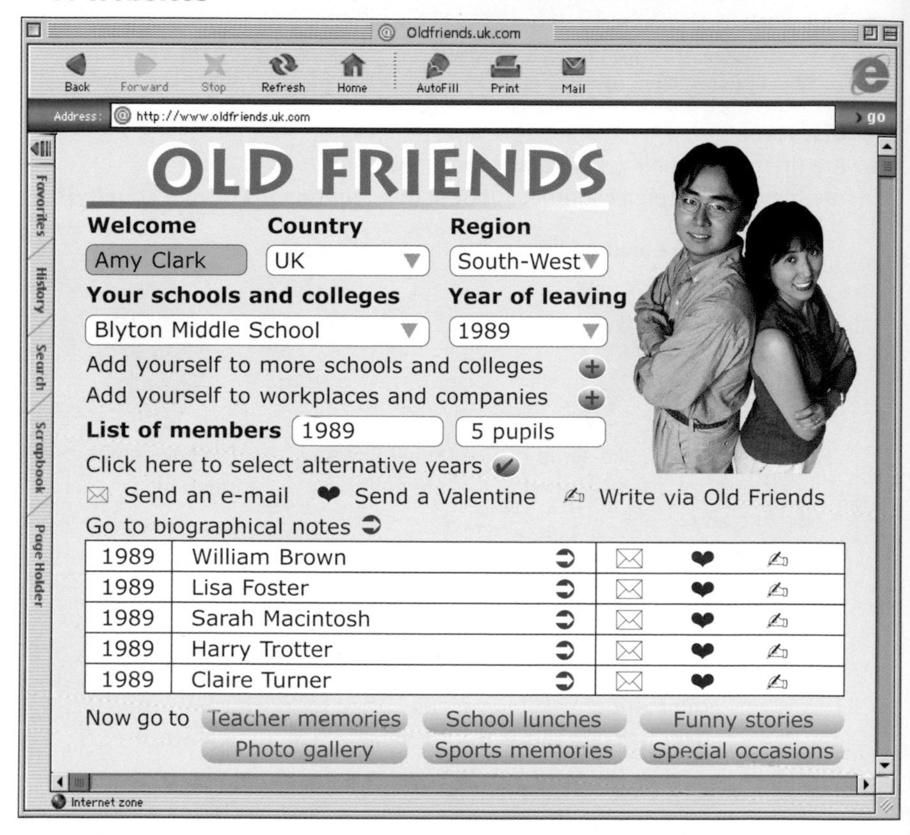

1 **There are websites in many countries where you can find old school friends. Amy Clark is looking at the website for her middle school (8 to 12 years old). Find this information.**

Which school did she go to? Which country was the school in?

When did she leave? Which region was the school in?

2 **Listen. Amy's talking to a friend about the website.** (✳ 1.35)
Look at the past forms of verbs, and write the present forms.

past	present	past	present	past	present
was		left		happened	
were		went		got married	
sat		saw		liked	

What can you remember about the people in her class?

e.g. Sarah – *She was Amy's best friend. She sat next to Amy.*

B Biographies

1 List the past verbs in the text. Which ones are regular?

2 Lisa didn't write complete sentences, she wrote notes.
Make complete sentences.

Left Blyton Middle School – 1989. *She left Blyton Middle School in 1989.*

Listen and check. (✳ 1.36)

3 Write notes for your autobiography. You can use these words.

Education / work		**Life events**
started went to left studied passed got (a job)	primary school middle school secondary school college university work	passed exam / driving test met (someone) got engaged / married / divorced had children travelled to / went on holiday to moved to / emigrated to

Read your partner the notes, but do not say the dates.
Your partner asks you questions about your life with *When ...?*

C Memories

1 Ask and answer.

subject questions Who taught music? Miss Kennedy did.
object questions What did Miss Kennedy teach? She taught music.

What did Miss Kennedy teach?
What was Miss Kennedy like?
Did she like William?
Where did Harry sit?
Who sang songs?
Who told tales about William?
Who sat behind Amy?
Who had a crush on Amy?
Who still hates singing?

2 Share your early school memories. Use these adjectives:

strict kind patient shy funny boring
friendly frightening popular unpopular

I remember a teacher called Mr Dodds. He was very strict and he was always angry. He was very unpopular. Nobody liked him.

You can: tell a story / tales / a lie / the truth / a joke

D The past simple

Did you know the answer? Yes, I did. / No, I didn't.
I knew the answer. / I didn't know the answer.

1 New verbs are regular. You can always guess the endings. Put the past form of the highlighted verb in these sentences.

1 Did you e-mail her? Yes, I .... her yesterday.
2 He didn't text me last night, but he .... me this morning.
3 Can you fax me the letter? I .... it five minutes ago.
4 Where did you download it from? I .... it from image.search.com.
5 I .... the programme last week, but I didn't video it last night.
6 Where did you post the message? I .... it on their website.

2 Regular *–ed* endings have three pronunciations, /t/, /d/, /ɪd/

Say the past forms in exercise 1 aloud. Are they /t/, /d/ **or** /ɪd/ **?**

Say the past forms of these verbs aloud then listen and check. (✳ 1.37)

believed	happened	liked	shouted	studied
dropped	hated	moved	started	travelled
emigrated	helped	passed	stopped	wanted

3 Learning verbs. Say aloud.

Irregular verbs with only one change in the vowel-sound and spelling:

become – became, drink – drank, get – got, give – gave,
know – knew, meet – met, sing – sang, sit – sat, write – wrote

Irregular verbs with one change in the vowel-sound but the spelling is different:

eat – ate, fly – flew, see – saw, wear – wore

Irregular verbs with a /t/ **or** /d/ **consonant sound at the end of the past form:**

buy – bought, go – went, have – had, hear – heard, leave – left,
sell – sold, send – sent, teach – taught, tell – told, think – thought

Irregular verbs which are the same in present and past forms:

cost – cost, let – let, put – put

Note: read /riːd/ (present) read /red/ (past) – the spelling is the same, but the pronunciation is different.

4 Find pairs of irregular verbs which are similar in the past.
e.g. *sold / told*

E Stories

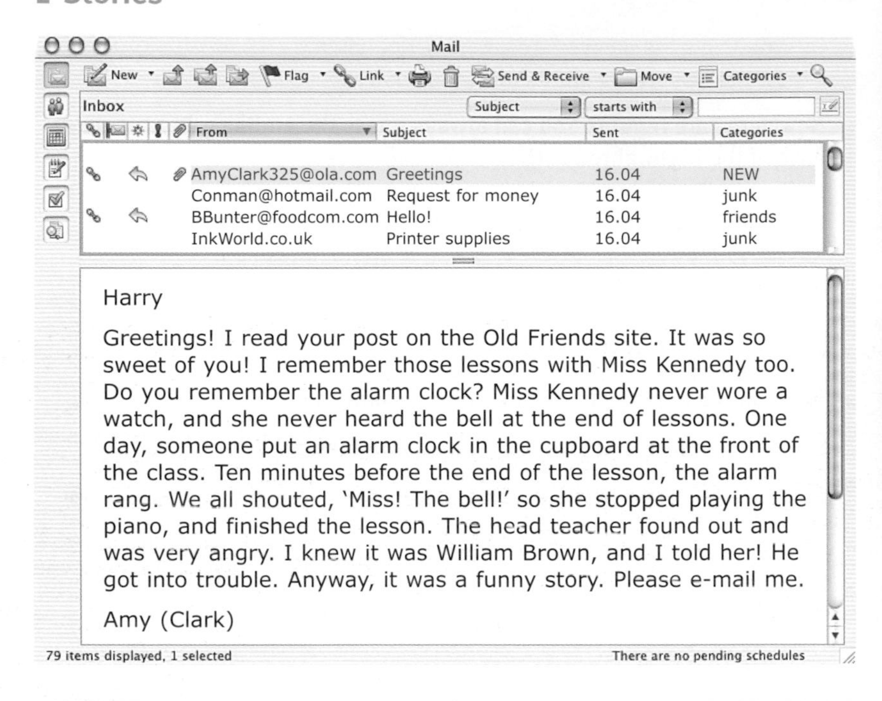

Mail

New Flag Link Send & Receive Move Categories

Inbox Subject starts with

From	Subject	Sent	Categories
AmyClark325@ola.com	Greetings	16.04	NEW
Conman@hotmail.com	Request for money	16.04	junk
BBunter@foodcom.com	Hello!	16.04	friends
InkWorld.co.uk	Printer supplies	16.04	junk

Harry

Greetings! I read your post on the Old Friends site. It was so sweet of you! I remember those lessons with Miss Kennedy too. Do you remember the alarm clock? Miss Kennedy never wore a watch, and she never heard the bell at the end of lessons. One day, someone put an alarm clock in the cupboard at the front of the class. Ten minutes before the end of the lesson, the alarm rang. We all shouted, 'Miss! The bell!' so she stopped playing the piano, and finished the lesson. The head teacher found out and was very angry. I knew it was William Brown, and I told her! He got into trouble. Anyway, it was a funny story. Please e-mail me.

Amy (Clark)

79 items displayed, 1 selected There are no pending schedules

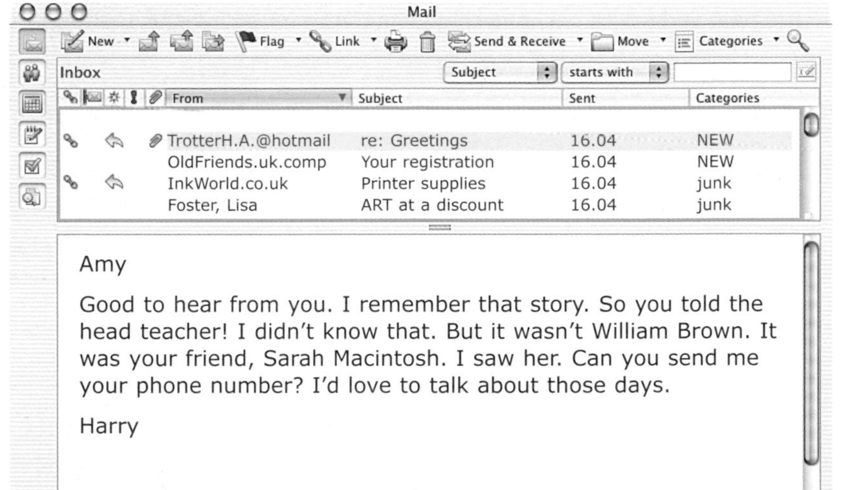

Mail

New Flag Link Send & Receive Move Categories

Inbox Subject starts with

From	Subject	Sent	Categories
TrotterH.A.@hotmail	re: Greetings	16.04	NEW
OldFriends.uk.comp	Your registration	16.04	NEW
InkWorld.co.uk	Printer supplies	16.04	junk
Foster, Lisa	ART at a discount	16.04	junk

Amy

Good to hear from you. I remember that story. So you told the head teacher! I didn't know that. But it wasn't William Brown. It was your friend, Sarah Macintosh. I saw her. Can you send me your phone number? I'd love to talk about those days.

Harry

1 **Find the past forms of verbs in the e-mails.**

2 **In the past, we use *that* / *those* not *this* / *these*. Find three examples.**

3 **Close your books and re-tell the story. Begin *One day* ...**
Have you got a funny story about school or work? Tell your partner.
When did it happen? How old were you? Where were you?

See **Extension 6** p.195

7 Ambitions

A Ten things to do ... before you die

1 **What would <u>you</u> like to do before you die?**
I'd like to climb Mount Everest.

2 **Tell your partner. React to your partner's ideas.**
Would you? / I wouldn't! / That sounds frightening!
Me, too. / I'd love (hate) to do that.

B Work and play

What kind of person are you?

Tick the boxes. Do not tick more than two in each section.

1 I like ...

- ☐ working on my own.
- ☐ working with other people.
- ☐ having a routine.
- ☐ being in control.

2 I enjoy ...

- ☐ making things.
- ☐ doing new things.
- ☐ travelling.
- ☐ looking after people.

3 I'd rather ...

- ☐ be happy than rich.
- ☐ be the boss than be popular.
- ☐ be at work than at home.
- ☐ do a satisfying job than a well-paid job.

4 I'd like ...

- ☐ to earn a lot of money.
- ☐ to change my appearance.
- ☐ to have more free time.
- ☐ to have a better life.
- ☐ to live somewhere else.
- ☐ to travel to different countries.
- ☐ to develop my spiritual interests.

5 I want ...

- ☐ to emigrate.
- ☐ to get a different job.
- ☐ to stay in the same place.
- ☐ to stay in the same job.
- ☐ to make new friends.
- ☐ to start my own business.

1 **Complete the questionnaire for yourself. Tell your partner your choices. Tell them some negative points too, using:**

I don't like ... I don't enjoy ... I'd rather not ...
I wouldn't like ... I don't want ...

2 **In what ways are you the same as your partner? In what ways are you different? Tell your class.**

I like working on my own, but she doesn't. She likes working with people.
I want to emigrate, but he wants to stay here.
I'd rather be rich than happy, but he'd rather be happy than rich.
I'd like to earn a lot of money, but she'd rather have more free time.

3 Collocations. Which words follow *do* and *make*?

friends aerobics a noise homework a mistake an exam
a cake cars the cooking your hair your bed a job
a dress yoga an offer love the washing-up

make / made ——

do / did ——

COMMUNICATION

Student A Look at Activity 2 on p. 210.
Student B Look at Activity 9 on p. 213.

4 Barney Jones is talking about his old career. Listen. (✳ 1.38)

Ask and answer.
What did he do?
How old is he?
What does he do now?
What did he love about his old job?
What doesn't he like about his life now?

5 Barney's talking about his plans. Choose verbs from the box.

'd like to want to 'd rather 'm going to hope to

I .... start college next September. I'm taking a degree in Sports Science, because I .... get a coaching certificate. I .... be a football manager one day. I .... do some television work too, if possible. I was on several sports programmes last year, and I enjoyed it. I think I'm good at it, too. But I .... be a manager. That's my ambition now.

Listen to Barney. Were your choices the same? (✳ 1.39)

base form or bare infinitive (*do*)
*I can **dance**. I'd rather **be** at home now.*
*I could **swim** when I was three.*

the infinitive (*to do*)
*I want to **be rich**. I'd like **to speak** to Ms Park.*
*She's going **to have** a baby. I hope **to get** married one day.*
*I plan **to get** a qualification in English.*

–*ing* form (*doing*)
*I enjoy **travelling**. I hate **doing** housework.*
*I prefer **shopping** in supermarkets. I can't stand **being** on my own.*

C Personality types

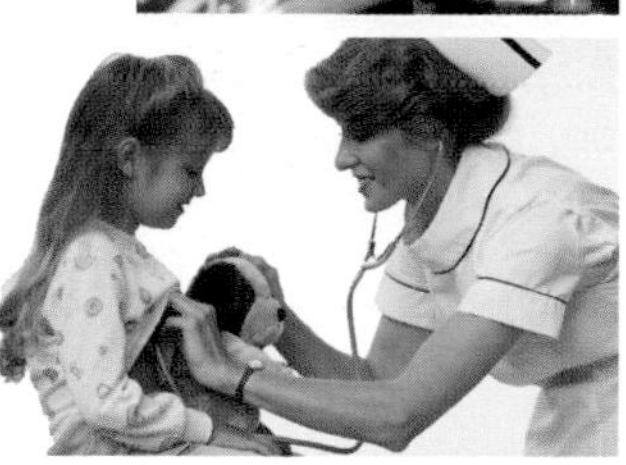

leaders are good at giving instructions. They like being in control.

manipulators persuade people, and change situations to get what they want.

social types enjoy being with lots of people, and like meeting new people.

carers enjoy looking after or helping others. They get job satisfaction from this.

creative types like expressing themselves in art, music, etc.

seekers have questions about life and are trying to find the answers.

conventional types like routines. They don't like being different to other people.

producers like making things, or working with their hands.

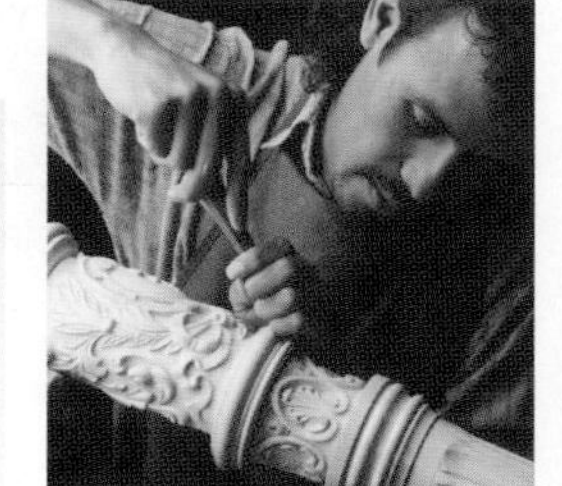

1 **Match the types to the pictures. Then match an adjective to each type. You can add more.**

charming practical artistic sensible kind
serious friendly confident

2 **Which types describe you best? What about your partner? What are suitable jobs for your personality type? Make positive and negative sentences.**
I'd like to (work in a hospital) because I like (looking after people).
I wouldn't like to (be a flight attendant) because I (hate flying).
When I leave college, I want to be a (salesperson).
I work in a (bank), but I'd rather be a (painter).

D Pronunciation

1 Putting words together. Listen and practise. (✳ 1.40)

Written English	What it sounds like
A Do you want to dance?	A D'you wanna dance?
B Yes, OK.	B Yeah, OK.
A Would you like to go for a drink?	A Would ya like to go for a drink?
B No, I've got to go now.	B No, I gotta go now.
A What are you doing tomorrow?	A Whatcha doin' tomorrow?
B I'm going to meet someone.	B I'm gonna meet someone.
A OK. See you.	A OK. See ya.

2 Even when we try to write contractions, we can't write all the sounds. Try saying these sentences. Listen and repeat. (✳ 1.41)

D'you /dʒə/ wanna /wɑnə/ dance?
Would ya /wʊdʒə/ like to /laɪktə/ go for a /fərə/ drink?
No, I gotta /gɑtə/ go now.
Whatcha /wɒtʃə/ doin' /duːɪn/ tomorrow?
I'm gonna /gənə/ meet someone.
OK. See ya. /jə/

E Song

I Want To Stay Here
by Gerry Goffin and Carole King

Woah-oh-oh-oh-oh
Woah-oh-oh-oh-oh
I don't wanna go to the party with you.
I don't wanna go to ______.
I don't wanna go anywhere with you.
I just wanna stay here and love you.
Woah-oh-oh-oh-oh
Now that I can be alone with you,
I won't throw away ______.
There's no place I'd go with you,
So I want to stay here and love you
All through the week
I miss you so.
So now that I've got you
I'm gonna hold you
closer and closer and closer and oh oh …
I don't wanna go for a walk with you.
And now that I am in ______,
I don't even know if I'll talk to you.
I just wanna stay here and love you.

1 **Read and guess where these words go. Don't use a dictionary.**

this trance the dance the chance

Deduce:
You go **to** a place or an event.
You throw **away** something.
You are **in** a state or mood.

Now check in a dictionary. Then listen. (✻ 1.42)

2 **Listen again and sing.**

See **Extension 7** p.196

8 Humour

A Comic cards

1 **Match the sentences to the pictures.**
Where have you been?
Has anyone seen the dog's dinner?
It's been the best day of my life!
Have you read them all?

2 **Your sense of humour.**
Which of these pictures are funny?
☐ all of them ☐ three of them ☐ two of them
☐ one of them ☐ none of them
Do they make you laugh? Which one is your favourite?
Are there any that you don't like?

B Embarrassing moments ...

This is a scene from the BBC TV comedy series 'Only Fools and Horses'. Del and Rodney have just arrived at a party. They thought it was a fancy-dress party and they've come in Batman and Robin costumes. However, their host has died and no one has told them. So it isn't a fancy-dress party any more, it's a funeral.

1 **Find someone who can answer *yes* to these questions.**

Have you ever ...
... worn the wrong clothes to a social event?
... gone out without any money?
... forgotten an important birthday or anniversary?
... said 'hello' to a stranger? (thinking they were someone else)
... made a mistake in a team sport?
... fallen over or been sick in a public place?

Can you add another question?

2 **Find more information.** (✳ 1.43)

► Have you ever gone out without any money?
◄ Yes, I have.
► What happened?
◄ I went to the supermarket. When I got to the checkout, I didn't have any money. I felt so embarrassed!

Ask your partner the questions in 1 again.

If they answer *yes*, continue: *What happened? How did you feel?*

C The present perfect

Present perfect
I, You, We, They + have / haven't + **past participle**
He, She, It + has / hasn't + **past participle**

Have you ever been to Scotland? Yes, I have. / No, I haven't.
He's seen the film three times. She hasn't seen it.
We've been to Florida. They haven't been there.

1 **Pronunciation.**

There are two pronunciations for *have* and *has*.
Stressed (strong): *have* /həv/, *has* /hæz/.
Unstressed (weak): *have* /həv/, *has* /həz/.

There are two pronunciations for *been*.
Stressed (strong): /biːn/.
Unstressed (weak): /bɪn/.

Listen to these sentences. Put *S* stressed, or *U* unstressed. (✳ 1.44)

1 Have ☐ you seen the film yet?
2 Yes, I have. ☐
3 She hasn't ☐ met his parents yet.
4 Has ☐ the post arrived yet?
5 Yes, it has. ☐
6 I haven't ☐ read 'War and Peace'.
7 I've only been ☐ once.
8 Where have you been ☐?

2 **Make guesses about your partner's day. Write three positive sentences and three negative sentences.**
You've had a cup of coffee today.
You've listened to the news on the radio.
You've read the newspaper.
You haven't watched TV yet.
You haven't had lunch yet.
You haven't made any mistakes in English yet.

3 **Interview your partner and find out if you were correct.**
► Have you listened to the news yet? (✳ 1.45)
◄ Yes, I have.
► When did you listen to it?
◄ I listened to it in my car on the way to work.

► Have you had a lunch yet? (✳ 1.46)
◄ No, I haven't. Not yet.
► When are you going to have lunch?
◄ I'm going to have lunch after this lesson.

4 **Change partners. Ask about your previous partner with *Has he ...? Has she ...?***

D It's gone!

1 Listen and practise. (✱ 1.47)

Gina What's the matter?
Sam I've lost my mobile phone. Have you seen it anywhere?
Gina No, I haven't.
Sam Well, it was here before lunch, and now it's gone!
Gina Where was it exactly?
Sam Here. On my desk.
Gina Where have you looked?
Sam Everywhere! It's gone!
Gina Well, don't panic. Take it easy. Think. Where have you been today?
Sam Nowhere. Just here in the office.
Gina You haven't been out of the office all day?
Sam Well, I've been to the photocopier room twice. But it isn't there. I've already looked.
Gina Look in your desk drawers.
Sam I've already looked there. I've taken everything out, and put it back in again ... three times. It's brand new. It cost over two hundred pounds. I haven't paid for it yet!

2 Role-play the conversation. Gina makes more suggestions. Sam has already done all of these things.

- Look on the shelf.
- Why don't you look in your car?
- Why don't you ask Sarah?
- Have you looked in your briefcase?
- Have you left it in the canteen?
- Is it in the filing cabinet?

already / yet
*Have you done it **yet**? Have you finished **yet**?*
*No, I haven't done it **yet**. / Yes, I've **already** done it.*

3 How are they going to find the phone? Have you got any ideas? Listen and check. (✳ 1.48)

4 Complete the spaces with *been* or *gone*.

1 I've got some money. I've just .... to the bank.
2 Oh, no! We're too late! It's 5.45. The post has already ....
3 Sorry, she isn't here. She's .... out.
4 Have you ever .... to a classical concert?
5 My wallet isn't in my pocket. It's .... !
6 The weather has .... very good recently.

E Past tense or present perfect?

I've seen a lot of kung-fu films. (in my life until now)
I saw a good film last week. (finished time, past)

1 Complete the sentences with time expressions from the box.

this month | recently | yesterday | at 3 o'clock
three times | in (her) life | last night | in 2003

1 He's played football for his country ....
2 I've been to the cinema twice ....
3 We've been very busy ....
4 She was busy ....
5 I didn't go out ....
6 They played tennis ....
7 She's never flown ....
8 We went to New York ....

2 Look at the dictionary definition. What do *pp* and *pt* mean?

take /teɪk/ verb [T] (pt **took** /tʊk/; pp **taken** /teɪkən/) **1** to carry sb/sth or to go with sb from one place to another: *Take your coat with you – it's cold.* • *Could you take this letter home?*

Learning past tenses and past participles

These are the basic types (base form / past tense / past participle):

A B B	**regular:** listen / listened / listened	All regular verbs are A B B
A B B	**irregular:** teach / taught / taught	About 60 irregular verbs
A B C	do / did / done eat / ate / eaten	About 60 irregular verbs
A A A	cost / cost / cost	About 20 irregular verbs
A B A	come / came / come	3 irregular verbs
A A B	beat / beat / beaten	This is the only example

3 Put these verbs in the correct groups.

cut have say go watch write wear play know
run feel give forget put see take leave make
become fall

F The funniest joke?

You can: tell / understand / get / know / remember / forget **a** / **the joke**
You can't: ~~say a joke, ask a joke~~

Psychiatrists wanted to find the funniest joke in the world.
In 2002, they told jokes to two million people from 70 countries.
This joke was the funniest. (✳ 1.49)

Two hunters are out in the woods. Suddenly one of them falls to the ground. He doesn't seem to be breathing, and his eyes are closed. Immediately, the other guy takes out his cell phone and calls the emergency services. He shouts, 'My friend is dead! What can I do?'
The operator says, 'Calm down. Take it easy. I can help. First, let's make sure he's dead.' There is a silence, then there's the sound of a gun shot. The guy comes back on the phone, and says, 'OK, I've done that. Now what?'

1 Ask and answer.

Do you get the joke?
Have you heard it before?
Is it the funniest joke in the world?
Who tells more jokes? Men or women?

COMMUNICATION

Tell a joke.

Student A Look at Activity 1 on p.210. Canada's favourite joke.
Student B Look at Activity 8 on p.213. Australia's favourite joke.
Student C Look at Activity 13 on p.216. Scotland's favourite joke.
Student D Look at Activity 19 on p.219. The USA's favourite joke.

What do you think of the jokes?

1 Are they ...? ☐ not funny ☐ quite funny ☐ funny ☐ very funny ☐ really funny
2 Are any of them offensive? Why?
3 Which is the funniest joke?

2 Translate a joke from your language. Tell it.

See **Extension 8** p.196

9 Sport

sky guide 7.14 Mon 18th March
SPORTS

TODAY	8.00 p.m.	8.30 p.m.	9.00 p.m.
401 SKY SPORTS 1	International football Brazil v Italy		Golf
402 SKY SPORTS 2	Live Tennis	Formula One Motor-Racing	
403 SKY SPORTS 3	World Athletics: Javelin		Windsurfing
412 EUROSPORT GB	Ten-pin bowling	Ice Dancing	Darts
499 EXTREME SPORTS	Monster Trucks	Snowboarding	Wrestling

Page up   Page down   + 24 hours   - 24 hours

Press SELECT to set reminder

A TV Guide

1 **Pair work. Think about these categories. Can you find examples of each type in the TV guide? How many more sports can you list?**

- sports that end in *-ball*
- racing sports
- table sports
- combat sports
- winter sports
- water sports
- target sports
- sports where you hold something (a bat, a club, a raquet)
- achievement sports (e.g. climbing)

I **play** football / darts / golf / tennis.
I **do** athletics / wrestling / exercise.
I **go** bowling / windsurfing / swimming.

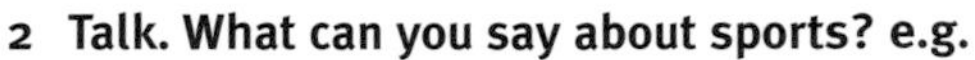

2 **Talk. What can you say about sports? e.g.**

I (do /play) (this sport) regularly.
I've never (played /done /gone) ... .
I've never heard of (this sport).
I often go to watch (this sport).
I watch (this sport) on TV.
I've never watched (this sport).

B Vocabulary

1 Match these verbs to the pictures.

catch
throw
pass
head
kick
hit
aim
save

Someone who runs is a **runner.**
Someone who plays football is a **footballer**.
Someone who plays tennis is a **tennis player**.
Someone who cycles is a **cyclist**.
Someone who does athletics is an **athlete**

2 Make similar sentences with these words:

swim skate dance climb box wrestle drive play golf

C Intonation

1 You are listening to the football results. Unfortunately the radio reception is bad. Listen to the intonation and guess the results. Write *1* – home team wins, *2* – away team wins, *X* – draw. ✱ 1.50

FA Cup Fifth Round

Home		*Away*	*Result*
Manchester United	v	Manchester City	
Arsenal	v	Swindon	
Liverpool	v	Newcastle	
Cambridge	v	Oxford	
Bournemouth	v	Brighton	
Tottenham	v	Birmingham	
Southampton	v	Northampton	
Leeds United	v	Bristol City	

2 Listen again. The reception is better now. Write the scores. 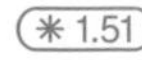

D Martial arts

1 Read about Josh's summer holiday.

"I didn't enjoy sport at school. We had to play football in the winter. When it was too cold and wet to play football, we had to do cross-country running, and I was always last. In the summer we had to play cricket, and I was never any good at it. I watched a lot of Jackie Chan movies when I was a kid, and I started doing martial arts when I was fifteen. Last summer I went to one of the kung-fu schools at the Shaolin Temple in China. There were thousands of students at the schools. We had to get up at 5 a.m. every morning and go for a run. Then we trained until midday. We couldn't train in the afternoon. We couldn't speak Chinese, but it didn't matter. We understood the instructions. It was hard work. I don't know why they don't teach martial arts in British schools."

2 Where can you insert these phrases into the text? Think and choose.

A because I couldn't hit the ball.
B but there were only a few Westerners.
C because it was too hot.
D but I really enjoyed it.

Listen and check. (✳ 1.52)

3 Correct the information.

At school ...	**In China ...**
he had to play football in the summer.	he had to get up at 8 a.m.
he didn't have to play cricket.	he had to train in the afternoon.
he was good at cricket.	he couldn't understand the instructions.

4 Ask and answer.

Did you have to do sport at school?
Which sports did / do you have to do?
What sports are / were you good at?
What sports aren't / weren't you any good at?

*He **had to** play football.* *She **didn't have to** play basketball.*
***Did** you **have to** play football at school? Yes, I did. / No, I didn't.*

E Sport or entertainment?

1 Match these words to the pictures.

ballroom dancing darts ice dancing
greyhound racing boxing rodeo

2 What is a sport? Does a sport need ...?

- a referee or judge
- human contestants
- spectators
- teams
- rules
- a score
- to be in the Olympic Games
- competition (winners and losers)

Do the players need ...?

- physical skill
- physical fitness

Yes, definitely. Yes, I think so. No, not at all.
No, not necessarily. No, I don't think so.

3 Pronunciation: stressed syllables. Listen and repeat. (✱ 1.53)

• ● •	• • ●	• ● • •	● • • •
con•test•ant	ref•er•ee	pro•fes•sion•al	def•i•nite•ly
spec•ta•tor	● • •	• • ● •	• • ● • •
a•chieve•ment	phys•i•cal	en•ter•tain•ment	in•ter•na•tion•al
o•lymp•ic	am•a•teur	com•pe•ti•tion	ne•ces•sar•i•ly

4 Listen. Tina and Steve are discussing ice dancing. (✳ 1.54)

Who thinks it's a sport?
Who thinks it's entertainment?
Who do you agree with?

5 Listen to the second part of their conversation. (✳ 1.55)

Tina thinks ...

boxing is .... horse-racing is .... greyhound racing is ....

6 Listen to both parts of the conversation.

Who says it? Write *S* for Steve, *T* for Tina.

☐ What do you mean, not a sport?
☐ I don't get it.
☐ That's not a sport at all, in my opinion.
☐ I get your point.

7 Do you agree with these statements?

Dancers have to be fit.
Darts players don't have to be fit.
Dancers have to train regularly.
Jockeys have to be skilful.

Discuss the pictures. Are they sport or entertainment, in your opinion?

See **Extension 9** p.197

10 *When* and *while*

A Two things at the same time

1 **What's she doing? Make sentences.**
She's having a bath. She isn't washing her hair.

have a bath	wash her hair	whistle	listen to music	sing
read a magazine	clean the bath	blow bubbles	chew gum	

2 **Join your sentences with *while*.**

She's reading a magazine. She's having a bath.
She's reading a magazine *while* she's having a bath. **or**
She's reading a magazine *while* having a bath.

3 Do you ever do two or more things at the same time? Make questions with *while*, then listen and check. (✱ 1.56)

listen to music / have a bath
Do you listen to music while you're having a bath? **or**
Do you listen to music while having a bath?

listen to music / work
read the newspaper / eat breakfast
read / watch TV
use a mobile phone / drive
do homework / travel to (work / school)
chew gum / drive
smoke / have a meal

4 Ask and answer the questions.

No, never. Yes, occasionally / sometimes / always.
It depends. I like listening to music while I'm doing housework.
But I hate listening to music while I'm working on the computer.

5 Read the text. (✱ 1.57)

You can't use your mobile while you're driving in Britain. Everybody knows that, but a van driver got a shock on the M4 motorway last week. Police stopped 32-year-old Matthew Wilson and charged him with 'Driving without due care and attention'. Matthew was eating a chicken sandwich while driving his white Ford Transit towards Heathrow Airport. A police officer said, 'He only had one hand on the wheel, and a sandwich in the other. It's the same as using a mobile phone.' Matthew asked, 'So why do all the petrol stations sell chocolate, sandwiches and cans of drink? This is crazy!'

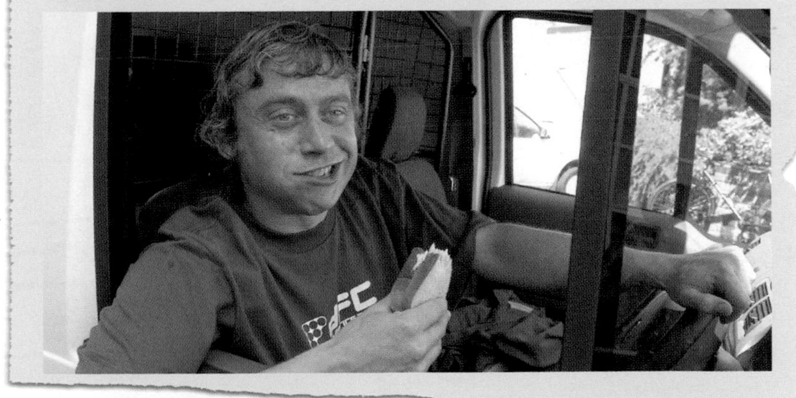

Answer the questions.

Who stopped him?
What was he eating?
Where was he going?
What kind of van was he driving?

Make a sentence with *while*.

B On the beach

It was a lovely summer day. The sun was shining, the sea was warm, and the beach was crowded. People were sunbathing. Some of them were swimming, someone was fishing, and children were playing on the beach. A lifeguard was watching the sea.

Suddenly, the lifeguard shouted 'Shark!'

The fisherman saw the shark's fin, and stood up.

The boat turned over and the fisherman fell into the sea.

Everybody ran out of the sea.

Everybody on the beach ran away from the sea.

'Where's everybody gone?'

Listen to the story. (✳ 1.58)

We use the past continuous to describe a scene.

Underline the examples of the past continuous.

We use the past simple to talk about a sequence of actions.

Circle the past simple verbs.

C Describing a scene

The past continuous
What were they doing? They were sunbathing.
What was she doing? She was reading a book.
Was he fishing? Yes, he was. / No, he wasn't.
Were they swimming? Yes, they were. / No, they weren't.

1 What was happening before the lifeguard shouted 'Shark!'? Study the large picture on page 62 for one minute. Correct these statements. Emphasize the words you change.

- A boy was burying his mother in the sand.
  No, a boy was burying his father in the sand.

1 A woman was lying on a blue towel.
2 A girl was standing on a donkey.
3 Two women were playing with a frisbee.
4 Two dogs were running towards the sea.
5 Two old women were sitting in the sea.
6 A girl was building a small sandcastle.
7 A photographer was taking a photo of a donkey.
8 The lifeguard wasn't looking through binoculars.

2 Make more sentences about the picture.

	while	
1 Two women were listening to music		A it was eating an ice-cream.
2 A boy was burying his father in the sand		B the photographer was taking their photo.
3 A girl was sitting on the donkey		C they were sunbathing.
4 The couple were smiling		D his mother was reading.

3 Pronunciation.

There are two pronunciations for *was* and *were*.
Stressed (strong): was /wɒz/, were /wɜː(r)/.
Unstressed (weak): was /wəz/, were /wə/.

Listen to these sentences. Put *S* (stressed), or *U* (unstressed). (✳ 1.59)

1 She was ☐ sunbathing.
2 Was ☐ the sun shining?
3 Yes, it was. ☐
4 What was ☐ happening?
5 Were ☐ they swimming?
6 Yes, they were. ☐
7 What were ☐ you doing?
8 We were ☐ working.

D Talking about a sequence

1 What happened when the lifeguard shouted 'Shark!'? Look at page 63.

The lifeguard saw the fin. He shouted 'Shark!'
Which happened first? Did he see the fin first, or did he shout first?
The lifeguard saw the fin, then he shouted 'Shark'.

When + first action , second action
When the lifeguard saw the fin, he shouted 'Shark!' (note the comma)

Second action + when + first action
The lifeguard shouted 'Shark!' when he saw the fin. (no comma)

Join these sentences in two ways. Start with *when*.
Then connect with *when*.
The fisherman saw the fin. He stood up.
The fisherman stood up. The boat turned over.
The boat turned over. The fisherman fell into the sea.
The people heard the lifeguard. They ran out of the sea.

2 Look at Section B. Connect these sentences with *when*.

- The lifeguard was looking through his binoculars. He saw the fin.
  The lifeguard was looking through his binoculars ***when*** *he saw the fin.*

1 The old women were standing in the sea. They heard the lifeguard.
2 The fisherman was sitting in his boat. He saw the fin.

Can you make more sentences about Section B?

- *while* joins two continuous verbs *I was reading* ***while*** *I was watching TV.*
  when joins two simple verbs *I turned off the TV* ***when*** *I heard the phone.*
- You can use *when* or *while* to join a simple verb and a continuous verb
  The phone rang ***while*** *I was having a bath.*
  The phone rang ***when*** *I was having a bath.*
- You can begin the sentence with *while* or *when*.
  While *I was having a bath, the phone rang.*
  When *I was having a bath, the phone rang.*
- Don't use *while* before a simple verb.
  ~~***While***~~ *the phone rang, I was having a bath.*

3 Look at the spaces in these sentences. Write:

A – *while* B – *when* C – *when* or *while*

1 ☐ I met her, I was walking to work.
2 They're having a drink ☐ they're waiting for some friends.
3 We got a shock ☐ we heard the news.
4 I was reading a magazine ☐ I was waiting to see the doctor.
5 We were talking ☐ the teacher came in.
6 The postman arrived ☐ I was having breakfast.

E Film script

<u>SCENE 16: AN INTERVIEW ROOM</u>

<u>POLICE OFFICER</u> Admit it, Chris. You were driving the car.

<u>CHRIS</u> No way. I don't know anything about it. I wasn't even in the city.

<u>POLICE OFFICER</u> So, what were you doing last night?

<u>CHRIS</u> What time?

<u>POLICE OFFICER</u> Between nine and ten.

<u>CHRIS</u> Uh, I was in New Jersey. I was playing pool with some guys in a club.

<u>POLICE OFFICER</u> Oh, really? Who were they?

<u>CHRIS</u> I don't remember their names.

<u>POLICE OFFICER</u> When did you get to the club?

<u>CHRIS</u> Eight. Maybe eight-fifteen.

<u>POLICE OFFICER</u> And what time did you leave?

<u>CHRIS</u> After eleven. I saw the TV news at eleven, then I left.

<u>POLICE OFFICER</u> So you weren't driving the car?

<u>CHRIS</u> I've never driven a Jaguar in my life.

<u>POLICE OFFICER</u> Uh huh. And who told you it was a Jaguar?

1 **Listen and practise.** (✱ 1.60)

2 **Role-play a similar interview. Someone was in the school last night and wrote 'I hate learning English' on every board. Find out where everyone was at 9.30 last night, and what they were doing.**

See **Extension 10** p.197

11 Phoning

A Phone etiquette

1 Do any of these things annoy you about telephones?

1. People who don't switch off their mobiles during films.
2. People who take mobile calls during a conversation.
3. People who eat or drink while they're talking on the phone.
4. People who talk loudly into mobiles in public places.
5. Calls from companies that are selling something.
6. People who phone during mealtimes, or very early or late.
7. Long recorded messages when you are paying for the call.
8. Famous tunes or silly sounds as ringtones.
9. Loud music while you're waiting to get through.
10. People who never check their voicemail.

Choose comments:

That really annoys me.
I don't mind that.
I do that myself!

2 Match the things in 1 to the recordings. You can match more than one to a recording.

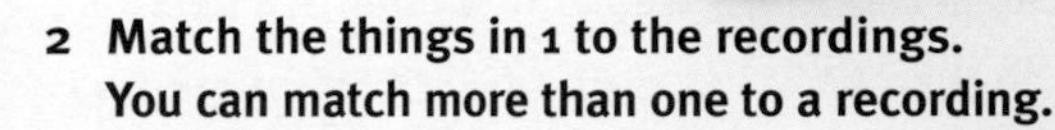

B Phone problems

B Good afternoon, Mrs Graham. My name's Colin, and I'm calling from Edinburgh Mail Order. You ordered a catalogue from us ...
A ....
B Of course. This is Colin from Edinburgh Mail ...
A ....
B Sorry, Mrs Graham, I'll start again. I'm calling from Edinburgh Mail Order ...
A ....
B Edinburgh Mail Order.
A ....
B Edinburgh ... E for Echo, D for Delta, I for India, N for November, B for Bravo, U for Uniform, R for Romeo, G for Golf, H for Hotel ...
A ....
B Oh, good. I was just checking. Have you looked at it yet?
A ....
B I'll hang up and call you back.
A ....

1 Listen. You can hear only B. Decide where A's sentences go in the conversation. (✳ 1.67)

1 Sorry. The reception isn't very good. Could you spell that?
2 Sorry, Colin. Could you speak more slowly?
3 Oh, yes! Edinburgh Mail Order. Your catalogue arrived this morning.
4 Could you repeat that?
5 Hello? Hello?
6 Sorry. I didn't catch that. Could you speak up a bit?
7 Sorry, you're breaking up.

Listen and check, then practise the conversation. (✳ 1.68)

2 These are the standard English words for spelling on the phone.

A Alpha	**H** Hotel	**O** Oscar	**V** Victor
B Bravo	**I** India	**P** Papa	**W** Whisky
C Charlie	**J** Juliet	**Q** Quebec	**X** X-Ray
D Delta	**K** Kilo	**R** Romeo	**Y** Yankee
E Echo	**L** Lima	**S** Sierra	**Z** Zulu
F Foxtrot	**M** Mike	**T** Tango	
G Golf	**N** November	**U** Uniform	

Write down the name of a city, a country, a weekday, a month, a person. Spell them to a partner using the system.

3 Work with a partner. Design a new list. You can't use two words which sound the same (e.g. *Paul* and *ball*). Spell words to another pair.

C I'll call you back ...

1 Listen. Try and match the sentences with the photos. (✱ 1.69)

1. Great! Saturday at eight. I'll be there.
2. Sorry, I'm really busy right now. I'll call you back.
3. Hold on. I'll just look in the catalogue for you.
4. Don't call me on this number. I'll ring you back from a payphone.
5. Yes, sir. I'll give her your message.
6. Yes, all right, I'll hold.

2 Imagine. Who are they speaking to? What is the conversation about?

5 *I think she's a personal assistant. Someone wants to speak to her boss. She is taking a message.*

D Getting through

1 Match the beginnings and endings of these sentences.

1 Thank you for
2 You can book online
3 Please choose from
4 For all other enquiries
5 Your call
6 Please hold. Your call will

A one of the following options.
B be answered shortly.
C calling Super Jet.
D is important to us.
E at www.superjet.co.uk
F please press four.

Listen and check. (✳ 1.70)

2 Mr Lawrence is calling Super Jet.
Listen and find the following information. (✳ 1.71)

His membership number: ....
His postcode: ....
His house number: ....
His date of birth: ....
His flight number: ....
Lost property phone number: ....

What is Mr Lawrence's problem?

3 Listen again. What does the operator say?

(Can / May / Could) I have your membership number?
(Could / Would / Can) you confirm your postcode, Mr Lawrence?
(Can / May / Could) I have the first line of your address?
As a security check, (can / may / could) I have your date of birth?
And how (can / may) I help you today?

Note: all the options are possible.

Polite requests
Can* / *Could* / *Would* / *Will you (give me the information)? NOT ~~*May you*~~ ...
May* / *Can* / *Could I (have the information)? NOT ~~*Would I*~~ ... ~~*Will I*~~ ...

4 Put the prepositions in the sentences. Then listen and check. (✳ 1.72)

to of with in on by

1 Please call Super Jet Customer Services .... 0845 300 300.
2 Please press star, followed .... the extension number.
3 Please press one .... the following numbers.
4 You are through .... the lost property office.
5 Your call is being held .... a queue.
6 Bear .... me while I check our lost property records.

5 Ask and answer.

Where was he flying from?
Where was he sitting?
Where was he flying to?
What's Tracy's suggestion?
Where did he put the documents?

COMMUNICATION

Student A Look at Activity 4 on p.211.
Student B Look at Activity 14 on p.216.

See **Extension 11** p.198

12 Quantity

Everyone has the right to a standa
health and well-being of themselve
food, clothing, housing and medic

A Necessities

1 **Read these sentences and list the necessities.**

We can live for many weeks without food, but only a few days without water.

There are a lot of edible plants, but just four – wheat, rice, maize and potatoes – provide 60% of the world's food.

Oil, gas and coal will not last forever. We need new sources of energy to provide electricity for heat, light and power.

Too many people have too little food. Farmers need pesticides to produce enough food.

In many countries people are living longer because of immunization and antibiotics.

There is too much pollution in many towns, and not enough clean air.

After natural disasters, like earthquakes, people need shelter and sanitation. Without sanitation, disease spreads quickly.

f living adequate for the
nd their families, including
are. *(Universal Declaration of Human Rights, United Nations)*

countable nouns have singular and plural forms.
They are used with words like *a / an, many, few.*
In dictionaries, countable nouns are marked with [C].

uncountable nouns don't have plural forms.
You can't put *a / an* or numbers in front of them.
They are used with singular verbs and words like *much, little.*
In dictionaries, uncountable nouns are marked with [U].

Some words can be [U] or [C].

There are many different pesticides. [C]
There's pesticide on these apples. [U]

2 **How many countable nouns can you find in the texts?**
How many uncountable nouns can you find in the texts?

In China, schoolchildren learn an old rhyme about the seven everyday necessities: firewood, rice, cooking oil, salt, soy sauce, vinegar and tea.

3 **Make a list of your seven everyday necessities.**

B Peace and quiet?

1 Ask and answer.

Do you live in the town or in the country?

Which do you prefer, the town or the country?

What words do you know for farm animals in English?

2 Look at the picture and listen to Helen. (✳ 1.73)
What were her complaints about city life? Choose the correct words.

1 There (was / were) too many problems with city life.
2 There was too (much / many) crime.
3 There (wasn't / weren't) enough policemen.
4 There was far too (many / much) traffic.
5 There was (too / very) much pollution.
6 There (wasn't / weren't) enough fresh air.

too much, too many	... more than you need
enough	... what you need, and no more
not enough	... less than you need

*far: There's **far** too much traffic. / There are **far** too many cars.*

3 Listen to Helen speaking about life in the country. (✳ 1.74)
Match her complaints with the reasons.

We wake up at five		the farmer sprays pesticide on the wheat.
We can't go back to sleep		the cows chase you.
The children can't play outside	**because**	there's pig manure on the fields.
Our cottage is full of smoke		the cockerel starts crowing.
There's a disgusting smell		the farmer has a lot of fires.
You can't walk across the fields		the farmer starts his tractor at 5.30.

C The farmer

1 Look at the picture and listen to the farmer's reply. (✳ 1.75)

Complete these sentences.

1 I've had a lot of ....
2 They complained about a little bit of ....
3 I don't use much ....
4 She's frightened of a few ....

2 Who do you sympathize with, Helen or the farmer? Role-play a conversation between Helen and the farmer.

Uncountable	**Countable**
Is there any water?	*Are there any glasses?*
How much water is there?	*How many glasses are there?*
There's a lot of (water).	*There are a lot of (glasses).*
There isn't much (water).	*There aren't many (glasses).*
There's (only) a little (water).	*There are (only) a few (glasses).*
There's a little bit of (water).	

3 Choose the correct words to complete the sentences.

1 Organic farmers don't use (some / any) pesticide.
2 A lot of the world's oil (come / comes) from the Middle-East.
3 (Many / Much) rivers are full of pollution from factories.
4 We are cutting down too (much / many) trees.
5 Many countries don't have (some / enough) clean water.
6 Only a (few / little) people live in Antarctica.
7 How (many / much) coal is there in Japan?
8 Immunization (have / has) saved children's lives.
9 Hospital doctors have to work too (much / many) hours a week.

D The world today

1 Are these words countable [C] or uncountable [U]?

oil money farms forests coal factories people
clean air jobs food rain pollution fresh water dams
houses schools gas work oil wells doctors traffic
cars noise crime police officers weapons

2 Put the words in the table.

There	's is	too much a lot of some enough a little no	rain.
	isn't	any enough much	
	are	too many a lot of some enough a few no	
	aren't	any enough many	

Don't confuse *too much / many and very much / many.*
I like it very much. NOT ~~*I like it too much*~~.
Fact: *There are a lot of oil wells* ... NOT ~~*There are too many oil wells*~~ ...
Opinion: *There are too many oil wells.* (i.e. There should be fewer)

Think about the world. Make true sentences.
There are too many weapons in the world.
There isn't enough food.

3 Talk about your country.

We haven't got enough ...
We've got a lot of ...
There aren't many ...
There isn't much ...
We've only got a little / few ...
We need more ...
We produce some / a lot of / a little / a few ...
We use a lot of / too much / too many...

E Save it!

1 Interview a partner and complete the questionnaire.

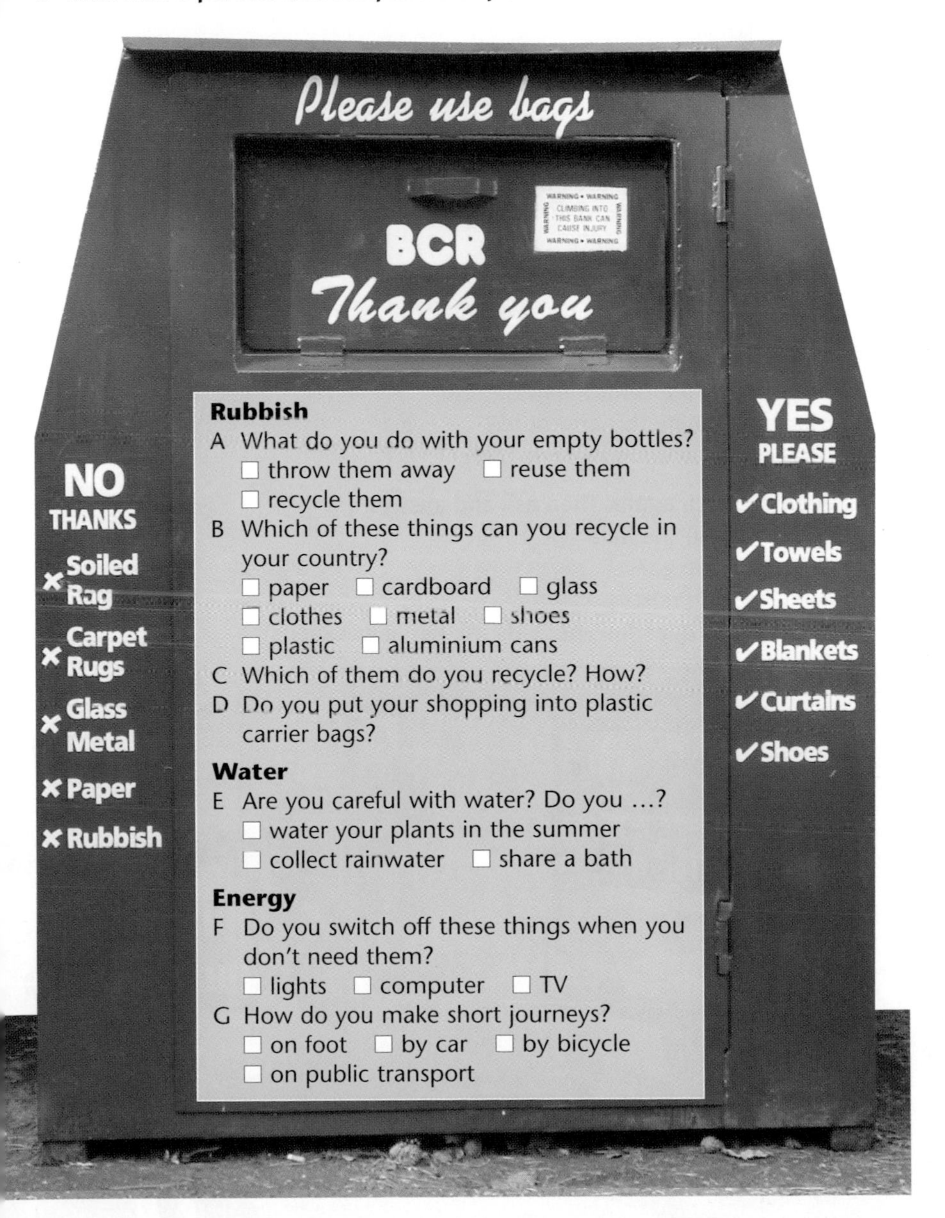

Rubbish

A What do you do with your empty bottles?
- ☐ throw them away ☐ reuse them
- ☐ recycle them

B Which of these things can you recycle in your country?
- ☐ paper ☐ cardboard ☐ glass
- ☐ clothes ☐ metal ☐ shoes
- ☐ plastic ☐ aluminium cans

C Which of them do you recycle? How?

D Do you put your shopping into plastic carrier bags?

Water

E Are you careful with water? Do you ...?
- ☐ water your plants in the summer
- ☐ collect rainwater ☐ share a bath

Energy

F Do you switch off these things when you don't need them?
- ☐ lights ☐ computer ☐ TV

G How do you make short journeys?
- ☐ on foot ☐ by car ☐ by bicycle
- ☐ on public transport

2 How many people in the class try to save energy? Does it make a difference? Will there be rules about saving energy in the future?

See **Extension 12** p.198

13 Futures

A The Office

1 Listen to four of the people in the picture. Identify them on the picture.

(✳ 1.76) Kevin (✳ 1.77) Zoe (✳ 1.78) Debbie (✳ 1.79) Brian

2 Kevin. Listen again. Then ask and answer. (✳ 1.76)
What's he doing tomorrow?
What's he doing tonight?
What are they going to do?
What'll they do while they're watching the match?

3 Zoe. Listen again. Then ask and answer. (✳ 1.77)
What are her plans for the future?
What's she doing this afternoon?
What does she think she'll do tonight?

4 Debbie. Listen again. Then ask and answer. (✳ 1.78)
What time will she finish work?
Where will she go?
What'll she do next?
What are the questions her kids ask her at weekends?

5 Brian. Listen again. What does he actually say? Choose his words. All the choices are correct English. (✳ 1.79)

1. We're planning (to move / on moving / to go) to the country.
2. I ('m going to / 'll / will) play golf everyday.
3. I (will / shall / 'll) have the time at last.
4. I certainly (won't / will / shan't) miss this office.
5. (I'll visit / I'm going to visit / I'm visiting) my wife in hospital.
6. But she ('s going to / 'll / will) be home by the weekend.

6 Imagine. Write a similar text for the fifth person in the picture. Compare your ideas with the class.

7 Talk about your plans for the future, and your plans for this evening.

***shall* in British English**

Shall I ...? / Shall we ...? are used when asking for decisions or instructions.

Shall we ...? is used for suggestions.

Some speakers prefer *shall / shan't* instead of *will / won't* after *I* and *we*. This is formal, and a little old-fashioned.

B *Shall we …? / Shall I …?*

Listen and practise.

(✻ 1.80)

A What shall we have for dinner?
B I don't mind. I don't feel like cooking.
A Nor do I. Let's get a pizza.
B OK.

(✻ 1.81)

C Hi, what are you doing this morning?
D Not much.
C Shall we meet for coffee?
D Good idea. How about Starbucks at eleven?
C Great. See you then.

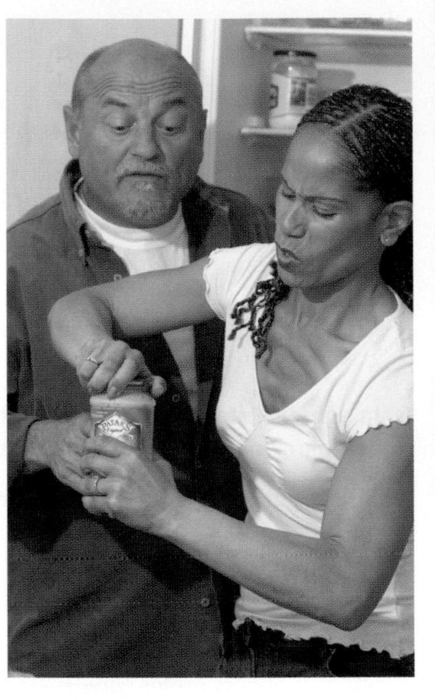

(✻ 1.82)

E I can't open this.
F Shall I have a go?
E It's impossible.
F Well, let me try.

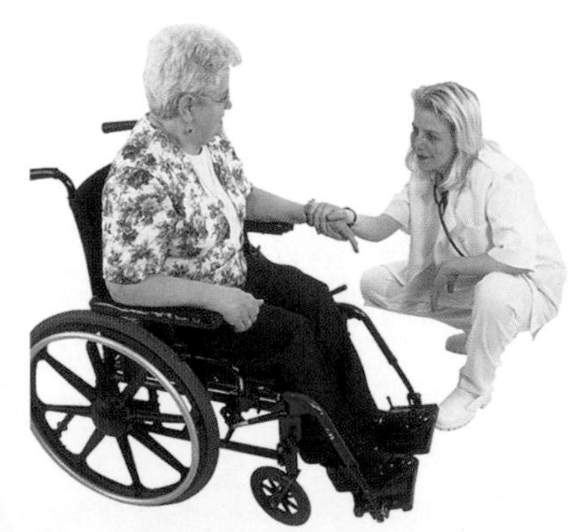

(✻ 1.83)

G How are you today?
H Not too bad. I'm feeling a bit cold.
G Shall I get you a blanket?
H Please. That's very kind of you.

Asking for decisions and instructions:
What *shall we have for dinner?* ***Where*** *shall we go?* ***What*** *shall I do?*
Shall I open the window? NOT ~~*Will I open the window?*~~
Shall I do it? = Let me do it for you. = Do you want me to do it?

Suggestions:
Shall we do it? = Let's do it. = Why don't we do it?
Shall we go out for dinner? NOT ~~*Will we go out for dinner?*~~

C Pronunciation

'll is called the 'dark l' and you hear it at the end of words (like *travel*, *bottle*) as well as the contraction of *will / shall*.

1 Sometimes /l/ is difficult to hear. Listen and underline the sound you hear in the sentences. ✻ 1.84

1	A I	B I'll
2	A What'll	B What
3	A It	B It'll
4	A We'll	B We
5	A Shall	B She'll
6	A You'll	B You
7	A They	B They'll
8	A Who'll	B Who

2 Practise saying *'ll* /l/. If you find it difficult, put an /ʊ/ sound with it, and then say the /ʊ/ sound more and more quietly:

/ʊl/ /ʊl/ /ʊl/ /ʊl/ /l/

Listen and say these sentences. 

1 I'll see you tomorrow.
2 You'll get my letter next week.
3 He'll be at the dance on Saturday.
4 She'll be there too.
5 We'll watch TV this evening.
6 They'll be at the meeting.
7 It'll be dark soon.
8 What'll you see?

shall is used mainly in British English for suggestions.
shall is used in British and American English for laws.
No car ***shall*** *exceed the speed limit.*
The President ***shall*** *be Commander-in-Chief of the Army and Navy* (Constitution of the USA)
shall is used for emphatic statements, as in the song titles.
We Shall Overcome, I Shall Be Released, We Shall Not Be Moved.

D *will, going to*

Decisions with *will* and *going to*
will – we are making a decision. *I'll answer the phone.*
going to – we have already made a decision. *I'm going to buy a new car,* and predictions from information we have now, *It's going to rain.*

I think I'll do it / I don't think I'll do it.
NOT ~~*I think I won't do it.*~~

1 Complete the sentences with *I'll* or *I'm going to.*

1 'Shall we go out tonight?' 'No. I'm tired. I think .... have an early night.'
2 Can I try these shoes on? Great, they're my size. .... take them.
3 'Let me pay for the drinks.' 'No, you paid last time. .... pay.'
4 It's my sister's wedding next week. .... be a bridesmaid.
5 'I don't understand this.' 'OK, ... help you.'
6 I'm graduating from university in June. .... have a big party.
7 I haven't finished yet, but I'm tired. .... finish it later.

2 Group work. Complete three of these sentences about yourself. Write them on a piece of paper.

During the next year ...
I'm definitely going to ...
I'll probably ...
I think I'll ...
I don't think I'll ...
I'm sure I won't ...
I'm definitely not going to ...

Don't show anyone. Put the pieces of paper in a bag. Take them out one at a time. Guess who wrote them.

E *Stay*

Stay
by Maurice Williams

Stay! Ah, just a little bit longer
Stay!
Please! Please, please, please, please
Tell me you're going to.

Now, your daddy don't mind
And your mommy don't mind
If we have another dance
Yeah, just one more time

Oh, won't you stay?
Just a little bit longer
Please let me dance and
Say you will!
Say you will!

Won't you place your sweet lips to mine
Won't you say you love me all of the time

Stay! Just a little bit longer
Stay!
Please! Please, please, please, please
Tell me you're going to.

Oh, won't you stay?
Just a little bit longer
Please let me dance and
Say you will!
Say you will!

Come on, come on,
come on and stay!

Note: In some regional accents (in Britain and America), people say *don't* instead of *doesn't* with *he* / *she* / *it*. You often find this in song lyrics.

Listen, then listen and sing. The class can take different parts of the song. (✳ 1.86)

F Future forms

Look at the grammar notes. There are two examples for each point. Add a third and fourth example from the box below.

Present simple: Timetables (See unit 4)

1 Their train arrives at 8.15. 3 ....
2 The film doesn't start until 7.30. 4 ....

Present continuous: Future plans (See unit 4)

1 I'm playing tennis tomorrow. 3 ....
2 We're meeting her at 10.45. 4 ....

***Going to* (*do*): Intentions (See unit 4)**

1 I'm going to buy a new car. 3 ....
2 They're going to get married. 4 ....

***Going to* (*do*): Predictions from information you have now. (See unit 4)**

1 It's going to be cold tonight. 3 ....
2 She's going to have a baby. 4 ....

***'ll* / *won't* for future reference**

1 We'll be there at nine thirty. 3 ....
2 What time will you get here? 4 ....

***'ll* / *won't* for decisions and promises (See unit 11)**

1 It's OK, I'll answer the door. 3 ....
2 Sorry. I won't do it again. 4 ....

***Will ... ?* for requests and instructions**

1 Will you marry me? 3 ....
2 Will you open your books, please? 4 ....

***Shall ... ?* for asking for decisions / instructions and for suggestions**

1 Which way shall we go? 3 ....
2 Shall we have a drink? 4 ....

I'm going to write to you every day.	The hotel serves dinner from 7.30.
Shall I carry your suitcase?	Will you phone me on Friday?
I'll pay you tomorrow. I promise.	I think it's going to rain.
When does your flight leave?	The taxi will be here soon.
Oh, no. We'll be late for the party!	Shall we get a take-away?
Which doctor are you seeing tomorrow?	I'll have that one.
Will you please be quiet!	He's going to get a new job soon.
England aren't going to win the game.	I'm having lunch with her on Sunday.

See **Extension 13** p.199

14 Men and women

A Stereotypes?

What are the stereotypes of men and women in your country? Are these statements stereotypical? Are they true?

Men are stronger than women.

Men hate shopping.

Men never change the baby's nappies.

Women always do the housework.

Pretty women are more successful in life.

Women don't start wars.

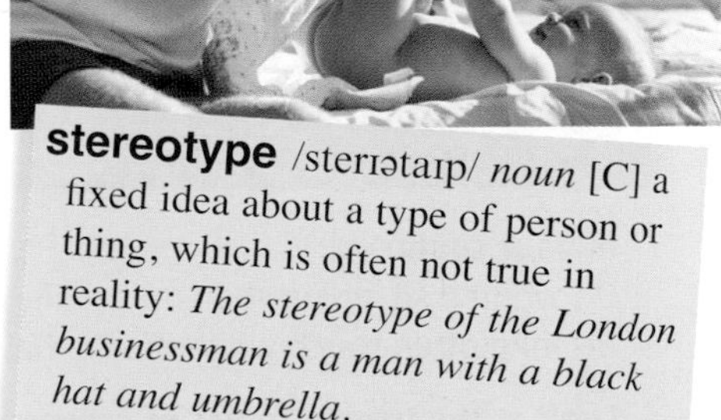

stereotype /steriətaɪp/ *noun* [C] a fixed idea about a type of person or thing, which is often not true in reality: *The stereotype of the London businessman is a man with a black hat and umbrella.*

stereotype *verb* [T] to have or show a fixed idea about a type of person or thing: *In advertisements women are often stereotyped as housewives.*

B Conversation topics

1 In your country ...

Do women sit closer than men while they're having a conversation?
Do men often touch while they're having a conversation?

2 Look at the twenty topics of conversation on page 87. Listen. What are the topics in these five conversations?

audio	✻ 1.87	✻ 1.88	✻ 1.89	✻ 1.90	✻ 1.91
topic					

3 How often do you talk about the topics in the table? Complete the table with numbers 0–6.

6 = all the time 5 = frequently 4 = quite often 3 = sometimes
2 = occasionally 1 = hardly ever 0 = never

The Top Twenty Topics of conversation (not in order)	to men friends	to women friends
current news and politics		
relationships and feelings		
work: business or academic		
health, diet		
sport, exercise		
sex		
family: children, parents, pets		
hobbies		
fashion, clothes, cosmetics, etc.		
music		
culture: art, literature, film, etc.		
religion, spiritual topics		
food, drink and recipes		
TV programmes		
things: cars, hi-fi, appliances, etc.		
money		
celebrities, royalty		
gossip (informal talk about other people's private lives)		
travel, holidays		
jokes, funny stories		

4 Look at the scores. Discuss:

What are the most popular three topics?
What are the least popular three topics?
Are the popular topics different for men and women?
What do you most like talking about?
What do you least like talking about?

COMMUNICATION

Find the results of a British survey on topics of conversation.
Student A Look at Activity 5 on p. 212.
Student B Look at Activity 15 on p. 217.

sad

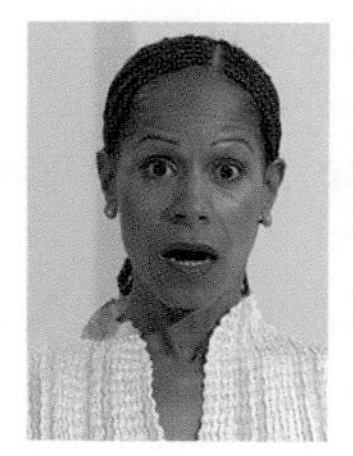
surprised

angry

happy

afraid

C Men and women

(✱ 1.92)

WOMEN AND MEN

- On average, men are taller and heavier than women.
- Women talk more than men (23,000 words a day v 12,000 words a day).
- Men have greater spatial awareness. They are better at reading maps than women, better at parking cars, target sports and playing video games.
- Women are better at multi-tasking. This means doing several things at the same time. Men prefer doing a single task.
- At school, girls are more co-operative. Boys are more competitive.
- Women apologize more often in conversation.
- The most important thing in life? Most men chose their work. Most women chose being a mother.
- When they're listening, women smile more, use more facial expressions, and use a greater number of sounds. Men use fewer sounds, and nod their heads.
- Women are less aggressive drivers. 92% of car horn 'toots' come from men drivers. Women have fewer accidents than men while driving.
- Women are better at hearing small sounds, but worse at saying where the sounds are coming from. More women than men can sing in tune.

1 **Look at the points in the text. Do you agree with them? If not, why not?**

2 **Here is an example of multi-tasking.** Stand up next to a table. With one hand, mime cleaning your teeth, moving the toothbrush up and down. With the other hand, mime polishing the table, moving your hand in circles. Count aloud backwards from ten to one. Do these actions at the same time.

Do men or women find this easier?

sad

surprised

angry

happy

afraid

3 Rewrite these sentences so that the meaning stays the same.

On average, men are taller than women.	Women *are shorter than men.*
On average, women are lighter than men.	Men ...
Women talk more than men.	Men ...
Men are worse at multi-tasking.	Women ...
Women are less aggressive drivers.	Men ...
Women have fewer accidents.	Men ...
Women use more facial expressions.	Men ...
Men are better at parking.	Women ...
Men apologize less often than women.	Women ...

superlative	**comparative**		**comparative**	**superlative**
the smallest	smaller	small / big	bigger	the biggest
the worst	worse	bad / good	better	the best
the least important	less important	important	more important	the most important

comparatives are for **comparing** things.
This one is better than that one.
She's taller than anyone else in her class.

superlatives are for **selecting** things from a group, and placing them first.
It's the best film I've ever seen. (Selecting from all the films I've seen)
I'll take the red one, not the pink one. The red one's the nicest.

We usually put *than* after a comparative and *the* before a superlative.

4 Think about your family and friends. Tell your partner.

Who is the oldest / the youngest?
Who's got the most children?
Who speaks the best English?
Who talks the most / the least?
Who tells the best jokes?
Who's the worst driver?
Who's had the most jobs?
Who do you see the most / least often?
Who's the tallest? / the strongest? / the shyest? / the kindest?
Who is the most generous? / the most aggressive?

D A man's world

1 Read this story. How is it possible?

There was a terrible road accident. A man and his son were in the car. An ambulance took them both to hospital, but the father died on the way. They took the son straight to the operating theatre. The surgeon looked at the boy and said, 'Oh, no! This is my son! I can't do the operation!'

It's a man's world ...

- 100% of British bricklayers are men.
- 89% of politicians in the world are men. (But in China and Sweden 50% of politicians have to be women.)
- 98% of the richest people in the world are men.
- 80% of children with reading difficulties are boys.
- 88% of murderers are men.
- 96% of burglars are men.
- 100% of British dental nurses are women.
- 75% of foreign language teachers in Britain are women.
- 82% of physics teachers are men.
- More than 50% of medical students are women, but 91% of the best-paid senior doctors are men.
- In Britain, girls get higher grades in school exams.
- Women doing the same jobs as men earn less. On average they earn 88% of the male salary.

2 Read the statistics. They all come from different surveys. Do you think they're accurate? If so, what are the reasons for these differences? Do you think some jobs are more suitable for men / women?

> There are three kinds of lies: lies, damned lies, and statistics.
>
> *Mark Twain.*

See **Extension 14** p.199

15 Obligation and advice

A Signs

You must do it. = You have to do it. = strong obligation.
You mustn't do it. = You can't do it. = prohibition.
You should do it. / *You shouldn't do it.* = advice or weak obligation.
You can do it. = It is permitted.

Read the signs. Complete the sentences with *must* / *mustn't* / *can* / *should* / *shouldn't.*

1 You .... park on the access road.
2 You .... remove valuable items when you leave your car.
3 You .... wear smart clothes when you visit this pub.
4 You .... play ball games on the road next to the beach.
5 Cars in the right lane .... go straight on.
6 You .... play ball games on the beach.
7 You .... leave litter in this tourist area.
8 Cars in the right lane .... turn right.

B Warnings

When you choose *must* or *should*, it depends on these things:

- Who are you speaking to? (*must* is stronger than *should*)
- Are you giving an order? (*must*)
- Do you want to be more polite? (*should*)
- Are you warning someone or giving advice? (*should*)

You mustn't smoke! You can't smoke here! (It's dangerous / illegal)
You should check your tyres. (It's a good idea)

Imagine: You're the attendant at a petrol station.
What are you going to say to the driver? Begin:

You must ... *You mustn't ...* *You can't ...*
You should ... *You shouldn't ...*

C Rules

THE ENGLISH MUSEUM

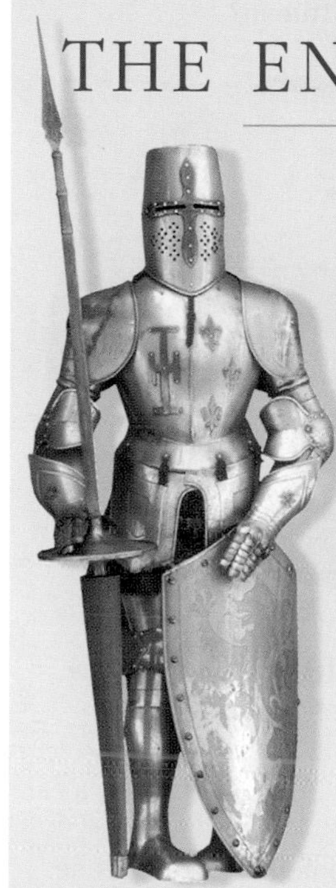

- Admission is free. Please make a donation. We suggest £5 per adult and £3 per student or child.
- Children under 16 are not allowed in the museum without an adult.
- No dogs allowed.
- Please leave bags and umbrellas in the cloakroom.
- Smoking, eating and drinking is prohibited in the museum, but is permitted in the Cromwell Café.
- Do not touch any of the exhibits.
- Flash photography is strictly forbidden.

1 Ask and answer.

Do you have to pay to get in?
Should you make a donation?
Can you take bags into the museum?
Where do you have to leave them?
Are photos without flash permitted?
Where can you eat and drink in the museum?

2 Put the letters into the table.

A *You can do it.*
B *You mustn't do it. / You can't do it.*
C *You must do it. / You have to do it.*

1 It is allowed. / It is permitted.	A
2 It is not allowed / It is not permitted.	
3 It is prohibited.	
4 It is forbidden.	
5 Do not do this.	
6 Do this.	

3 Tell someone about the museum rules. Begin:

You must / You have to ... *You mustn't / You can't ...* *You should ...*

D Obligation

1 Do you know which countries these things are true in?

- You must wear a seat belt in cars.
- You should take off your shoes when you enter someone's home.
- You shouldn't give people things with your left hand.
- You mustn't drink and drive.
- You must not carry an open bottle of alcohol in the street or in a car.
- You should never touch people on the head.
- You should use two hands when you pass something to someone.
- You must not smoke in restaurants.
- On trains, you must give your seat to people who were injured in wars.
- You must display your insurance certificate on your car.
- You mustn't chew gum in the street.
- You can cross a red traffic light if you are turning right.

COMMUNICATION

Student A Look at Activity 3 on p.211. Tell your partner the answers.
Student B Look at Activity 16 on p.217. Tell your partner the answers.

must = have to (obligation)
*American visitors to the UK **must** have a passport.*
mustn't is for an obligation **not** to do something.
*You **mustn't** travel without a passport.*
needn't = don't have to (there is no obligation)
*American visitors to the UK **needn't** have a visa.*

2 Compare your country.

You can (do this).
You should (do this) too. / You must (do this) too.
You shouldn't (do this) either. / You mustn't (do this) either.
You needn't (do this) / worry about (this) in my country.

E Opinion

We use *They should* ... to give opinions. Often we don't know who 'they' are. Sometimes it's the government, or the town council, or the management of a company, or people in authority.

1 **What are they protesting about?**
Find the slogans to match these opinions:
They should stop killing whales.
They should pay women the same as men for the same job.
They should ban weapons of mass destruction.
They should pay teachers more.
They shouldn't build the new road.
They should ban genetically-modified food.
Rich countries should cancel the debts of poor countries.

2 **What do you feel strongly about? Give your opinions.**
They should spend more on ... / less on ...
They should build more ... / fewer ...
They should stop ... / ban ...
They should help ...
They shouldn't ...

F 'The Money Doctor'

1 **Damian has an expensive lifestyle. He spends far more than he earns, and he's in debt. He owes his credit card company a lot of money. These are some of the things that he has spent money on this week. How can he save money?**
He should stop smoking. / He shouldn't buy cigarettes.

'The Money Doctor' is a TV programme. Every week Liz Patterson gives financial advice to someone with money problems. This week she's with Damian.

2 Listen. (✳ 1.93)
Complete the sentences.
Damian is spending ....
He can earn .... or he can spend ....
He can't take a second job because he doesn't have .... free time.
He must cut .... his spending.
He must give .... some of his expensive habits.
He .... afford the monthly payments on his credit card.

3 Listen.
What is Liz's solution? (✳ 1.94)

LIZ'S ANALYSIS
Problem: *Gym membership is expensive.*
Solution:
Savings: *Gym membership, petrol, car park.*

4 Listen.
Complete the box. (✳ 1.95)

LIZ'S ANALYSIS
Problem:
Solution:
Savings:

5 Listen.
Complete the box. (✳ 1.96)

LIZ'S ANALYSIS
Problem:
Solution:
Savings:

6 Listen. What does Liz say? (✳ 1.97)
You (☐ shouldn't ☐ mustn't) buy lottery tickets.
You (☐ should ☐ must) cut up your credit card.

7 Role-play Liz and Damian. Talk about the other things in the pictures and give advice.

8 List the things you spend too much on. Look at your partner's list. Role-play Liz and give advice.

See **Extension 15** p.200

16 Starting a conversation

A Questionnaire

Interview your partner and complete the questionnaire.

Are you an introvert or an extrovert?

1 You're in a class. The teacher has just asked a question. You know what the answer is. What do you do?
A answer immediately **B** wait for the teacher to ask you
C hope the teacher won't ask you

2 A new person started work today. You've just finished work. The new person sees you and says, 'Let's go for a coffee.' What do you say?
A 'Great!' **B** 'I'm sorry. I can't.' **C** 'I'm busy now, but how about tomorrow?'

3 When you meet new people, how do you feel?
A Shy and quiet. **B** Interested. You like meeting people. **C** You try to impress them.

4 You're at a party. You've just met three new people. Suddenly there's a silence in the conversation. Do you ...?
A speak first **B** wait for someone else to speak first **C** feel embarrassed and say nothing

5 Which of these statements best describes you?
A I'm happiest by myself **B** I'm happiest with a few close friends **C** I'm happiest with a crowd of people

6 You're learning a new expression in English. Would you rather ...?
A Say it aloud straight away
B Listen, then repeat it **C** Just read it

COMMUNICATION

Activity 20 on p.219 – find your partner's score.

B Starting a conversation

1 We often ask questions at the beginning of a conversation with strangers. Can you think of three questions to ask in these situations?

You're flying home. The British person next to you is travelling to your country.

You're meeting a foreign business visitor. She's just arrived.

You're talking to a tourist in your country.

You're at a friend's party. You're talking to a stranger.

2 Match three questions to each situation in 1. Are they the same as the questions you thought of?

How was the flight?	How do you know (my friend)?
Are you travelling on business or for pleasure?	What do you think of (my town)?
How long have you been here?	Is this your first visit to (my country)?
What do you do?	Have you known (my friend) long?
Have you seen (the castle) yet?	What was the weather like when you left?
Do you speak (my language)?	Excuse me, are you (Mr / Ms Smith)?

3 Role-play the conversations in the situations.

C Indirect questions

Direct *wh-* question	**Indirect *wh-* question**
question + verb + subject	question phrase + subject + verb
What is it?	*Do you know what it is?*
Where did he go?	*Could you tell me where he went?*
Direct question	**Indirect question**
Is the train late?	*Do you know if the train is late?*
Does this bus go to London?	*Can you tell me if this bus goes to London?*

1 **Listen. Then change the indirect questions in the cartoons to direct questions.** (✳ 2.02)

Listen and check. Which sound more polite, the direct questions or the indirect questions? (✳ 2.03)

2 Negative polite replies. Ask the questions in the cartoons and reply politely. (✳ 2.04)

► Do you know what it is?

◄ No, sorry. I don't know what it is.

► Can you tell me if this bus goes to London?

◄ No, sorry. I don't know if this bus goes to London.

3 Put the subjects in the correct place.

subject	direct question	indirect question
1 the bank	Where is?	Can you tell me where is?
• *Where is the bank?*		*Can you tell me where the bank is?*
2 this ring	How much does cost?	Could you tell me how much costs?
3 they	Will be there?	Do you know if will be there?
4 Tom	Where does live?	Do you know where lives?
5 the train	When did leave?	Could you tell me when left?
6 Anna	Is at home?	Can you tell me if is at home?

D Getting a response

The weather is a good neutral starting point for conversations. One of the most famous expressions in English is *It's a nice day, isn't it?*

... *isn't it?* is a tag question. We add question tags to sentences because the listener has to respond (usually they agree with the speaker!).
We add negative tags to positive sentences. *It is nice, isn't it?*
We add positive tags to negative sentences. *It isn't nice, is it?*

1 Match the tag questions to possible responses.

1 It's a nice day, isn't it?	A No. Brrr!
2 It was a cold morning, wasn't it?	B Yes, it has, really lovely.
3 It won't rain this afternoon, will it?	C Yes, it certainly did.
4 It isn't very warm today, is it?	D Yes, I hope it will.
5 That wasn't thunder, was it?	E Yes, it is. Very nice.
6 It rained all day yesterday, didn't it?	F No, it wasn't. I don't think so.
7 The weather's been lovely, hasn't it?	G Yes, it was. Freezing!
8 It'll be hot again tomorrow, won't it?	H No, I don't think so./I hope not.

Listen to the conversations. (✳ 2.05)

2 Tag questions have a falling intonation when they're asking for agreement (this is most of the time).
It's a lovely day, isn't it?

Add question tags. Then listen and practise the falling intonation.
(✳ 2.06)

1 You'll be here tomorrow, ... you?
2 You can come to the meeting, ... you?
3 You don't know the answer, ... you?
4 It's a great restaurant, ... it?
5 He didn't phone, ... he?
6 We should leave soon, ... we?

E Being a better listener

1 Match the sounds in red to the meanings.

1 **Uh-huh** ... What happened next?	A What a surprise!
2 **Eh**? Can you repeat that?	B I understand.
3 **Ah**! Now I get it. Very funny.	C Pardon? I didn't hear.
4 **Oh**! I thought he was married!	D I'm not sure. Let me think.
5 **Um** ... the answer's ... **er** ... **um** ... 62?	E This is very nice!
6 **Ooh**! It's lovely! Thank you.	F I'm listening. Go on ...

Listen and check. (✱ 2.07)

2 Act out this conversation from a soap opera.

A You never listen to me, do you?
B Eh? What did you say?
A You never listen to me!
B Ah. Sorry. I was reading the paper.
A Do you know what I was talking about?
B Um, yes, you ... er ... um ...
A I was telling you about Carol Foster.
B Yeah?
A She's getting married.
B What, Carol?
A Yes, Carol.

B Oh! I thought she was about seventy.
A No, she isn't. She's only fifty-five.
B She looks seventy.
A Well, she met this man in the supermarket car park ...
B Uh-huh.
A She crashed into his car.
B Mmm ...
A She was so nervous. He took her into the café and bought her a cup of tea.
B Uh-huh.
A They started talking, and he asked her out. That was two weeks ago.
B Eh?
A He's bought her a beautiful diamond ring. It cost two thousand pounds.
B Oh! Do you know how old he is?
A Yes. Thirty-seven.
B I don't believe it! I just don't believe it.

See **Extension 16** p.200

17 Possessions

A *How long?*

Jean

We decorated this room when we got married. Most of the things were wedding presents, so we didn't choose them ourselves. We've been married for thirty years, and we haven't changed very much. We aren't planning to change anything either. Actually, I don't like the furniture. And the carpet's a horrible colour. I've never liked it, but it hasn't worn out yet. I hate throwing good things away. The newest thing in the room is the television. We bought that ten years ago. We've looked after everything. I would like a new sofa one day, but I'll keep this one until it has worn out.

1 Listen, then match the questions and answers. (✱ 2.08)

1 When did they get married?	A For thirty years.
2 How long have they been married?	B Ten years old.
3 When did they buy the TV?	C Thirty years ago.
4 How long have they had the TV?	D Ten years ago.
5 How old is the TV?	E For ten years.

2 Ask and answer.

Did they choose the furniture? Why not?
Have they changed much? Why not?
Why hasn't she thrown the carpet away?
When will they buy a new sofa?

Darius

I really must have the latest gadgets. I love buying new things. I've had my phone since last January, and I'll probably keep it until next January. Then I'll get a newer model. I don't keep things for long. I get bored quickly. It's a throwaway society. I've had loads of computers. I usually change them once a year. You know, the next one will be twice as powerful and half the price! I've only had my car for a year, but I've just seen the new Volkswagen. I'll probably get one. I bought this flat in 2004. It's great, but I'm planning to move soon. I'd like a bigger place.

3 Listen, then match the questions and answers. (✳ 2.09)

1 When did he buy his phone?	A Since last January.
2 How long has he had his phone?	B In 2004.
3 How long will he keep the phone?	C Since 2004.
4 When did he buy his flat?	D In January.
5 How long has he had his flat?	E For a year.
6 How long has he had his car?	F Until next January.

4 Ask and answer.

How many computers has he had? How often does he change them?
Which new car has he just seen? Is he going to get one?
Why doesn't he keep things for long?

5 Imagine.

What kind of people are Jean and her husband?
Do you know anyone like them?
What kind of person is Darius?
Do you know anyone like him?

B *for, since, until*

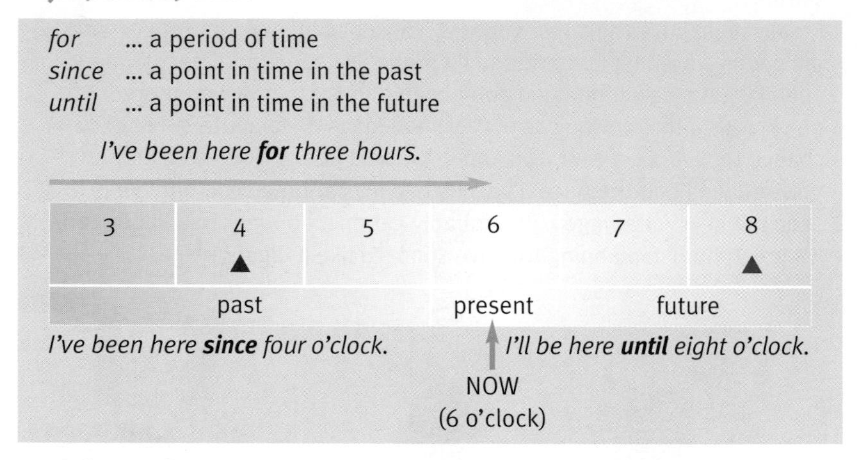

1 Make two lists: words with *for* and words with *since*.

two weeks   a long time   five years   June 21st   six months
Thursday   Christmas   two days   July   4 o'clock   2003

2 Make two lists: words with *until* and words with *since*.

next February   last March   tomorrow   yesterday   2025
last Saturday   2004   next weekend   next summer   last winter

3 Pronunciation of *for*. Unstressed /fə/ or stressed /fɔː/ (✳ 2.10)
Listen. Which words in bold are /fə/? Which are /fɔː/?

1 I've been here **for four** years.
2 Who is this **for**?
3 We've been friends **for** years.
4 What do you want it **for**?
5 I'd like a table **for four** people.
6 Sorry, **for** how many people?

Say the sentences, then listen again and repeat.

4 Pair work. Ask and answer the questions.

What's your oldest possession? How long have you had it?	What was the first music album that you bought? Have you still got it? How long have you had it?
What's your most recent purchase? How long have you had it? How long will you keep it?	What's your oldest item of clothing? How long have you had it / them? Is it / Are they worn out yet?
Which male friend have you known the longest? How long have you known him? Ask about a female friend.	Who sits next to you in class? How long have you known him / her?

C Possessions

1 How many of these items do you own? Tick the boxes.

☐ a watch	☐ a hairdryer	☐ a mobile phone	☐ trainers
☐ glasses	☐ sunglasses	☐ a purse	☐ a wallet
☐ a personal stereo	☐ a camera	☐ gloves	☐ a penknife

2 The questions below are for a singular item (e.g. a watch). Rewrite the questions for a plural item (e.g. glasses).

1 How long have you had it?
2 Did you buy it or was it a present?
3 Was it cheap or expensive?
4 Is it the latest model / fashion?
5 Is it already out-of-date / old-fashioned?
6 Has it worn out yet?
7 How often do you usually replace this item?
8 How long will you keep this one?
9 When you get a new one, what will you do with the old one?

3 Pair work. Ask your partner about the items they have ticked in 1.

D Jackie Chan

1 Ask and answer.

Have you seen any Jackie Chan films?
Which ones have you seen?
Have you bought any of his videos or DVDs?

2 Listen and read. (✻ 2.11)

3 Give titles to the three paragraphs in the text opposite.

An International Star / Early Days / Injuries

4 Paragraph 1. Complete the spaces with words from the box.

when then in after for

1 He was born .... 1954.
2 He was six .... he moved to Australia.
3 He lived in Australia .... a year.
4 He left the Dance Academy .... ten years.
5 He worked as a stunt man, ... he became a star.

5 Paragraph 2. Point to these parts of your body:

fingers leg shoulders ribs brain
jaw arm nose knee ankle

Ask and answer.

1 Which bones has Jackie Chan broken?
2 How many times has he broken his nose?
3 How many fingers has he broken?
4 What happened while he was filming *Armour of God*?
5 What other things have happened to him?
6 Have you ever broken any bones?

6 Paragraph 3. Ask and answer.

1 Who does the stunts in his films?
2 Why couldn't the studio get insurance?
3 How many films has he made?
4 How do audiences know that the stunts are real?

Past participle groups (see unit 8)

A B B live / lived / lived	A B C know / knew / known
A B A come / came / come	A A A put / put/ put

7 Which groups are these verbs in?

become, break, buy, do, have, hit, jump, make, see, walk, win

Jackie Chan has won fans all over the world with his unique mix of action, drama and comedy and has become an international star. He was born in Hong Kong in 1954, and moved to Australia for a year when he was six. On his return to Hong Kong he joined the city's China Drama Academy and studied classical Chinese dance theatre. He left after ten years when he was seventeen. His ability in martial arts got him work as a stunt man, then he became a star in kung-fu films.

During his career, Jackie has broken his jaw, his nose three times, two fingers, his knee, his ankle, several of his ribs, his shoulders and he has had brain surgery. During the film *Armour of God* (1986), he had to jump from a castle onto a tree. He missed, fell ten metres, and hit his head on a rock. He almost died, and still has a small hole in his head. A helicopter has hit him, he has walked across burning coals (he burned his hair) and has jumped from a mountain onto a hot-air balloon.

He has always done his own stunts, and when he started making films in Hollywood, the studio couldn't get insurance for him. Since then he has starred in films like *Rush Hour, Shanghai Knights* and *Around The World in 80 Days.* Jackie Chan has made more than one hundred films. Audiences know that his stunts are real, because the closing credits of his films show the stunts that went wrong. He said, 'Because so many children see my films, all my action films have lots of fighting, but no blood. There's no sex, or violence or politics in my films.'

See **Extension 17** p.201

18 Speech

A *say, tell, ask*

1 Listen and practise. (✱ 2.12)

Rachel	Oh no! The phone ... can you get it, Kelly? I can't talk to anyone at the moment.
Kelly	Hi, Kelly here.
Oliver	This is Oliver. Is Rachel there?
Kelly	Hang on ... it's Oliver.
Rachel	Not now. Tell him I'm busy.
Kelly	Sorry, Oliver, she's busy ...
Rachel	Ask him to ring back in an hour.
Kelly	Sorry, hang on, Oliver ... What did you say?
Rachel	Ask him to ring back in an hour.
Kelly	Can you ring her back in an hour?
Oliver	Mmm, that's a bit difficult. I've got an appointment.
Kelly	He says he's got an appointment.
Rachel	Tell him I'll call him tonight.
Kelly	She says she'll call you tonight.
Oliver	Ask her what time.
Kelly	What time?
Rachel	Oh, give me the phone. I'll speak to him now. You finish the cooking.

say, tell, ask

- After *tell*, put an object pronoun or name.
  Tell ***him / Oliver*** *I'm busy.* NOT ~~*Tell I'm busy.*~~
- *ask* and *tell* + infinitive is used for instructions.
  Ask / Tell *them to wait.* (*ask* is more polite) But NOT ~~*Say them to wait.*~~
- Don't put an object pronoun or name directly after *say*.
  Say *I'm very sorry.* NOT ~~*Say him I'm very sorry.*~~
- You can use *to / from* with *say* and an object.
  Say hello ***to her****. Say hello* ***from me****.*

2 This is a description of a phone conversation. Choose the correct word in brackets.

A Mrs Cook answers the phone and (says / tells) her name.

B Simon (tells / says) Hello.
C Simon (asks / tells) to speak to Mandy.

D She (says / tells) him Mandy's out.

E Simon (says / asks) when she'll be back.

F She (says / tells) she doesn't know.

G He (asks / tells) for Mandy's mobile number.

H She (says / asks) him for his name.

I He (says / tells) her his name.

J She (tells / says) him the number.

K He (tells / says) thank you, and goodbye.

L She (tells / says) goodbye to him.

3 Match the sentences below to the descriptions above.

1 Oh, dear. When will she be back?
2 Could you give me her mobile number?
3 Hello. Belinda Cook speaking.
4 Sorry. I'm Simon Nolan, a friend from college.
5 Goodbye.
6 Hello, Mrs Cook.
7 I don't know. She didn't tell me.
8 Uh, well ... who's speaking?
9 Can I speak to Mandy, please?
10 Ah, yes. Simon. It's 07973 081254.
11 I'm afraid she's out.
12 Thank you very much, Mrs Cook. Goodbye.

4 Listen and check. Practise the conversation. 

B Fiction (✻ 2.14)

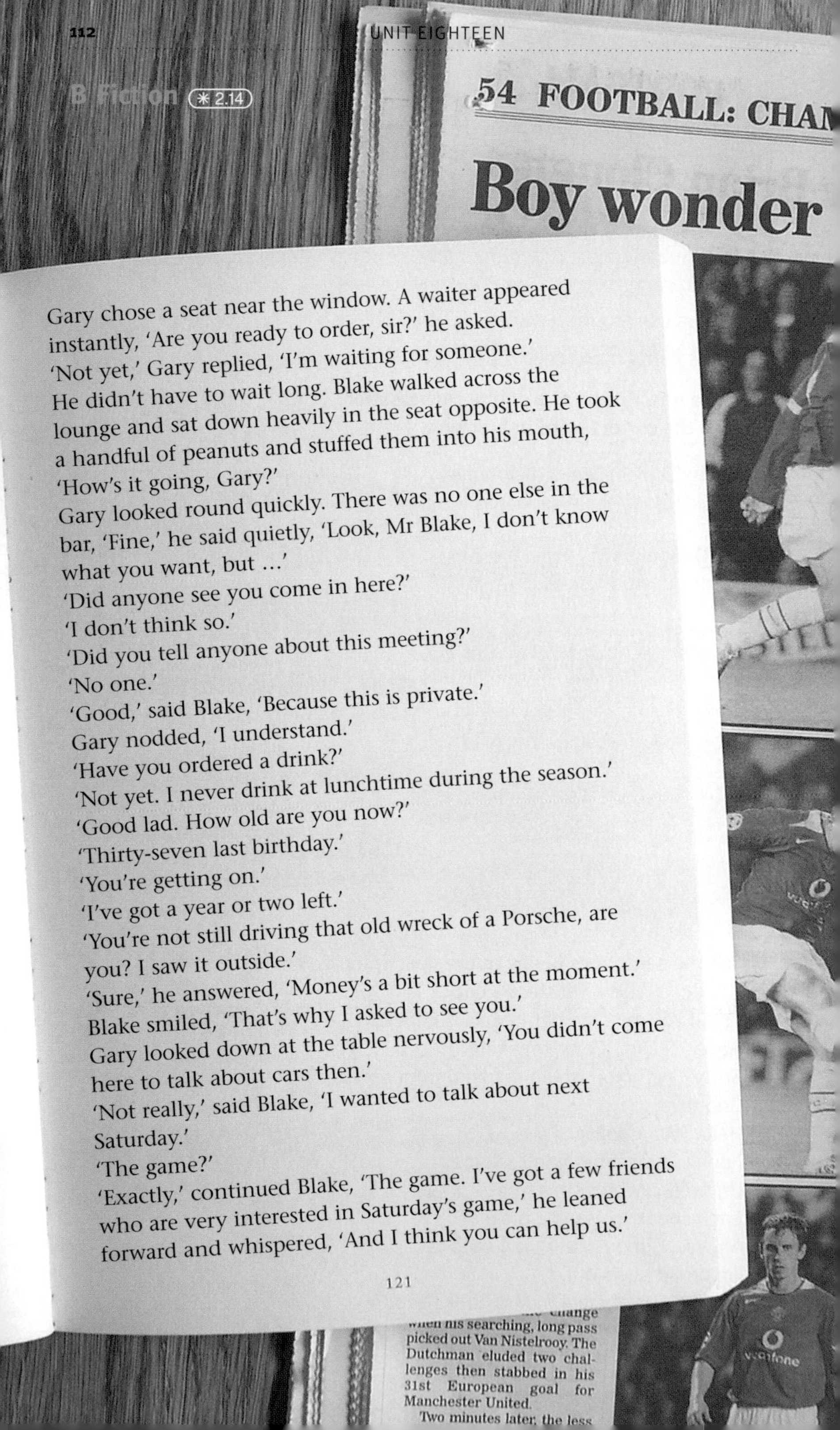

54 FOOTBALL: CHAM

Boy wonder

Gary chose a seat near the window. A waiter appeared instantly, 'Are you ready to order, sir?' he asked.
'Not yet,' Gary replied, 'I'm waiting for someone.'
He didn't have to wait long. Blake walked across the lounge and sat down heavily in the seat opposite. He took a handful of peanuts and stuffed them into his mouth, 'How's it going, Gary?'
Gary looked round quickly. There was no one else in the bar, 'Fine,' he said quietly, 'Look, Mr Blake, I don't know what you want, but …'
'Did anyone see you come in here?'
'I don't think so.'
'Did you tell anyone about this meeting?'
'No one.'
'Good,' said Blake, 'Because this is private.'
Gary nodded, 'I understand.'
'Have you ordered a drink?'
'Not yet. I never drink at lunchtime during the season.'
'Good lad. How old are you now?'
'Thirty-seven last birthday.'
'You're getting on.'
'I've got a year or two left.'
'You're not still driving that old wreck of a Porsche, are you? I saw it outside.'
'Sure,' he answered, 'Money's a bit short at the moment.'
Blake smiled, 'That's why I asked to see you.'
Gary looked down at the table nervously, 'You didn't come here to talk about cars then.'
'Not really,' said Blake, 'I wanted to talk about next Saturday.'
'The game?'
'Exactly,' continued Blake, 'The game. I've got a few friends who are very interested in Saturday's game,' he leaned forward and whispered, 'And I think you can help us.'

121

… change when his searching, long pass picked out Van Nistelrooy. The Dutchman eluded two challenges then stabbed in his 31st European goal for Manchester United.
Two minutes later, the less

You're getting on = You're getting older
Money's a bit short = I'm short of money = I haven't got enough money
an old wreck = an old car in bad condition

Fiction uses **direct speech** more frequently than non-fiction texts.

1 **Read this extract from a novel. Put *G* next to things Gary says, and *B* next to the things that Blake says.**

2 ***Said* is a reporting verb. Underline the other reporting verbs.**

3 **How do they do / say it? Find the adverbs of manner (e.g. *quietly*).**

Adverbs of manner tell us **how** someone did something.
'OK,' he replied ***quickly****.* *She looked at him* ***sadly****.*
'Yes,' he said ***softly****.*
Regular adverbs of manner end in *–ly*: *badly, slowly, angrily*

4 **Act out the conversation. Act out the words they say and the actions too.**

C Writing

Quotation marks (quotes)
In English, quotations marks are like this: 'Hello' or "Hello".
In handwriting, we often use double marks ("..."). In typing, single marks ('...') are more frequent. Both are correct.

Put a comma, a question mark, a full stop or an exclamation mark at the end of the direct speech.

'What?' she asked. 'I don't know,' he said. 'Nonsense!' she replied.
He said, 'I don't believe it.'

1 **Read the text in 1 again. Circle the commas.**

2 **Punctuate these sentences.**

"..." , ? ! .

1 Don't say any more said Gary quickly
2 No said Blake Can you just listen for a minute
3 There's £100,000 for you if you do it he added
4 He looked into Gary's eyes It's easy You just let the ball go past you
5 Gary stood up and spoke angrily I won't do it he said
6 We're 3rd in the league he said And City are 20th
7 That's why we're going to do it replied Blake
8 You see continued Blake Nobody thinks City can win, but they will

3 **Act out the conversation.**

D Reporting verbs

1 Guess which words go in the spaces. There are several possible correct answers.

said whispered warned answered begged told called added suggested shouted promised replied hissed complained

2 Listen, then complete the spaces from memory. (✳ 2.15)

Romeo looked up at the dark balcony, 'Julie,' he .... softly.
There was no reply.
'Julie!' he ....
The door opened and Julie came out onto the balcony, 'Keep your voice down!' she .... , 'You'll wake them.'
'I couldn't sleep,' he .... , 'I was thinking about you.'
'Pardon?' she .... , 'You're too quiet. I can't hear you.'
'Can't you come downstairs?' he .... , a little more loudly.
'What? Now? I was asleep,' she .... , 'And you woke me up,' she ....
'I've brought a ladder,' he .... , 'Climb down.'
'I can't,' she ....
'Please ...' he ....
'No! But I'll speak to you tomorrow,' she ....
Suddenly they heard her mother's voice, 'Julie! Who are you talking to?'
'Hurry! She'll see you!' Julie .... him.
'Goodnight Julie!'
'Go now! Before my father wakes up!' she .... him.

Listen again and check.

This is a practice text. No real story would use this many reporting verbs.

3 Act out the conversation.

See **Extension 18** p.201

19 Made in ...

A Labels

1 **Read the labels and guess what items they are from. Check.**

COMMUNICATION

Activity 7 on p.212.

2 **Ask and answer.**
What things are manufactured in (name of country)?
What is produced in (name of country)?

Evian water ***is*** *produced in France.* (uncountable)
Boeing planes ***are*** *made in the USA* (countable)

B Film locations

1 Read

For many years most American films were made in Hollywood. Studios were built in Southern California for two reasons. The weather was good all the year round, and near Hollywood a great variety of locations could be found; city, desert, countryside, forest, ocean and mountains. Nowadays film companies look for new locations and films are made all over the world.

2 Match the photos to the places on the map.

Do you know which films they are from?
Complete the last column on the table.

3 Talk about the films.

Who was *Lord of The Rings* directed by?
When was it made?
Where was this scene filmed?

Scene
The Planet Tatooir
The ship
Rydell High Schoo
The Misty Mounta
Hogwarts school
Gladiator school

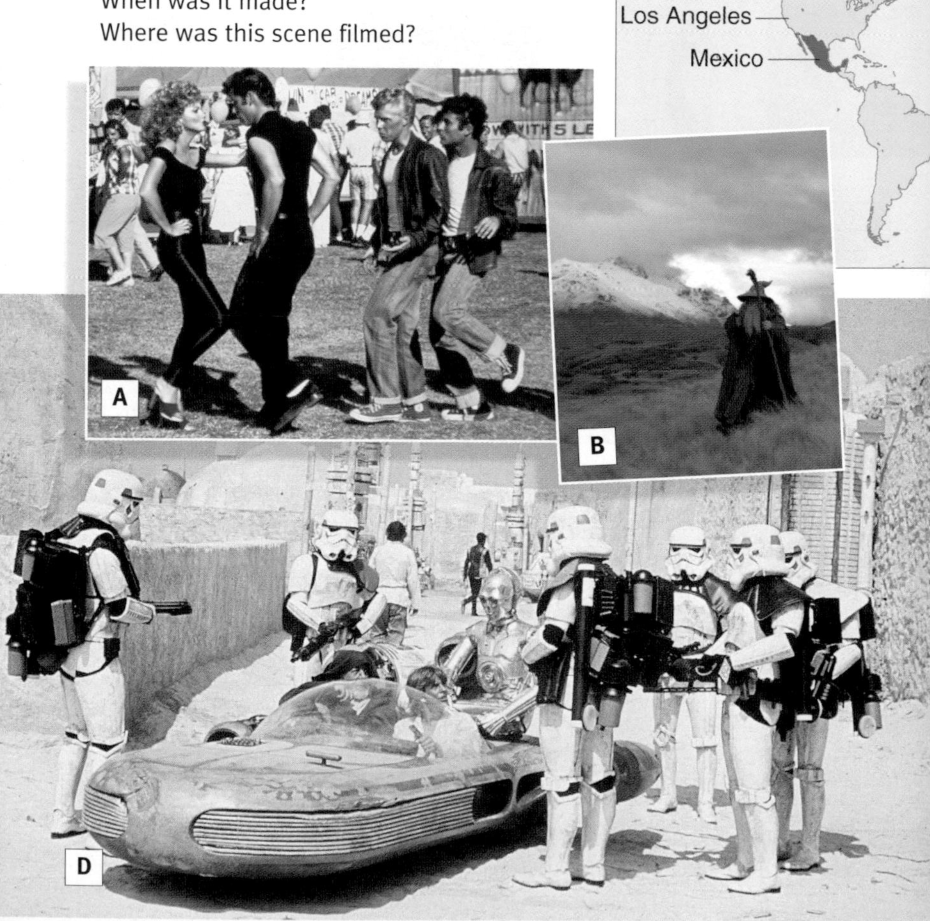

m	Director	Date	Location
ar Wars- Episode II	George Lucas	2002	
anic	James Cameron	1997	
ease	Randal Kleiser	1978	
rd of The Rings	Peter Jackson	2001	
rry Potter and e Philosopher's Stone	Chris Columbus	2001	
adiator	Ridley Scott	2000	

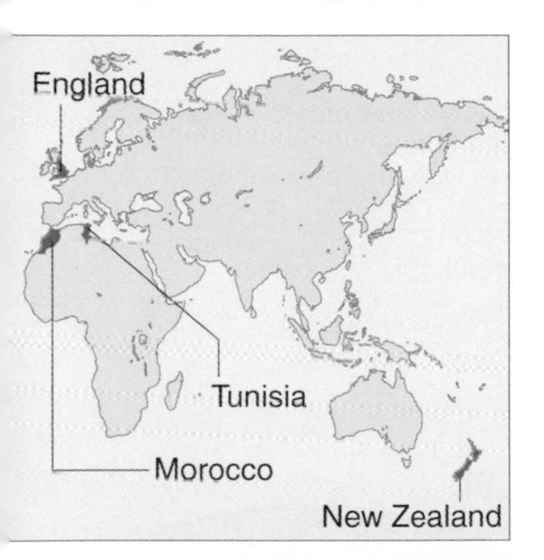

C The passive

What is the passive?

Somebody	***made***	***the film***	***in 2003.***
subject	active verb	object	
The film	***was made***	***in 2003.***	
subject	passive verb		

We use the active to say what the subject does / did.
We use the passive to say what happens / happened to the subject.

We form the passive with **to be + past participle.**
We use the passive when we are more interested in something than the person who did / made it.
Jurassic Park was made in 1993. *Jurassic Park was filmed in Hawaii.*

We can also say the same things in an active way or a passive way. We make the choice.

George Lucas *is one of the most successful film directors ever.*
George Lucas *directed* ***Star Wars***. (active)

Grease *is the most successful musical film ever.*
Grease *was directed by* ***Randal Kleiser***. (passive)

1 Are these sentences active (*A*) or passive (*P*)?

1 My watch was made in Switzerland.
2 My friends call me Peter.
3 *Grease* starred Olivia Newton-John and John Travolta.
4 Scenes for *Grease* were filmed at two Los Angeles high schools.
5 Special effects are called *SFX* in the film industry.
6 They make a lot of chocolate in Belgium.

2 Choose the correct words.

1 Shakespeare (wrote / was writing / was written) *Romeo and Juliet*.
2 Premier League football games (play / playing / are played) on Saturdays.
3 English and French (speak / spoken / are spoken) in Canada.
4 Paul McCartney (was born / born / is born) in Liverpool.
5 Those houses (built / are built / were built) 200 years ago.
6 They (make / are made / making) a lot of films in Hollywood.
7 This shirt (is making / is made / made) of cotton.
8 The United States (produced / is produced / produces) a lot of cotton.

D *Ben Hur* (1926)

The 1926 version of *Ben Hur* was the most expensive silent film ever .... Filming started in 1924 in Italy. There is a sea battle in the film, and several full-size ships were .... Many extras were .... for the battle scene, and they were .... real metal armour to wear. During the filming, the ships really caught fire. The extras jumped into the sea, but many of them couldn't swim in the heavy armour. Fortunately there were small boats all around the ships to rescue them.

After the battle, the extras went back to the beach and got dressed in their own clothes. But there were three piles of clothes left on the beach. The film company destroyed the clothes and told no one. They thought the extras were dead. Two days later, three very unhappy extras arrived on the set. During the battle, they were .... by a fishing boat, and they were .... to a town farther along the coast. They were still .... in Roman armour and they were looking for their clothes.

The filming of the battle scene was .... with model boats. There were problems with the weather, and in 1925 the film company moved back to Hollywood, leaving all the expensive sets behind. All the sets were .... again in California. That is why it was the most expensive film of its time.

1 **Read the text, and complete the spaces with past participles from the box.**

completed taken given employed
made dressed rescued built (x 2)

Listen and check. (✳ 2.16)

2 **How many of the past participles are irregular?**

E Win a million

cheat /tʃiːt/ *verb* [I] to act in a dishonest or unfair way in a game or an exam because you want to win the game or pass the exam • *Sam was cheating in the exam. The answers were written on his arm. When we play cards, she always cheats.*

1 **Listen to part of a quiz show.** (✻ 2.17) **Do you think the contestant is cheating?**

2 **Role-play the TV show. One person asks the questions. The contestant can do each of these things once, and only once:**

- Ask the group or class to vote on the correct answer.
- Ask one student only for advice (in 20 seconds).
- Ask the teacher to tell you two wrong answers.

If the contestant gets an answer wrong, someone else becomes the contestant and continues.

2,000	
Where are kangaroos found?	
1 Asia	3 Australia
2 Africa	4 Europe

4,000	
Where is champagne produced?	
1 Germany	3 France
2 England	4 Canada

8,000	
Who was E.T. directed by?	
1 Spielberg	3 Hitchcock
2 Lucas	4 Ford

16,000	
How is a line of Arabic written? From …	
1 top to bottom.	3 bottom to top.
2 left to right.	4 right to left.

32,000	
What is pasta normally made from?	
1 rice	3 corn
2 wheat	4 potatoes

64,000	
When was President John F. Kennedy assassinated?	
1 1953	3 1973
2 1963	4 1983

125,000	
When was the Great Pyramid of Giza built in Egypt?	
1 9000 years ago	3 4500 years ago
2 1000 years ago	4 2200 years ago

250,000	
What is steel made from?	
1 iron & gold	3 iron & silver
2 iron & copper	4 iron & coal

500,000	
When was penicillin discovered?	
1 1898	3 1948
2 1928	4 1978

1,000,000	
In which studio were most of The Beatles' albums recorded?	
1 Lime Street	3 Oxford Street
2 Abbey Road	4 Penny Lane

See **Extension 19** p.202

20 *If* ...

A Possibilities

1 Find these things in the picture.

a ledge a tree branch an eagle
a nest a snake a goat a clifftop

2 What's going to happen? Give your ideas with the expressions in the box.

It'll definitely happen	certain	He'll definitely fall.
It'll probably happen	probable	He'll probably fall.
I think it'll happen		I think he'll fall.
It might happen	possible	He might fall.
It might not happen		He might not fall.
I don't think it'll happen		I don't think he'll fall.
It probably won't happen	probable	He probably won't fall.
It definitely won't happen	certain	He definitely won't fall.

You can use these verbs.

attack bite break eat through fall rescue

B *might*

- *might* is a modal verb (like *must, can, should, will, would*).
- We use *might* to talk about possibility.
  *It **might** rain tomorrow.* *I **might** go out this evening.*
- The negative is *might not* (no contraction).
- The question form (*Might I ...?*) is not very frequent.
  We usually ask with *will*.
  ***Will** you do **it**?* and answer with *might Yes, I **might**. / No, I **might not**.*
- Use *will / won't / going to* if you are more sure about a future event.
- *may* is an alternative to *might*. It is a little more certain, but is less frequent especially in American English.
  Don't worry about the difference.
  *I **may** look for a new job, I don't know.* *I **may not** be at the party.*

1 Choose the correct verbs.

1. I ('m going / might go) to Paris next week. I've booked my flight.
2. I ('m going / might go) away for a few days. I haven't decided yet.
3. I'm going to the bank later, so I (might / 'll) get some money from the cashpoint.
4. It ('ll / might) snow tomorrow, but I don't think it will.
5. I don't know, it (is / may be) the right answer but I'm not sure.
6. I ('ll / might) definitely phone you later.
7. We (will / may) have to work on Saturday. We won't know until Friday afternoon.
8. She (won't / might not) come to the party. It depends on how busy she is.
9. He (will / might) go to university. It depends on his exam results.

2 Say what you might do ...

- tonight
- next weekend
- next summer
- when this class finishes
- when you finish this book
- when you have your next day off work

Remember! If you have definite plans, don't use *might*.

3 Think about your answers in 2.

Will your answers be different ...

- if you're tired?
- if the weather's good?
- if the weather's bad?
- if you have to do some extra work?
- if friends arrive unexpectedly?

C When I get home

As soon as I get home ...

When we get to Florida ...

If it lands on twenty-one ...

While I'm watching TV tonight ...

After this dance ...

Before I get a job ...

1 **Complete the sentences with your ideas, then compare with other students.**

2 **Listen to the examples. Are they the same as your ideas in 1?** (✻ 2.18 - 2.23)

We use a present tense after *when, if, as soon as, before, after, while*
I'll get some bread ***when*** *I go to the supermarket.*
We'll have a cup of tea ***before*** *we go to bed.*
She'll take an umbrella ***if*** *it rains.*
If *you've finished, I'll take your plate.*
I'll have a beer ***while*** *I'm watching the football on TV.*

3 **Circle the future forms in the language box. Underline the present forms.**

D Consequences

***If* word order**
Start with *if* and use a comma:
***If** we miss the bus**,** we'll be late.*
Put **if** between the two parts of the sentence:
*We'll be late **if** we miss the bus.*

1 Say these sentences in the reverse order.

1 If you watch that horror film, you won't sleep.
2 He'll be angry if we're late.
3 She'll have to move to London if she gets the job.
4 If you marry me, I'll make you happy.

***If* + present tense / future tense**
If we don't hurry, we'll miss the bus.
If we miss the bus, we'll be late.
If we're late, we'll miss the beginning of the film.
If we miss the beginning, we won't understand the story.
If we don't understand the story, we won't enjoy the film ...

2 Listen and follow the consequences. Can you continue the chain? (✳ 2.24)

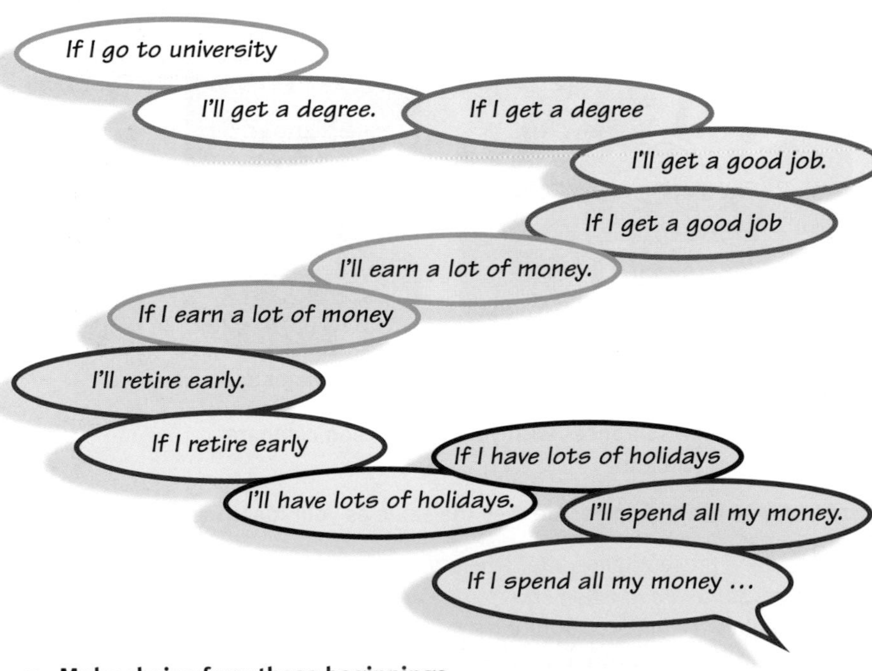

3 Make chains from these beginnings.

If you work harder ...
If you use your credit card ...
If you lend me some money ...
If I fail my exams ...
If I can't sleep tonight ...
If my alarm clock doesn't work ...

E Safari

1 A safari guide in South Africa is giving instructions to a group of tourists before they go out looking for lions. Match the parts and make sentences.

1. If you stay close to me
2. You won't see me use the rifle
3. Even if I have time to fire the rifle
4. If we don't have lions
5. What do you do
6. If you move away slowly
7. She doesn't know if she's going to attack
8. You only need to worry about the male lion
9. If a leopard decides to attack

A I'll probably miss.
B we don't have tourists.
C she'll walk away.
D you'll be safe.
E you'll be dead before you know it.
F unless I really have to.
G if you step on him by accident.
H if a lioness attacks?
I until she sees your reaction.

Listen and check. (✳ 2.25)

2 Read the questions, then listen again and find the answers.

1. Why are they leaving early?
2. How fast can a lioness run?
3. How does a lioness give a warning?
4. What will the guide do if a lioness attacks?
5. Do leopards run faster than lions?

F Things we say to kids ...

- We often use *if* with imperatives.
  ***If** you see her, say hello from me.*
- We can use the present in both parts of the sentence.
  What do you do if a lioness attacks?
- *must, can, might, should* often replace *will.*
  If you're busy, I ***can*** *call back later.*
  If you go to Paris, you really ***must*** *see the Mona Lisa!*
  If you buy a lottery ticket, you ***might*** *win millions.*
  If you're unhappy about it, you ***should*** *complain.*

1 Child psychologists say we shouldn't use bribes, threats or warnings to children. Look at the three groups of sentences. Label them Bribes, Threats, Warnings.

If you don't eat your lunch, you won't get any dinner.
If you don't wear your seat belt, a policeman will take you to prison.
When your father gets home, you'll be in trouble.
If you don't behave at school, the teacher will smack you!
If you hit your baby sister again, I'll hit you.
If you do that again, you'll be sorry!
If you don't keep quiet, you'll have to wait outside.
If you're not good, you won't go to heaven.

If you don't clean your teeth, they'll fall out.
If you climb that tree, you might fall off and break your arm.
If you go near the water, you might fall in.
If you kiss boys, you'll get pregnant.
If you don't eat your meat, you won't grow.

If you stop shouting, I'll buy you an ice-cream.
If you eat all your vegetables, you can have a dessert.
If you finish your homework, you can watch TV.
If you go to bed now, I'll read you a story.

2 Think about when you were a child.
Did you hear any bribes, threats and warnings like these?
Can you remember them?
Did they frighten you?
Did they worry you?
Have they made you a better person?
Can you think of examples?

3 Have you ever said things like these to children?
What did you say?
Did you feel sorry about it afterwards?
Do you think the child psychologists are right or wrong?

Dot always offered
the children a choice:
Fishfingers or unimaginable violence.

See **Extension 20** p.203

21 Health

A What's wrong?

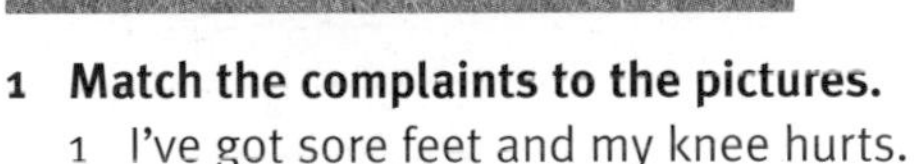

1 Match the complaints to the pictures.

1 I've got sore feet and my knee hurts.
2 Ouch! I've burnt myself.
3 I've cut myself. Get me a plaster!
4 I've got stomach-ache, and I feel sick.
5 Ow. My back aches.
6 I've got toothache.
7 I've got a temperature. I think I'm getting a cold.
8 My arm hurts and I've got a pain in my shoulder.

2 Match the complaints to the reasons below.

A I've had too much to drink.
B I was cooking sausages and I touched the grill.
C I've been painting all day.
D I've been carrying heavy boxes all day.
E I was cutting flowers and I was careless.
F I got very cold and wet yesterday.
G I've just run a marathon.
H I've just bitten into a hard apple.

Listen and check. 

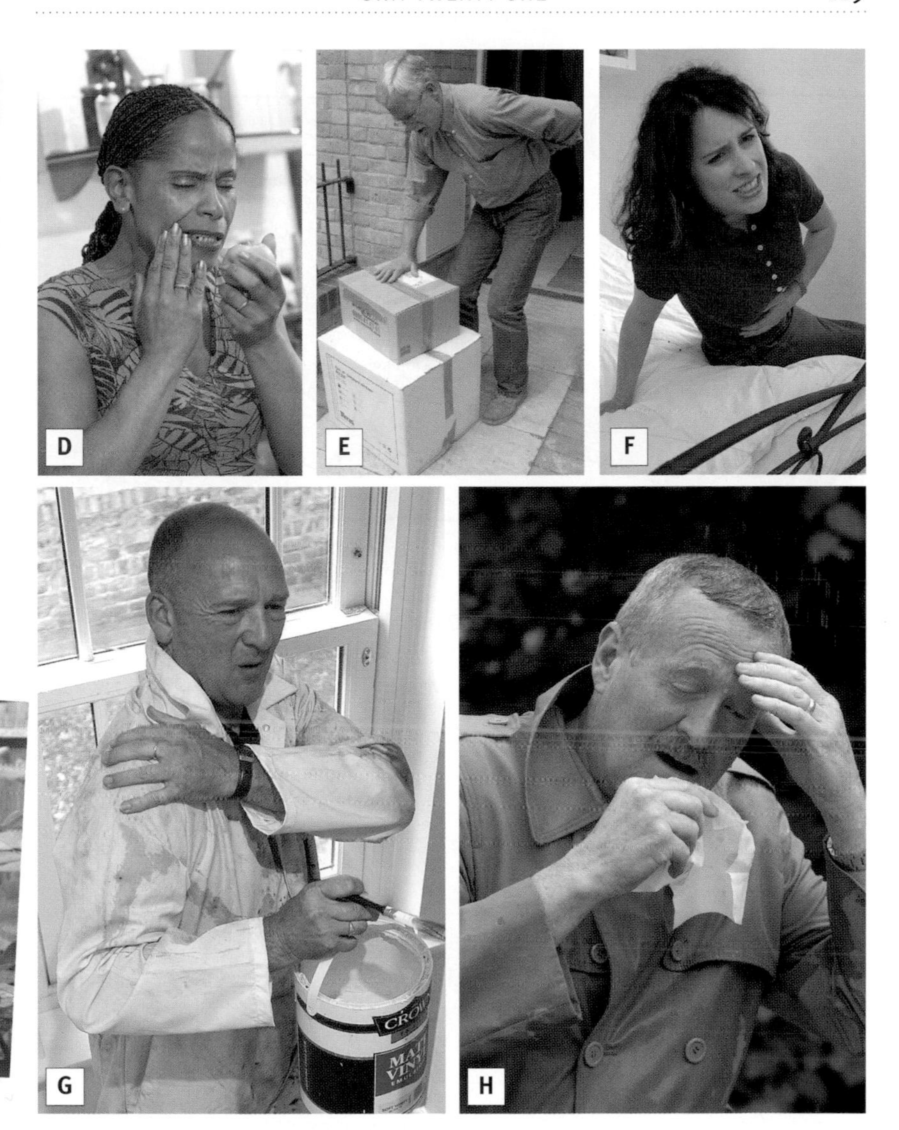

3 How many parts of the body can you name?

What's the matter? *What's wrong?*

-ache

I've got backache, earache, headache, stomach-ache, toothache

For all other parts of the body:

I've got a ***pain*** *in (my / the) foot, knee, leg, etc.*

I've got a ***sore*** *foot, sore feet, a sore knee.*

My feet ***hurt*** */* ***ache****. My knee hurts / aches.*

bad: *I'm feeling bad, I've got a bad back / stomach / cough / chest.*

B *How long?*

1 Listen and practice. (✱ 2.27)

Nurse	Who's next?
Man	Me. I've been waiting since nine o'clock.
Woman	I've been waiting longer than that!
Nurse	How long have you been waiting?
Woman	For over an hour.

Ask and answer.

Are they waiting now?
Who has been waiting the longest?
How long has he been waiting?
How long has she been waiting?

Present perfect continuous
***have / has + been* + present participle**
We've been living here ***since*** *January.* = and we're still living here.
They've been travelling ***for*** *an hour.* = and they're still travelling.
How long has it been raining? It has been raining all day. = and it is still raining.

I've read 'Lord of the Rings'.
(I've finished it. I'm not reading it at the moment.)

I've been reading 'Lord of the Rings'. (I haven't finished. I'm still reading it.)

2 Ask your partner. Answer with *for* or *since*.

1 How long have you been learning English?
2 How long have you been studying this book?
3 How long have you been sitting in this classroom?
4 How long have you been living in your present home?

3 Change partners. Ask about the previous partner.

C At the pharmacy

1 Look at the remedies. Have you got any of these at hom Which ones can you use for a cut?

2 Listen and practise. (✻ 2.28)

Pharmacist	Can I help you?
Woman	Have you got anything for hay fever?
Pharmacist	Yes, we've got some antihistamine tablets, or some eye drops.
Woman	I'd like the tablets, please.
Pharmacist	Have you taken antihistamines before?
Woman	No, I haven't. How often do you take them?
Pharmacist	Twice a day, morning and night. You might feel tired when you're taking them. If you do, you shouldn't drive.
Woman	OK. Thank you.

3 Listen. (✻ 2.29)

► Have you got anything for insect bites?
◄ Why don't you try this spray?
► Fine. How often do you use it?
◄ It doesn't matter. Whenever you need it.

Look at the remedies. Make conversations like 2.28 and 2.29.

. the doctor's

1 Pronunciation: stressed syllables. Listen and repeat. (✱ 2.30)

• ● •	● • •	● • • •	• • ● •
pre•scrip•tion	phar•ma•cy	tem•pe•ra•ture	in•di•ges•tion
al•ler•gic	al•co•hol	● • ● • •	● • • ● •
in•fec•tion	rem•e•dy	an•ti•his•ta•mine	an•ti• bi•ot•ic

2 Check the meaning of these symptoms.

a sore throat   a temperature   a runny nose   a cough
swollen glands   aches and pains

3 Listen. Look at 2. What symptoms does the patient have? 

4 Are these statements true or false?

1 He's had a sore throat for two days.
2 He's been shouting and singing.
3 He doesn't smoke.
4 If it's a virus, antibiotics will help.
5 He isn't allergic to antibiotics.
6 He might have mononucleosis.
7 She isn't going to send him for a blood test.
8 If he feels better, he needn't take all the tablets.
9 He shouldn't drink while he's taking the tablets.

5 Read the chart from a medical website, then listen again.

6 Role-play this situation at the doctor's.

haven't got / don't have, etc.
I've got a cold. / I have a cold.
You haven't got flu. / You don't have flu.
Have I got glandular fever? / Do I have glandular fever?

In British English *have got* is used more often in conversation.
In a formal text, you will see *have / don't* have more often.

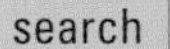

search **sore throat** GO

WEBDOCTOR

Start here

Do you have a fever? (a temperature of 38°C or above)?
- Fever
- No fever

Do you have swollen glands?
- Yes
- No

You might have mononucleosis (glandular fever).
✚ You will need a blood test. See your doctor.

Do you have any of these symptoms?
- headache
- cough
- runny nose
- aches and pains all over the body
- none of these

Sore throats

You might have a bacterial throat infection.
✆ Make an appointment to see your doctor.

Have you been …
- shouting or singing?
- smoking, or breathing in smoke or dust
- None of these

If you've been doing these things, you might have inflammation in your throat.

You might have a viral illness, (cold or flu). See your doctor if symptoms get worse, or if you don't get better after two days.

You might be getting a cold.

www.webdoctor.uk.com

E Questionnaire

1 Interview a partner. You can choose more than one answer.

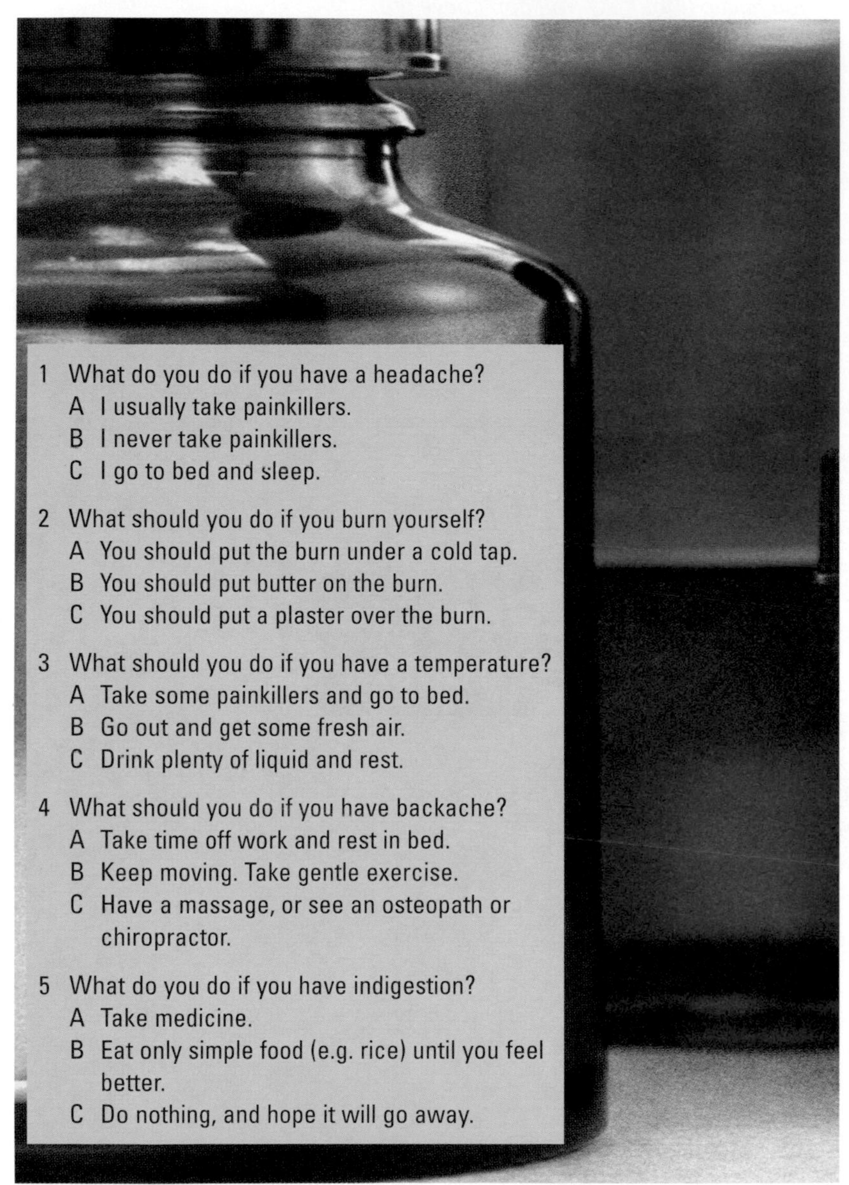

1 What do you do if you have a headache?
   A I usually take painkillers.
   B I never take painkillers.
   C I go to bed and sleep.

2 What should you do if you burn yourself?
   A You should put the burn under a cold tap.
   B You should put butter on the burn.
   C You should put a plaster over the burn.

3 What should you do if you have a temperature?
   A Take some painkillers and go to bed.
   B Go out and get some fresh air.
   C Drink plenty of liquid and rest.

4 What should you do if you have backache?
   A Take time off work and rest in bed.
   B Keep moving. Take gentle exercise.
   C Have a massage, or see an osteopath or chiropractor.

5 What do you do if you have indigestion?
   A Take medicine.
   B Eat only simple food (e.g. rice) until you feel better.
   C Do nothing, and hope it will go away.

2 Do you agree or disagree with these statements?

If you eat good food, you don't need extra vitamins.
Every child should be immunized against infectious diseases.
Life-saving medicines should be cheaper in poor countries.
If you want to lose weight, diet is less important than exercise.

See **Extension 21** p.203

22 People

A Guessing ...

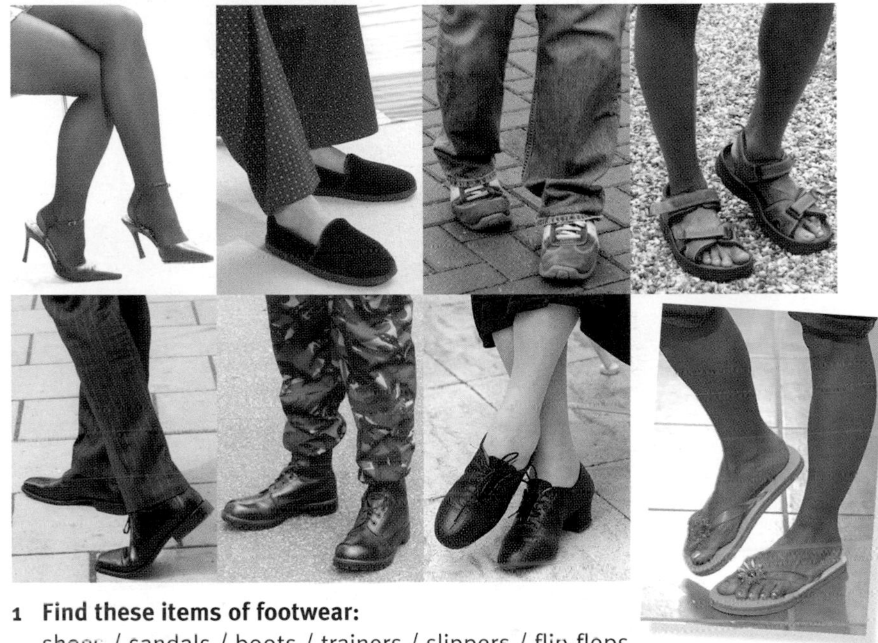

1 **Find these items of footwear:**
shoes / sandals / boots / trainers / slippers / flip-flops

2 **Guess what clothes these people are wearing.**
These are smart shoes.
I think he's wearing a business suit, with a shirt and tie.

3 **What other things can you guess about the people? Discuss with a partner.**
► *He must be a businessman. I guess he's about forty. He probably wears these clothes at work every day.*
◄ *No, he might not be a businessman. He might be at a wedding, or a funeral.*

I'm certain it's true:
He must be a businessman. / He's definitely a businessman.

I'm almost certain it's true:
He's probably a businessman.

I don't know if it's true:
He might be a businessman. / He could be a businessman.

I'm certain it's not true:
He can't be a businessman. / He's definitely not a businessman.

B Appearance

1 Point to these people:

The men who are wearing sunglasses.
The woman who's lying on a sofa.
The man who's playing the guitar.
The woman who's wearing a low-cut dress.
The people who are wearing formal suits.
The woman who's wearing boots.
The man who's wearing a wig.

2 Decide which people these are.

The one who looks scruffy.
The ones who look tough.
The ones who look serious.
The ones who look rich.
The ones who look glamorous.
The ones who look happy.
The ones who look smart.
The ones who look casual.

Compare with a partner. Have you chosen the same ones?

3 Pair work. Talk about the photos with words from 2 and the box.

► Look at the first man who's wearing sunglasses.
◄ He looks (serious). He looks like (a lawyer). He looks about (fifty).

gangster	author	athlete	disc jockey (DJ)	model
musician	accountant	bank clerk	billionaire	criminal
detective	actor	politician	police officer	chef
fit	handsome	about (forty)	aggressive	relaxed

* If you recognize any of the people, don't tell your partner yet.

look / looks like + noun *She looks like a (teacher).*
look / looks + adjective *She looks worried.*

4 Listen to the conversation. Which picture are they talking about? (✳ 2.32)
Now use the communication activities and make more conversations.

COMMUNICATION

Student A Look at Activity 10 on p.214.
Student B Look at Activity 18 on p.218.

C Relative clauses

1 Read the definitions and circle *who* and *that*.

athlete /æθliːt/ *noun* [C] a person who can run, jump, etc very well, especially one who takes part in sports competitions, etc

sandal /sændl/ *noun* [C] a type of light, open shoe with straps that people wear when the weather is warm

model /mɒdl/ *noun* [C] **4** a person who is employed to wear clothes at a fashion show or for magazine photographs

wig /wɪg/ *noun* [C] a covering made of real or false hair that you wear on your head, because you are bald or because you want to cover up your own hair

Relative clauses

Relative clauses give extra information about a person or thing.

two sentences.

A boot is a type of shoe. ***It*** *covers the ankle.*

(boot is a noun, ***it*** is a pronoun)

A chef is a cook. ***He / She*** *is the head cook in a restaurant.*

(chef is a noun, ***he*** and ***she*** are pronouns)

one sentence with a relative clause.

A boot is a type of shoe ***that / which*** *covers the ankle.*

A chef is a cook ***who*** *is the head cook in a restaurant.*

Note: we don't repeat *it, he, she,* so NOT:

~~*A boot is a type of shoe that it covers the ankle.*~~

~~*A chef is a cook who he is the head cook in a restaurant.*~~

We use the **relative pronouns** *who* (or *that*) for people, and *that* (or *which*) for things.

2 In the second sentence in each pair, there is a pronoun which refers to a noun in the first sentence. Highlight the matching nouns and pronouns.

- *I've got two sisters. They live in Australia.*

1 Last night I met a man. He knows you.
2 She's got long hair. It goes down to her waist.
3 These are the socks. They were a birthday present.
4 There's a girl in my class. She always wears jeans.
5 I saw a film yesterday. It really frightened me.
6 They're the people. They've been waiting the longest.
7 Have you seen the card? It arrived this morning.
8 Do you know the people? They live upstairs.

3 **Connect the sentences in 2 with *who* or *that*.**
I've got two sisters ***who*** *live in Australia.*

4 **Make true sentences beginning ...**
1 I've got a friend who ...
2 I've read a book that ...
3 I live in a town that ...
4 I've never met anyone who ...
5 There's a shop in my town that ...
6 I'd like to meet someone who ...

D *Have You Heard The News?*

1 **Read and complete the spaces with your guesses.**

Have you heard the news?
Have you heard the news?
Some people win, but others lose,
Have you heard, have you heard
the news?

Have you heard about the . . . . . .
who's been to outer space?
Have you heard about the . . . . . .
who's won every single race?
Have you heard about the . . . . . .
who's gone to Hollywood?
Have you heard about the . . . . . .
who haven't got any food?

Chorus

Have you heard about the . . . . . .?
They've killed them nearly all.
Have you heard about the . . . . . .
who were shot against a wall?
Have you heard about the . . . . . .
that give us the air we need?
Have you heard about the . . . . . .
with hungry mouths to feed?

Chorus

2 **Listen and check.** (✱ 2.33)

3 **Listen and sing.**

See **Extension 22** p.204

23 Numbers

A Does it add up?

1 Assess yourself. True or false?

A I'm confident about using numbers in English.

B When I see a number in English (e.g. 4,381), I think of it in my own language.

C I can say these numbers in English:

1,349	100,784
4/5	9.32
5,000,000	33%
32°	12th

Listen and check. (✻ 2.34)

2 How many ways can you make the number twelve?

Adding	+	Six plus six is twelve.
Subtracting	–	Twenty minus eight is twelve.
Multiplying	x	Three times four is twelve.
Dividing	÷	Twenty four divided by two is twelve.

How many ways can you make 32? Give yourself two minutes. Compare with a partner.

3 Try this. You can use a calculator.

Begin with the number of your house or flat. Multiply it by two. Add the number of days in a week. Multiply by fifty. Then add your age. Subtract the number of days in a year. Add fifteen. The result will be your house or flat number and your age.

B Number connections

1 How many connections can you find for the number seven?

Seven Voyages of Sinbad
lucky for some
septathalon
septagon
Seven-Up

Time to get up
a week
Seven wonders of the world
septet
September
July

Which ones mean:

Something which has seven sides
A musical group which has seven members
The seventh month of the Roman calendar
(but ninth month of the modern calendar)
An athletics contest which has seven seperate events

2 Which numbers do these words connect with?

a century	a decade	a kilogram	The Pentagon
a fortnight	a football team	midnight	a quartet
triplets	twins	an octopus	a dozen

3 How many things can you think of connected to these numbers?

$1/10$, $1/100$, 2, 3, 4, 5, 6, 8, 10, 11, 12, 13, 14, 20, 21, 100, 1000, 1,000,000

C The history of numbers

Until the fifteenth century, most of Europe used Roman numerals, which had letters for numbers:

M (1000)	D (500)
C (100)	L (50)
X (10)	V (5)
and I (1)	

They only used three fractions, $1/4$, $1/2$ and $3/4$, and had no concept of zero or decimal points. Numbers were made by adding the smaller number afterwards

XI = 10 + 1 = 11 LXX = 50 + 10 + 10 = 70

or subtracting the smaller number before

IX = 10 – 1 = 9 XC = 100 – 10 = 90

Modern numbers are called Arabic numbers. They arrived in Baghdad from India in 789 AD. The first recorded use of zero with Arabic numbers was in India in 876.

The next great invention was the decimal point which appeared in Italy in 1592. Without a decimal point it is impossible to make precise calculations, like the length of the year, which is 365.242199 days.

The metric system came from France during the 1790s. It uses prefixes like *deci* ($1/10$), *centi* ($1/100$), *milli* ($1/1000$), and *kilo* (1000). Metric measures are used in the United Kingdom and Canada, but you still hear the old Imperial measures, like *pounds* (lbs) and *ounces* (ozs), *gallons* and also degrees *Fahrenheit* (°F) in conversation. The USA doesn't use metric measures except in science and athletics.

1 What are these Roman numbers?

XII, MMVIII, MCMXCIV

2 Find examples of these in the text.

a fraction, a decimal number, the years 1400–1499, the symbol for degrees, a date, Imperial measures, prefixes

D Listening

1 Listen to the conversation in a restaurant and complete the credit card slip. (✳ 2.35)

The Cheddar Cheese Restaurant
Cranborne, Dorset
Card type: MasterCard
Number: **** **** **** 9101
Auth code: 1234567
Expiry date: 12 / 09
MEALS & DRINKS ....
VAT @ .... % ....
SUB-TOTAL ....
GRATUITY ....
Please debit my account with the sum of ....
SIGNATURE: ....

2 Look at the phone screen. Say the prize amounts aloud. (✳ 2.36)

3 Listen and check.
What number did Ed hear wrongly?
What number did Bella read wrongly?
What is the chance of guessing six numbers correctly out of 49 numbers?

E Facts and figures

1 Answer the questions. Guess. Compare with your class.

1 How much of an iceberg is under water?
A two-thirds B four-fifths C nine-tenths

2 You find twelve-inch rulers in the USA. What is this in metric countries?
A a twenty-centimetre ruler B a thirty-centimetre ruler
C a metre ruler

3 A one Gigabyte memory chip is ...
A one million bytes B one billion bytes
C one hundred thousand bytes

4 Water boils at 100° Celsius, which is the same as ...
A 100°F B 180°F C 212°F

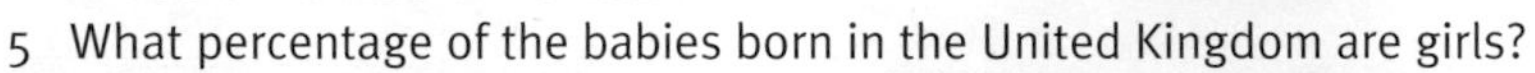

5 What percentage of the babies born in the United Kingdom are girls?
A Exactly 50% B 48.7% C 51.3%

6 What percentage of Americans travel to work by car?
A More than 85%
B Approximately 70%
C Less than 60%

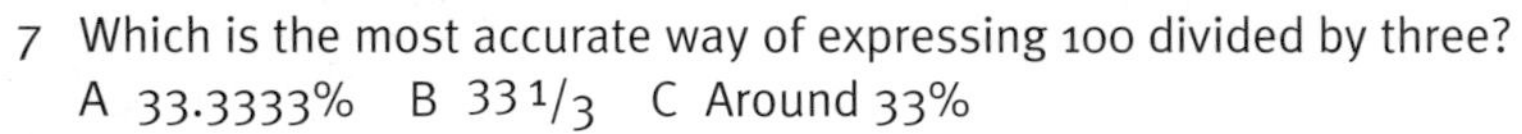

7 Which is the most accurate way of expressing 100 divided by three?
A 33.3333% B 33 1/3 C Around 33%

8 How big is a sheet of A3 paper?
A twice as big as A4 B half as big as A4 C four times as big as A4

COMMUNICATION

The answers are in Activity 17 on p.218. Choose someone to look them up.

2 Read the problem. Can you explain the answer?

THE MISSING EURO

Three men were eating in a café. They finished their meal and asked for the bill. The waitress said that it was €30. Each of the men gave her €10. When she got to the cash desk, she realized that the bill was only €25. The men seemed happy about paying €30, so she had an idea. She put €2 in her pocket, and gave them back €1 each. They were very pleased.

Each of them paid €10, and got €1 back, so they paid €9 each.Three nines are twenty-seven. The waitress took €2.

27 + 2 = 29

So, where did the 30th euro go?

COMMUNICATION

The answer is in Activity 6 on p.212.

See **Extension 23** p.205

24 Changes

A Things have changed ...

1 **Look at the picture. What can you guess about this man?**
How old is he?
What's the special occasion?
How long has he been working there?

Listen. Were your guesses correct? (✻ 2.37)

2 **Rewrite these sentences in the correct order.**
1 Acme Insurance / has / for / working / Graham / fifty years. / been / for
2 since / working / He / there / been / has / was / he / fifteen.
3 joined / ago. / company / years /He / the / fifty

3 **Make a list of equipment you can find in an office nowadays. How many items from your list were in offices when Graham started work?**

B Listening (1)

1 **Listen to the six parts of Graham's speech. Match the pictures A to F to the listening sections.**

	✱ 2.38	✱ 2.39	✱ 2.40	✱ 2.41	✱ 2.42	✱ 2.43
picture						
sentence						

2 **Match these sentences to the pictures.**

1 Computers used to be huge and slow.
2 We used to dress smartly for work.
3 The Managing Director used to come to the party every year.
4 Nearly everyone used to smoke in those days.
5 We used to have a special room for the photocopier.
6 The secretaries used to take notes in shorthand.

C
E
F

C Listening (2)

used to /juːst tə juːst tuː/ **+ bare infinitive** is for talking about repeated actions, states and feelings in the past.
*I **used to** get up at 6 a.m. everyday.* (repeated action)
*They **used to** live in London.* (state)
*I **used to** believe in Father Christmas.* (feelings)

used to is only for the past.
I used to smoke means also *but I don't smoke anymore.*

We form questions and short answers with *did.*
Did she use to live near you? Yes, she did / No, she didn't.
We often use *never* to form negatives.
I never used to do my homework when I was younger.
(or *I didn't use to do my homework*).

You are going to listen to (✻ 2.38 – 2.43) **again.**

1 **Do you remember what Graham said about the Managing Director?**
He / party every year.
He / all the food and drink.
We / 'sir' at all times.

Listen and check. (✻ 2.38)

2 **Choose the correct word.**
In (these / those) days computers used to be huge and slow.
They were (more / less) powerful than one modern laptop.
We used (have / to have) a special room for the photocopier.
Nowadays we send e-mails, so there are no postboys (anymore /now).

Listen and check. (✻ 2.39 – 2.40)

3 **Listen.** (✻ 2.41 – 2.43)
Did managers use to do their own typing?
Who used to dictate letters?
Who used to take notes?
What did men have to wear to work?
What did Graham use to wear?
Were women allowed to wear trousers?
What hours did they use to work?
How many cigarettes a day did Graham use to smoke?

4 **Does Graham smoke anymore? Did more people use to smoke in the past? Are there any rules / laws about smoking in your country?**
You aren't allowed to smoke on planes. You are allowed to smoke in bars.

5 **Discuss the photos in B. When were they taken? Guess.**
Talk about fashions, technology, male / female roles, employers / employees.

D ... years ago

I remember when I was a kid, I used to have an old teddy bear with one ear. I wonder what happened to it?

Before I got married, I never used to cook.

When I was younger, I used to love Britney Spears, but I don't listen to her anymore.

I used to play video games, but I don't have time anymore.

When I was little, I used to be terrified of monsters in cartoons.

1 Think back. How have you changed? Make sentences. You can use these ideas, or add other ideas.

When I was little ...	I used to ...	have (long hair).
When I was younger ...	I never used to ...	be (afraid of ...)
When I was a teenager ...	I didn't use to ...	be (a punk).
Ten years ago ...		live in ...
Before I ...		listen to ...
I remember ...		collect ...
		like ...
		play ...
		work ...

2 Pair work. Think of a question to ask your partner:

► Did you use to (listen to *Oasis*) when you were (younger)?
◄ Yes, I did. / No, I didn't.
► Do you still like them?
◄ Yes, I do. / No, not anymore.

E A memory

Don't count your chickens ...

When I was five or six, we used to keep chickens. They lived in the back garden, and each one had a different coloured ring around its leg. There were about a dozen, and I gave them all names out of comic books. Without any doubt my favourite was Minnie with the orange ring. My sister and I would feed the chickens, and we'd collect the eggs every day. They were like old friends, and they would come straight to us, clucking and pecking for food.

Back in those days, before factory farming, chicken for dinner was a luxury. We would eat it at Christmas, or Easter or when we had visitors. I did notice that we had fewer chickens as time went by, but my dad explained that some escaped, and some became ill and died. Then one cold December day, I counted. There were just three chickens left; my favourite Minnie, with Daisy and Olive.

I'll never forget that awful Christmas. The family sat down to dinner, and my mother brought out the golden roast chicken for my father to carve. That's when I saw the orange ring around its leg.

And then there were two.

From *Growing up in the Fifties* – Burt Northeast

1 Did the writer eat his Christmas dinner? What do you think?

would* and *used to
You can also use *would* to talk about repeated actions and habits in the past, especially in written English.
*We lived near the sea and we **used to** go to the beach at weekends.*
*We lived near the sea and we **would** go to the beach at weekends.*

You cannot use *would* for states or feelings in the past.
*I **used to** live in Scotland.* NOT ~~*I would live in Scotland.*~~
*He **used to** be in love with her.* NOT ~~*He would be in love with her.*~~

2 Is it possible to change *used to* to *would* in the text?
Is it possible to change *would* to *used to*? Try it.

3 Are these sentences true or false?
1 His house had a garden behind it.
2 He only liked Minnie, not the others.
3 Chicken used to be very expensive.
4 People only ate chicken on special occasions.
5 Some of the chickens escaped from the garden.
6 Mothers usually did the cooking in those days.
7 Fathers used to carve the meat.

4 Can you name a dozen colours in English?

5 Complete the spaces in this definition with a verb, a noun and an adjective from the text. Put *C* (countable) and *U* (uncountable) in the correct brackets [ ].

chicken / tʃɪkɪn / noun 1 [ ] a bird that people often .... for its .... and its meat 2 [ ] the meat of this bird: .... *chicken* • *cold chicken and salad*

6 Writing. Write an anecdote about your past.
Start with telling us about a 'state' (*My grandparents used to live in the country ...*).
Then describe some repeated actions (*When we visited them, we would play in the forest, and we would pick fruit ...*)
Then say what happened using the past simple (*One day ...*).

See **Extension 24** p.206

25 On holiday

A Going on holiday

1 **You're planning a holiday. Which three things are most important for you? Number them 1 to 3. Which things are least important for you?**

- Good weather
- Shopping
- Meeting the opposite sex
- Exciting nightlife
- A budget flight
- Theme parks
- Cheap accommodation
- Practising your English
- Luxury hotels
- Interesting places to visit
- Peace and quiet
- Activities (e.g. surfing, skiing)
- Beautiful scenery
- Food and drink
- Spending time with friends / family
- Beaches

2 **Make sentences. Discuss with your partner.**

- *A budget flight is the most important thing for me because I'm worried about the cost.*
- *I'm not interested in luxury hotels or shopping.*
- *I want to meet new people and make friends.*

3 **What do you like doing on holiday? Is there anything that you don't like doing?**

4 **Study the map on the right. How many words do you understand? Match the words to the definitions.**

A ripoff	1 Deliberately to give less change than you should
B hangover	2 A place where food, souvenirs, etc. are more expensive than they should be
C happy hour	3 The bad feeling a day after drinking too much alcohol
D short change	4 Something which is worth much less than its price
E tourist trap	5 A time of day when drinks are cheaper than normal

5 **Where will you find the things that most interest you?**

6 **Add these places to the map. You decide where to put them.**

1 Oil Refinery
2 Sunburn
3 Traffic jam
4 Hitch-hike
5 Bungee jump

Compare with your partner.

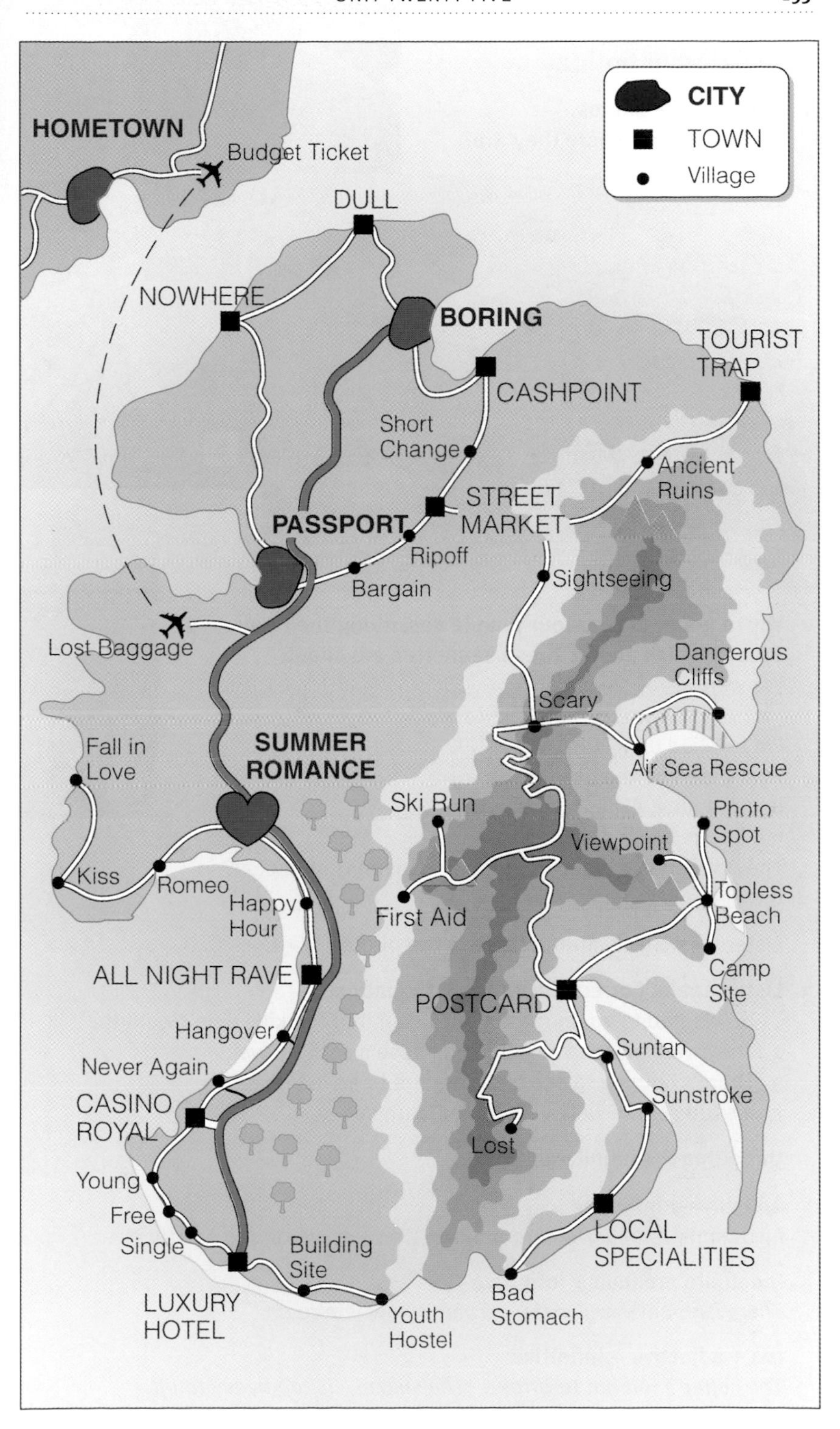
CITY
TOWN
Village
HOMETOWN
Budget Ticket
DULL
NOWHERE
BORING
TOURIST TRAP
CASHPOINT
Short Change
Ancient Ruins
STREET MARKET
PASSPORT
Ripoff
Bargain
Sightseeing
Lost Baggage
Dangerous Cliffs
Scary
Air Sea Rescue
Fall in Love
SUMMER ROMANCE
Ski Run
Photo Spot
Viewpoint
Kiss
Romeo
Happy Hour
First Aid
Topless Beach
Camp Site
ALL NIGHT RAVE
POSTCARD
Hangover
Suntan
Never Again
Sunstroke
CASINO ROYAL
Lost
Young
Free
Single
LOCAL SPECIALITIES
Building Site
LUXURY HOTEL
Youth Hostel
Bad Stomach

B My kind of holiday

1 Describe the photos.
Can you guess where they are?

B

C

2 You're going to hear four people describing their holidays.
Predict which photos these sentences are about:

We were really shocked!
I was a bit worried about the car.
I'm terrified of heights.
I get bored on the beach.
It was a long, exhausting flight.
It was a relaxing drive.
They have these really interesting Christmas markets.
It was really thrilling.

Listen and check. Match them to the photos. (✱ 2.44 – 2.47)

3 Listen again. Correct the wrong information.

1 He wanted to go on the roller-coaster, but the kids didn't want to.
2 They were pleased to get in and have a cold shower.
3 There's nothing to see and nowhere to go in Vienna.
4 It's too cold to walk very far in Death Valley.

Underline the infinitives.

Adjective + infinitive
I was sorry to hear the bad news. *We were pleased to see them.*

Indefinite pronoun + infinitive
There isn't anything to do. *There's nowhere to go.*

***too* + adjective + infinitive**
The coffee's too hot to drink. *The suitcase is too heavy to lift.*

4 Choose the correct words.

terrifying	exhausting	relaxing	exciting	interesting
terrified	exhausted	relaxed	excited	interested

1 I'm .... of heights. / But the ride wasn't ....
2 The flight was long and .... / We felt really .... when we got there.
3 We felt .... in the sunshine. / Lying on the beach was very ....
4 The plane landing was .... / We were .... by the landing.
5 I was .... in the museums. / I think art galleries are .... too.

Adjectives: *worrying* / *worried*, etc.
***–ing* adjectives** describe a person, a thing or a situation.
We met interesting people. *It was a frightening story.*
It was a tiring drive. *I had a relaxing bath.*

***–ed* adjectives** tell us how people feel.
I'm interested in museums. *They were frightened.* *He was tired.*

5 Which of the four holidays would you prefer? Why?

C Hotel problems

1 Look at the phrase book on page 157. Label the pictures with these words. Think! Are they countable or uncountable?

shampoo hot pillows noisy taps hairdryer cold
remote warm hangers quiet light shower big
blankets small soap radiator cool toilet paper

2 Add these words to the phrase book.

air conditioning glasses towels bathrobes fridge switch

3 Listen and practise.

(* 2.48)

Reception	Reception?
Man	This is Paul Jones in Room 34.
Reception	How can I help you, Mr Jones?
Man	There isn't any soap in the bathroom, and there aren't any towels.
Reception	I am sorry about that. I'll send some up straight away.

(* 2.49)

Woman	I wonder if you can help me.
Reception	Certainly, what's the problem?
Woman	It's the toilet. It's blocked. I can't flush it.
Reception	Oh, dear. I'm sorry. I'll send someone right away.

(* 2.50)

Woman	Hello? Is that the front desk?
Reception	Yes. How may I help you?
Woman	The air conditioning doesn't work. I think it's broken.
Reception	I'm sorry to hear that. I'll send an engineer.
Woman	Well, actually I'd like to change my room. It's much too hot in here.
Reception	I'm afraid we're fully-booked this evening. I'm sure the engineer will sort it out.

(* 2.51)

Man	Could you send an engineer to my room, please?
Reception	What's the problem?
Man	The TV's gone wrong. I can't change channels.
Reception	I'm sorry, the engineer's busy right now. He'll be there in twenty minutes.

4 Look at the phrase book. Make more conversations.

IN YOUR HOTEL ROOM ... PROBLEMS

There isn't any ...
There isn't enough ...
I need some (more) ...

1 .... 2 .... 3 ....

There aren't any ...
There aren't enough ...
I need some (more) ...

1 .... 2 .... 3 ....

The ... doesn't work.
The ... has gone wrong.
The ... is broken.
I can't turn on the ...
I can't turn off the ...

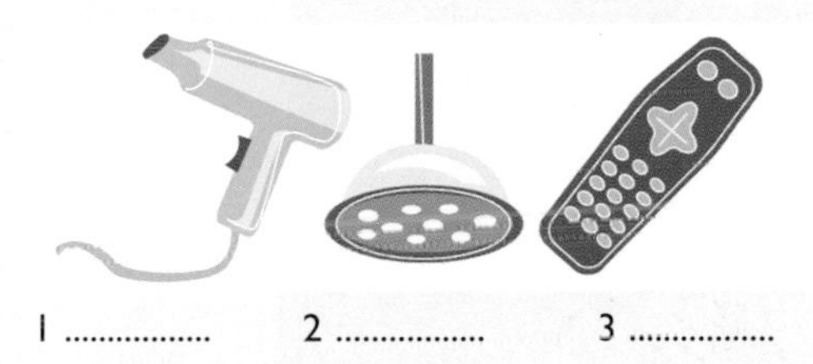

1 .... 2 .... 3 ....

The ... doesn't / don't work.
The ... has / have gone wrong.
The ... is / are broken.
I can't turn on the ...
I can't turn off the ...

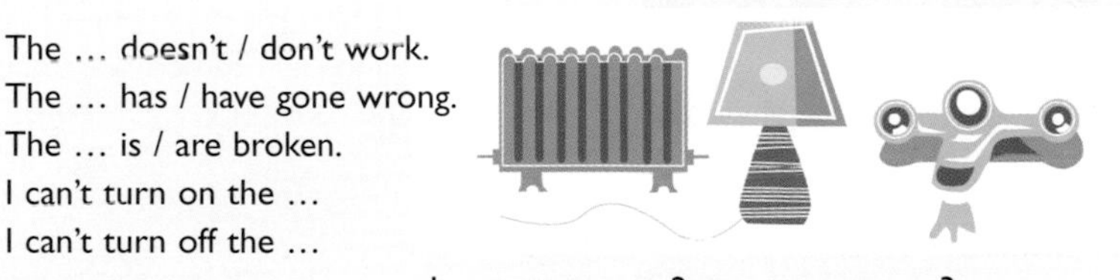

1 .... 2 .... 3 ....

My room's too ...

1 .... 2 .... 3 .... 4 ....

My room isn't ... enough.

1 .... 2 .... 3 .... 4 ....

In most holiday resorts you will find five types of postcard. They are:

1 a photo of your hotel on the only day the sun shone last year.
2 a photo of the view from your hotel which was taken five years ago before they built the oil refinery.
3 a faded photo of the town clock, with a few 1970s cars next to it.
4 an artistic photo of an animal, child or flower. This was actually taken in a different country.
5 a comic card which is so rude that you're worried for the rest of the holiday because you've sent it to your boss.

The worst thing about postcards is that you have to write on them, so you should always buy the smallest postcards you can find. Women buy one for everyone they've ever met, spend hours choosing exactly the right card for each person, then more hours writing something personal and interesting on each card. Men buy five cards with rude jokes and just sign their names. It doesn't really matter because men haven't brought their address books with them and can't remember the post codes, so the cards never get there.

D Postcards

1 Before you read, answer these questions.

1. Are you the kind of person who sends postcards?
2. When do you send them? At the start of your holiday? In the middle? At the end?
3. Do you write different messages on every card?

2 Read the text. Label the paragraphs.

Finding a stamp / Men v Women / Kinds of postcard / The Message

Is the writer being serious, or trying to be amusing?

3 Find words which mean:

1. having lost its colour or brightness
2. a person who receives something
3. a stronger word for *whole* or *complete*

So what should you write about? As little as possible, because you haven't written anything to anybody since your last holiday. But don't worry; nobody will be able to read your writing anyway. Always say where you are first. The recipient will be able to see this from the picture, but *"Hello, we're staying in St. Herbert, a lovely little town in ..."* takes up 25% of the card. *"We're having a lovely / boring / terrible time."* takes up 20% more. Then the most important things are weather, accommodation and food. You can write these in note form. *"Weather awful. Hotel noisy. Food disgusting."*

Finally you have to find a stamp. In holiday areas everywhere sells cards. Unfortunately, you can only buy stamps in the regional capital twenty kilometres away between 8.30 a.m. and 11.15 a.m. on weekdays (not including Tuesdays, Thursdays, or national holidays). So it takes an entire half-day of your holiday just to put stamps on the things. When you get back to work, everybody complains that you forgot to send them a card. That's because no one will receive their card until at least two weeks after your return.

4 Do you agree with the writer's opinions?
There are five types of postcard.
Women enjoy writing postcards. Men don't.
You should write the same things on every card.
It's difficult to find stamps in holiday areas.
Sending postcards is a waste of time and money.

will be able to ...
can does not have an infinitive form. We use *to be able to ...*
For the future, we use *will / won't be able to ...*

5 Describe a typical postcard from your area.
What are the popular subjects? Buildings? Scenery? Local customs?
Can you remember the last postcard you received?
Who was it from? Where were they? What was the photo on the card?

See **Extension 25** p.206

26 Imagine ...

A *Would you ...?*

1 **Match the questions to the pictures.**
Would you hang this on your wall?
Would you sleep in a haunted house by yourself?
Would you do this?
Would you eat this?
Would you wear this?
Would you give him any money?

2 **Ask and give true answers.** (✳ 2.52)
► Would you eat this?
◄ Yes, I would. Would you?
► No, I wouldn't!

Give reasons.

3 **Can you think of more questions like this?**

A

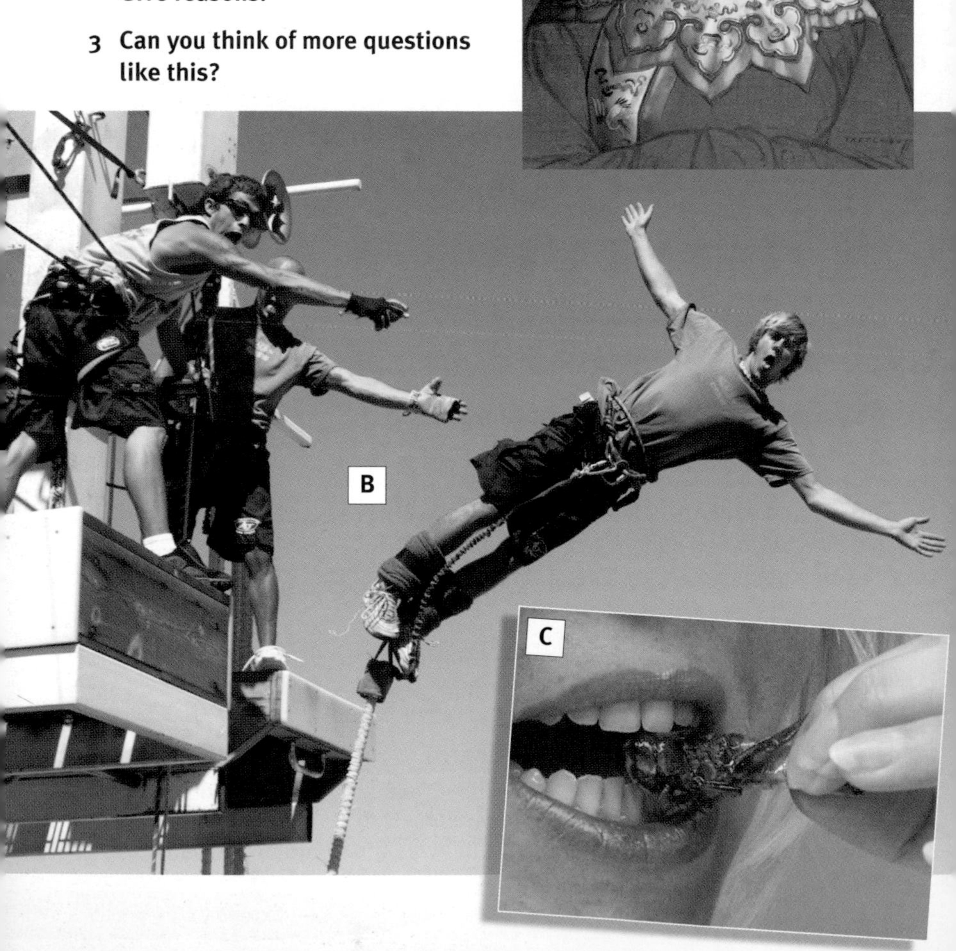

B *What if ...?*

1 If you answered *no*, would you change your mind?

If your grandmother gave you the picture, would you hang it on your wall?
If someone gave you a thousand pounds, would you eat the bug?
If you were freezing cold, would you wear the hat?
If the rest of your class did the bungee jump, would you do it?
If you were a celebrity, would you give him some money?
If your friends were with you, would you sleep in a haunted house?

Answer again with:

I might do it / I still wouldn't do it / I wouldn't do it (for a thousand pounds), but I *would* do it for (ten thousand pounds).

2 Look at the *if* part of the sentences (the 'conditions').

Underline the main verbs. What tense are they in?
Are they in this tense because ...

A you're talking about the past.
B you're talking about an imaginary situation?

3 If you thought of more questions in A 3, can you add 'conditions'?

C What would you do? (✻ 2.53)

They say that money can't buy you happiness, and there are many stories about people who have won a fortune and whose lives have been ruined.

When Patrick O'Donnell won ten million euros on the Irish lottery, the first thing he did was to phone his boss. 'I'm going to retire,' he said. His boss laughed, 'You haven't won the lottery, have you?'
'Indeed I have,' Patrick replied.
'I haven't checked my ticket yet,' said his boss.
'Don't bother,' Patrick told him, 'I've won the lot.'

Patrick is 62, and his wife Bridget is 59. Unlike other lottery winners, the money has made them happy. Why? Because they have given most of it away.

Patrick says, 'They say money changes you, but we haven't changed at all. We're happy because we have been able to make so many other people happy.' This is what they did with the money:

- They didn't move away, but they sold their three-bedroom house and bought a new four-bedroom house in the same area.
- They bought a new car, but not an expensive one.
- They got passports for the first time and went on a world cruise.
- They bought houses for their three children, Patrick's sister and Bridget's brother.
- They invested money for their seven grandchildren.
- They gave millions to their local hospital and to children's charities.
- They paid for all the children from their local school to travel to Dublin to see a show.

'I spent ten euros on lottery tickets that day,' says Patrick, 'And Bridget still owes me five euros for her half.'

1 Read the story. Choose words to describe Patrick and Bridget.

generous kind-hearted ordinary unselfish boring
dull nicer than me good extravagant stupid

Would younger people spend a lottery win differently?

2 If you won the lottery, what would you do? Discuss in pairs.
What would you do immediately?
Would you leave your job?
Would you buy a new house?
Would you move to a different area?
What would you buy for yourself?
Would you travel? Where to?
Would you give any away?
How much would you give away?
Who would you give it to?
Would you keep the same friends?
Do you think your friends would be jealous?

3 Look at the words in 1. How would you describe your partner?

D Unreal conditionals

Unreal conditionals (or Type 2 Conditionals) are for imaginary situations. We use:
If **+ a past tense /** ***would***, ***could***, **or** ***might*** **+ a bare infinitive**

If	I won the lottery I had ten million euros I became rich I were a millionaire	I	'd would (n't) could might	leave my job. buy a new house. travel round the world. give a lot of money away.

Choose the correct words to complete the sentences.
1 If I (found / find) some money in the street, I'd take it to the police.
2 If I (can / could) live anywhere in the world, I'd live in Hawaii.
3 If I (have / had) a cold, I'd take vitamin C.
4 If I (can / could) meet any celebrity, I'd choose Prince William.
5 If I (see / saw) someone shoplifting, I wouldn't say anything.
6 If I (have / had) more money, I could buy a better car.

Now make the sentences true for you.

Compare with Type 1 conditionals (unit 20):

Real (Type 1): *If I **meet** the Prince, I'll ask for his autograph.*
(said by someone waiting outside a building to see the Prince. It's possible / quite likely).

Unreal (Type 2): *If I **met** the Prince, I'd ask for his autograph.*
(said by someone reading a newspaper, who has no plans to meet the Prince. It's impossible / very unlikely).

E Giving advice

In unreal conditional sentences we often use *were* not *was*.
In formal English *were* is the better choice, especially with *I* ...
If I were you ... is a frequent formula for advice.

1 Listening (1).

'Stewart's Problem Hour' is a radio phone-in show. People phone the radio station with their problems, and other people call in with advice. You're going to hear a call from Josie. Try and guess her problem and fill in the spaces.

1 Josie has a problem with her ....
2 He .... helps her with the housework.
3 His room is a ....
4 He plays .... all night.
5 She's had ....

Listen and check. (✳ 2.54)

2 Listening (2). You're going to hear advice from four callers. Can you guess who says these things? Match them to the photos.

'I wouldn't worry about it.'
'If I were you, I'd throw him out.'
'If I were you, I'd stop complaining.'
'I'd stop doing his washing and his meals.'

Listen and check. (✳ 2.55 – 2.58)

3 What advice would you give to Josie? Begin:

If I were you ... I wouldn't ...
You should / shouldn't ... Why don't you ...?

F *Tower of Strength*

1 Listen and read. (✳ 2.59)

2 Listen and sing.

TOWER OF STRENGTH

by Burt Bacharach and Bob Hillard

If I were a tower of strength
I'd walk away

I'd look in your eyes
and here's what I'd say

and I'd walk out the door.

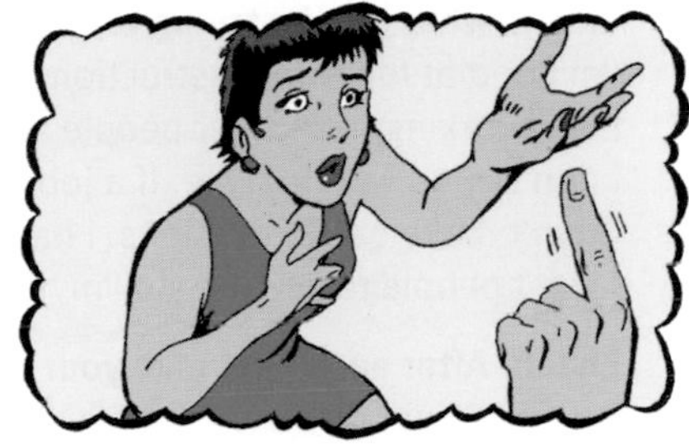

You'd be down on your knees
You'd be calling to me
But a tower of strength is
something I'll never be

If I were a tower of strength
I'd watch you cry

I'd laugh at your tears
And tell you goodbye

I don't want you, I don't need you
I don't love you anymore
and I'd walk out the door.

You'd be down on your knees
You'd be calling to me
But a tower of strength is
something I'll never be.

See **Extension 26** p.207

27 People talking

A Speech habits

1 Check the meaning of these words:

articulate inarticulate enthusiastic dull boring clever
confident over-confident likeable nervous shy assertive

2 You're going to hear four people at a job interview. They are all going to say the same thing, but they all have different speech habits.
This is what they're trying to say:
I'm good at following instructions.
I like working with other people and I'm a good team member.
I don't mind working late. If a job needs finishing, I'll stay until it's done.
I don't make quick decisions. I have to think about things carefully first.
I want people to like me, so I'm 'too nice'.

Listen. After each one, give your opinions about the speakers:
He / She sounds inarticulate. He / She doesn't sound very confident.
(* 2.60) Judy, (* 2.61) Terry, (* 2.62) Marcia, (* 2.63) Alvin

3 Complete these sentences.
.... sounds as if he / she's reading notes.
.... uses a lot of introductory adverbs (e.g. *Basically* ...)
.... uses a lot of qualifiers (e.g. *extremely*, *rather*)
.... uses a lot of hesitation words (e.g. *you know* ..., *I mean* ...)

You will hear all of these listening pieces again later in this unit.

B Attitude

1 Listen to Judy again. (✻ 2.60) **Which of these introductory adverbs does she use?**

- ☐ Basically ...
- ☐ Actually ...
- ☐ Hopefully ...
- ☐ Personally ...
- ☐ Fortunately ...
- ☐ Unfortunately ...
- ☐ Obviously ...
- ☐ Honestly ...

2 Match these words with the phrases you could replace them with.

A Honestly ...	1 As you know / can see ..., It is clear that ...
B Basically ...	2 It is / was good that ...
C Actually ...	3 Speaking for myself ...
D Fortunately ...	4 If the best thing happens ...
E Unfortunately ...	5 What I'm saying is true ...
F Personally ...	6 This might surprise you, but the truth is ...
G Obviously ...	7 The important thing is that ...
H Hopefully ...	8 It is / was bad that ...

3 Listen to the sentences and check. (✻ 2.64)

Attitude markers

Some **introductory adverbs** are **attitude markers**.
Look at exercise 2 above.
Frequency adverbs are often used in a similar way, especially:
Generally ... Normally ...

We use **attitude markers** to show our feelings about what we are going to say.

I'm afraid ... (*you've failed your exam.*) when we think the listener won't like what we're saying.
Sorry ... and ***Yes, but*** ... when we're going to disagree with something.
Of course ... and ***Obviously / Clearly*** ... when we want to strengthen what we're saying.

C Pausing

1 **Listen to Terry again.** (✳ 2.61)

2 **Terry didn't read the commas, so he didn't pause in the right places. Say these sentences aloud to yourself. Where should the commas be?**

1 She spoke slowly carefully and sensibly.
2 My home address is Flat 5 16 High Street Oxbridge Hampshire.
3 Yes I've met her mother her father and her brother.
4 If I won the lottery I'd buy a house a car a boat and a private plane.
5 When he was at school he used to wear a white shirt a red tie a blue jacket and grey trousers.

3 **Write these punctuation marks:**

question mark	brackets	quotation marks	slash
full stop (dot)	comma	exclamation	asterisk
colon	semi colon	dash	backslash

4 **This letter hasn't got any punctuation.**
Listen and add the punctuation. (✳ 2.65)

Dear Anna David and Sarah

Thanks for your postcard It was really great to hear from you again I've just bought a new computer printer scanner and CD burner Now you'll be able to e-mail me My new e-mail address is
richardjohnson family@btnet co uk

By the way I found a new website for family history The address is
http family history north uk com johnson 8975

You should try it Do you know what I found out Our family came from Sweden about two hundred years ago

Very best wishes

Uncle Richard

D Thinking time

1 Listen to Marcia again. (✳ 2.62)

People use *kind of ..., sort of ..., like ..., you know ...* a lot in spoken English. This is something to understand, but not to imitate because it makes you sound inarticulate.

Marcia was trying to get thinking time. Here are some strategies.

Ask the speaker for repitition	*Sorry? Pardon? Could you repeat that? What did you say?*
Repeat the question yourself	*What are my strengths and weaknesses?*
Just echo the end of the question	*Strengths and weaknesses?*
Delaying words / noises	*It depends (on) ..., Well ..., Um ..., Let me think ...*

2 You can repeat the end of a question to get extra thinking time. Listen, and repeat the echos. (✳ 2.66)

Which president was assassinated in 1963?	1963?
What's the capital of Scotland?	Scotland?
What's six times seven?	Six times seven?
Do you believe in ghosts?	Ghosts?
What's the meaning of 'prohibited'?	Prohibited?
What was your best school subject?	My best school subjects?

COMMUNICATION

Student A Look at Activity 11 on p.214.
Student B Look at Activity 21 on p.220.

E Qualifiers

1 Listen to Alvin again. What does he say? Match. (✻ 2.63)

very	quick
really	carefully
completely	good
particularly	too nice
rather	excellent
almost	finished

Adverbs of degree or **intensifiers** are a type of **qualifier**.
They make the following word stronger or weaker.
Stronger: *I'm **very** tired, I'm **extremely** tired*
Weaker: *I'm **rather** tired, I'm **quite** tired*

2 Listen and read. Does the highlighted adverb make the following word stronger (+) or weaker (-)? (✻ 2.67)

1 Sorry, you're totally wrong.
2 Well, yes, it's quite nice.
3 He was feeling rather annoyed.
4 I woke up, and I was terribly thirsty.
5 They were a bit late for the meeting.
6 She was only slightly hurt in the accident.
7 Throw it away. It's completely useless.
8 It was almost dark when we arrived.
9 He looked really surprised.
10 The film was absolutely fantastic!

3 Read this story, then choose where to add five (or more) qualifiers. Tell the story aloud to your partner. Did you choose different qualifiers?

It was late and we were tired. It was dark when we arrived at the hotel. It was big and old. We couldn't see any lights in the windows. I knocked on the door, and a light went on. It was starting to rain. We were cold and wet.

'Who's that?' shouted a woman, 'It's late.' She sounded angry. She opened the door, and looked surprised.

'We've got a reservation,' I said.

'We're full,' she replied, 'We haven't got any rooms.'

'But I phoned last week,' I said, 'Ben and Stella Lenton, from Bristol?'

The woman looked puzzled, 'But Mr and Mrs Lenton are already here,' she said, 'They arrived two hours ago. They're asleep.'

4 Can you continue the story?

See **Extension 27** p.207

28 Stories

Once upon a time, a handsome prince met a poor village girl and they fell in love. His name was Conrad and her name was Rose. They had to keep their romance secret from the King and Queen. Conrad gave Rose a gold ring with a large diamond. She gave him a silver ring with a small emerald. It wasn't expensive, but it was the only ring she had.

One day Rose was walking through the village when she saw Gloria, the innkeeper's daughter. She couldn't believe her eyes! Gloria was wearing the silver ring. Rose left the village that afternoon with a broken heart. Conrad never saw her again. They both lived unhappily ever after.

A A folk story

Listen and read. Then underline the verbs in the story. What tense are they? (✳ 2.68)

The story is told in a chronological sequence (*first* this happened, *then* that happened ...)
The story uses only the past simple and the past continuous.

If you want to explain the story, you may need another tense, the **past perfect** or 'the past of the past'. Turn the page and read the explanation.

Once upon a time, a handsome prince met a poor village girl and they fell in love. His name was Conrad and her name was Rose. They had to keep their romance secret from the King and Queen. Conrad gave Rose a gold ring with a large diamond. She gave him a silver ring with a small emerald which her mother had given her just before she died.

One day Rose was walking through the village when she saw Gloria, the innkeeper's daughter. She couldn't believe her eyes! Gloria was wearing her mother's silver ring.

There was a simple explanation. Earlier that day Prince Conrad had left the ring by an open window in his room, while he went hunting with his father. A magpie had seen the ring sparkling in the sunlight. It had flown down and taken the ring. Later, the magpie was frightened by the hunters, and dropped the ring just outside the village inn. Gloria found it a few minutes later.

Rose thought that the prince had given Gloria the ring. She left the village that afternoon with a broken heart.

When Conrad returned from hunting he went to his room. The ring had gone! He ran to the village to tell Rose, but she had already left. Conrad never saw her again. They both lived unhappily ever after, though they were both rich, because Rose sold the gold ring that the prince had given her.

B The whole story

1 Read the story. (✳ 2.69)

A *Rose **gave** Conrad a silver ring.*
B *Rose's mother **had given** her a silver ring.*

Which **action** happened first in time, and which happened second?
Which example is past simple? Which example is past perfect?

Underline the examples of the past perfect in the story.

2 Number these events in chronological order from 1 to 14.

	They gave each other rings.		Conrad met Rose.
	Gloria found the ring.		The magpie dropped the ring.
1	Rose's mother gave her the ring.		Conrad left the ring by a window.
	Rose left the village.		Rose saw Gloria with the ring.
	A magpie took the ring.		Rose's mother died.
	Conrad returned from hunting.		Conrad ran to the village.
	Conrad and Rose fell in love.		Conrad went hunting.

When events are in a chronological sequence, you only need the **past simple**. The order is already clear.
When the events are 'mixed up' in a story, you can use the **past perfect** to make the chronological sequence clear. It is the 'past of the past'.

3 Ask and answer.

1 When Conrad returned to his room, was the ring still there?
No. It had gone.
2 When the magpie flew into the room, was Conrad still there?
3 When Gloria found the ring, was the magpie still there?
4 When Conrad got to the village, was Rose still there?

4 Close your book and retell the story in your own words.

C Past perfect

We are talking about the past: *I arrived late at the airport ...*
This is the **point in time** of the story we're telling.
When we want to talk about something **earlier** than that point in time, we use the past perfect: ... *and my plane* ***had*** *already* ***taken*** *off.*

Past — 3.10 — point in time (3.15) — now

The plane took off. — I arrived at the airport ...

Past perfect	*When I arrived at 3.15, the plane had taken off.*
Past continuous	*He arrived at 3.10, just as the plane was taking off.*
Past simple	*She arrived at 2.45. The plane took off at 3.10.*

The past perfect often appears with *when*:
When *he* ***had finished*** *the book, he went to sleep.*

With *after* and *before* we can use the past perfect or the past simple because *after / before* make the time clear.
After *(**I'd seen** / **I saw**) the film, I bought the souvenir book about it.*

Starting point	*I got to work and I didn't have my keys.*
Question	*Oh, dear. Had you left them at home?*
Short answers	*Yes, I had. / No, I hadn't.*
Negative	*I hadn't left them at home.*
Contraction 'd	*They'd fallen out of my pocket.*

1 Choose the correct words.

1 When the Queen arrived, the concert (began / had begun).

2 When we arrived, the concert (began / had already begun).

2 Make sentences with *because* + past perfect.

They were very nervous. It was their first flight.
They were very nervous because they had never flown before.

1 We were really hungry. It was our first meal for 24 hours.
2 She was terribly thirsty after six hours on the beach.
3 We were a bit bored by the film. It was our third time!
4 He was sick after the 7-course meal. He ate too much.

D Don't forget ...

Last summer Andy and Cristine went on a weekend break. Their teenage son and daughter hadn't wanted to go with them, so they left them at home on their own Cristine left a note for the kids:

Don't forget ...
Water the plants daily
Wash-up after every meal
Put all your dirty clothes in the washing machine
Feed the dog and the cat
Put the rubbish out on Friday morning (before 8 a.m.)
Don't play loud music after 11 p.m.
Vacuum the carpet daily
and ABSOLUTELY NO PARTIES!!!

1 **This was the scene when they got back. Can you guess what had happened while they were away? What things hadn't their kids done? What had they forgotten to do?**

2 **Pronunciation: *had had***

When you use *had had*, it's best to use a contraction /ˈd/ on the first *had*. If you aren't using a contraction, the first *had* is a weak form. The second *had* is a strong form: /həd hæd/

She had had /həd hæd/ *the cat for four* /fə(r) fɔː(r)/ *years when it died.*

Look at these sentences. There is a highlighted sound that appears twice. Which one is stressed, and which one is unstressed?

1 He had had the cold for a fortnight before he went to the doctor.
2 Can you ask the shopkeeper for four stamps?
3 I'd like to buy two tickets, please.
4 Can you pass me that can of beer?
5 'Have you got the time?' 'Yes, I have.'
6 'The programme's on at eight.' 'Really? Which TV Guide are you looking at?'

Listen and check. Repeat the sentences. (✻ 2.70)

E Jesse James

1 Complete the stories. Change the verbs in brackets into the past perfect. Notice the position of the adverbs.

*He had **really** done it.* *I had **just** arrived ...* *She had **then** left ...*

(✻ 2.71)

The legend

Jesse and Frank James were the most famous outlaws in the Wild West. The James Gang robbed banks and trains, and like Robin Hood, they stole from the rich and gave to the poor. By 1881, Frank (have) enough of crime and left the gang. His wife (just have) a baby and Frank wanted to become a farmer. Jesse decided to quit too. In 1882, Bob Ford came to visit him. When Jesse turned to get him a drink, Ford shot him in the back. The gun that he used (be) a gift from Jesse. Ford collected the $10,000 reward for killing Jesse. But was that the end of the story?

(✻ 2.72)

The real story?

In 1948, newspapers found a 102-year-old man in Oklahoma called J. Frank Dalton. He told reporters that he was Jesse James. Dalton had exactly the same scars on his body that Jesse (have). Apparently, Bob Ford (kill) another man, Charlie Bigelow, who (look) just like Jesse. Jesse (then sing) at his own funeral, before leaving for South America. He (decide) to keep the secret until his 100th birthday. Dalton died peacefully in 1951 at the age of 104.

Frank James spent the rest of his life looking for one million dollars' worth of gold that he and Jesse (bury) in Oklahoma. He (forget) the exact location. Strangely, Frank never tried to kill his brother's murderer, and in fact a few years later he gave Bob Ford money to open a saloon. It seems that Ford was their first cousin, and, Frank James said, 'If Bob Ford (really shoot) Jesse James, he wouldn't have lived until sundown.'

2 Listen and check.

F Well-known stories

1 Discuss these stories:

Cinderella	Joan of Arc	Alice in Wonderland
Zatoichi	Helen of Troy	The Three Musketeers
Nasreddin	Romeo & Juliet	Billy the Kid
Frankenstein	Robin Hood	The Wicked Witch

1. Which of these characters have you heard of?
2. Which ones have you seen films about?
3. Which countries are the stories from?
4. What do you know about them?
5. Are the stories well-known in your country?

2 What are popular stories from your country? Can you tell one?

See **Extension 28** p.208

29 The news

MILLIONS HIT BY POWER BLACKOUT

DAILY EXPRESS

FREE ICE CREAM FOR EVERY READER

FREE FOR EVERY READER AERIAL PHOTO OF YOUR HOME

DIANA Fury over shocking new book about the night she died

Anger as Britain starts to run out of electricity

POWER CUTS BY CHRISTMAS

WE TOLD YOU SO: Daily Express, August 15

MILLIONS were last night hit by a massive power cut which plunged a wide area of England into darkness and chaos.

By John Ingham

Daily Express revealed that the electricity

the South-east were stranded. Nearly 400 trains allocated to carry 120,000 commuters across southern England ground to a halt.

Kent and Wimbledon in west London. Frightened commuters told how they feared London had been hit by an Al Qaeda attack.

London paralysed by electricity blackout

BY DANIELLE DEMETRIOU

... was Alan Basford, 52, a

BLACKOUT

POWER CUTS HIT 1 MILLION LONDONERS:

SEE PAGE 8

A Headlines

1 Answer the questions:

What happened?

Where did it happen?

What time of day did it happen?

2 Find these words in the headlines.

Which word does **not** mean the same as the others in the group?

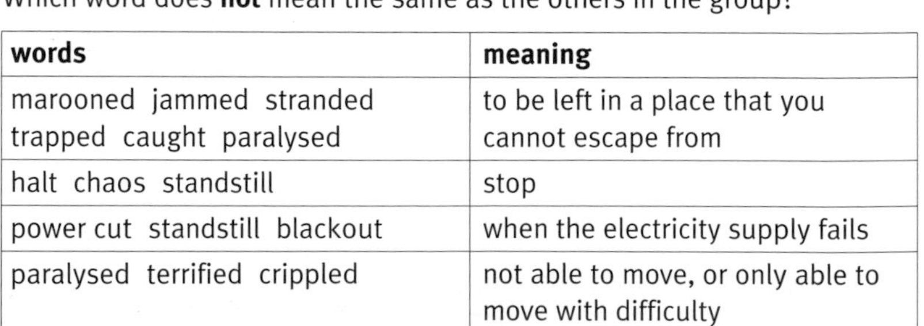

words	meaning
marooned jammed stranded trapped caught paralysed	to be left in a place that you cannot escape from
halt chaos standstill	stop
power cut standstill blackout	when the electricity supply fails
paralysed terrified crippled	not able to move, or only able to move with difficulty

3 Find words which mean:

a the busiest time of day for transport

b very big

c an underground train

d completely full with people (or things)

2G THE SUN, Friday, August 29, 2003

CHAOS IN THE DARK

Rescued at last . . . transport police and Tube worker with torch guide passengers to safety at Stockwell station in South London last night

500,000 stranded as Tubes and trains halt

HALF a million people were stranded on the Tube and rail-

WHAT A GREAT RECEP... STILL THE UK'S #1 MOVIE
EVEN THE UPPER
"STIFLER... ONE TRULY GRE...

Blackout Thursday

LONDON IS CRIPPLED BY RUSH HOUR POWER CUT

By GARY JONES, Chief Reporter

A GIGANTIC electricity failure last

PAGE TWO

TRAPPED AND TERRIFIED!

By Stephen Wright

- MASSIVE BLACKOUT BRINGS RUSH HOUR LONDON TO A STANDSTILL
- 250,000 PEOPLE MAROONED IN TUBE TRAINS DEEP UNDERGROUND

TERRORISM or not, it spread terror on an unprecedented scale.

Hundreds of thousands of commuters were trapped on trains, 250,000 underground. Others were stranded in lifts. The Mayor called it 'an absolute disgrace'.

Last night an urgent investigation was under way into a massive power

failed, bringing chaos at major junctions. Police CCTV cameras also failed. Coming just a fortnight before the second anniversary of September 11, the power failure raised fears of a terror attack.

Last night the cause was unclear. Theories ranged from sabotage to the simple collapse of a crumbling, archaic network.

Initial investigations were centred on transformer failures at three South London substations.

The blackout came just two weeks

London left in the dark by massive power cut

By Lewis Smith

A POWER blackout plunged large parts of London into chaos at the height of the rush

---

Thousands stranded as big power cut hits London

250,000 caught in Tube after power cut

By Catriona Davies and John Crowley

AN estimated 250,000 com-

Energy said: "We los... plies to large parts of London as a resul... National Grid failure

---

Blackout

Panic in the streets as Tubes trapped, stations jammed and traffic in chaos

B Newsflash

Newspaper headlines often use the **passive** without the **auxiliary verb**.
Headlines leave out other words too.
250,000 caught = 250,000 people **were** caught ...
Millions hit by blackout = Millions **were** hit by **a** blackout ...

The missing auxiliary verb depends on the time of the report:
(Radio news during the blackout) – 250,000 people **are** caught / 250,000 people **have been** caught ...
(News after the blackout) – 250,000 people **were** caught ...

**1 This is a radio report during the blackout.
Complete the spaces with words from the box.**

cut chaos deep massive power
rush-hour standstill tube without

This is a newsflash. London is in chaos following a .... power failure at six-twenty this evening. Five hundred .... trains have been halted by the .... , and another four hundred main line trains have been halted above ground. Tens of thousands of passengers are stranded in tube trains .... underground and many people are trapped in lifts. A spokesperson for London Underground says, 'Stations are being cleared, and passengers are being taken to safety by underground staff. The trains which are at a .... in the tunnels will be evacuated. Emergency power supplies cannot be switched on yet because passengers are walking along the lines.' More than 270 traffic lights have also failed, bringing .... to streets which are jammed with .... traffic. Thousands of homes have been left .... electricity. Police are asking people to remain calm while they are waiting for .... to be restored.

Listen and check. (✳ 2.73)

2 Highlight the auxiliary verbs in the text which come before past participles. Complete this table:

Active	**Passive**
The power cut has halted trains.	Trains *have been halted.*
They are clearing stations.	Stations ....
We will evacuate the trains.	The trains ....
We can't switch on the power.	The power ....
They are going to restore power.	Power is going ....

C Passives

Passives account for 25% of the verbs in academic and scientific writing.
Passives account for 15% of the verbs in news reports.
Passives account for 2% of the verbs in everyday conversation.

	active	**passive**
perfect	They have done it. They had done it.	It has been done. It had been done.
continuous	They are doing it. They were doing it.	It is being done. It was being done.
modal	They can / must do it. They will / might do it. They could / would do it.	It can / must be done. It will / might be done. It could / would be done.
infinitive	to do They had to do it. They're going to do it.	to be done It had to be done. It's going to be done.

Use this chart and make ten true sentences.

John Lennon	is not	found	in Canada.
The Earth's weather	are	translated	in the morning sky.
Safety-belts	was	changed	in the future.
Shakespeare's 'Hamlet'	were	allowed	in Liverpool.
Smoking	have been	worn	in New York in 1980.
The planet Venus	has been	born	in cars in Britain.
English and French	is being	made	into many languages.
Films	will be	murdered	by pollution.
A cure for cancer	can be	spoken	in this building.
The Beatles	must be	seen	in Hollywood since 1909.

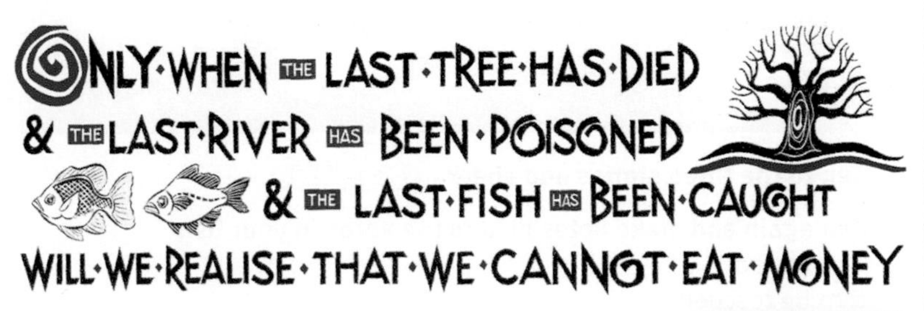

D TV news

1 **The passive forms of these verbs are all frequent in news stories.**

accused arrested burgled charged with discovered
found released injured jailed killed lost named
offered hurt rescued shot sold stolen trapped

You're going to hear three news stories. Can you guess which of the verbs you will hear in the stories? Make three lists with these titles:

Motorway chaos after crash
Self-defence or murder?
Priceless painting in phone box!

2 **Listen to the three stories and check.** (✱ 2.74 – 2.76)

3 **Listen again and make notes next to the verbs in your lists.**

were trapped
had to be rescued

Then retell the stories from memory.

E More news

"No news is good news"

1 **Many of the frequent verbs in section D describe bad news. But would anyone read a 'good news newspaper'?**

The Daily Smile

IN TODAY'S NEWSPAPER

Fewer people have been killed on the roads this year.
No one was murdered in London yesterday.
More schools and hospitals will be built next year.
A Hollywood star has been happily married for 30 years.
12,000 healthy babies were delivered in the UK last week.

Can you think of some good news stories?

2 **Imagine. Can you imagine the stories that might go with these headlines?**

Rock star arrested after concert

Influenza caused by viruses from outer-space

European football champions beaten by schoolboy team

Lost island of Atlantis discovered

Three injured in strange accident!

UFO SEEN OVER LONDON

See **Extension 29** p.209

30 Reporting

A *They said ...*

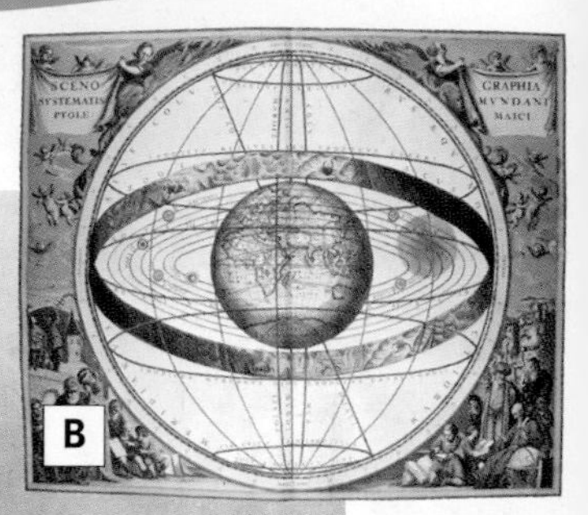

1 Match the sentences to the pictures.

They said the Earth was flat.
They said we would never fly.
They said it couldn't sink.
They said we had discovered everything.
They said the Sun moved round the Earth.
They said there would be no more wars.

2 The actual words were said a long time ago. What did they actually say?

"The Earth (was / is) flat."
"The Sun (moved / moves) round the Earth."
"We (had discovered / have discovered) everything."
"We (will / would) never fly."
"It (cannot / couldn't) sink."
"There (would / will) be no more wars."

Listen and check. (✳ 2.77)

B Reporting verbs

A He .... that *Eye Dolls* were playing in his town.

B He .... he would go and see them.

C The ticket office .... him that all the tickets had gone.

D He .... that tickets were for sale on the Internet.

E He .... that they were very expensive.

F He .... a friend to phone him from the concert.

1 Complete the spaces with reporting verbs from the box.

saw read told asked thought heard

2 Listen and check. (✻ 2.78)

3 Match these sentences to the pictures.

1. I'll go and see them!
2. Hmm, *Eye Dolls* are playing here next week.
3. Wow! They're very expensive!
4. Tickets are on sale at www.ticketsales.com
5. Can you phone me from the concert?
6. Sorry, I'm afraid all the tickets have gone.

C Reported speech

There are two ways of reporting.
You can use **direct speech** (see unit 18): *He said, "I'm tired."*

You can use **reported speech**: *He said (that) he was tired.*
Backshifting. In reported speech, the tense of the report often moves back one tense into the past.

am, is	➜	was
are	➜	were
have	➜	had
can	➜	could
will	➜	would

do, does	➜	did
go, like, see	➜	went, liked, saw
has, have (done)	➜	had (done)
did, saw	➜	had done, had seen
must	➜	had to

would, *could*, *should*, *might*, *had done* do not change
We do not always change the past into the past perfect.

direct: *'I saw a film,' said Rosie.*
reported: *She said she saw a film.* OR *She said she had seen a film.*

When the statement is still true at the time of the report, we don't have to change the tense.
'It's my favourite city,' he said.
He said it's his favourite city. (And it still is his favourite city).

time words sometimes change.
direct: *She said, 'I'll do it tomorrow.'*
reported (the same day): *She said she would do it tomorrow.*
reported (later): *She said she would do it the next day.*
yesterday ➜ the day before tomorrow ➜ the next day
last week ➜ the week before next year ➜ the next year

1 **Put your name on a piece of paper. Write three true statements, one past, one present and one future:**

Maria
I met some friends on Saturday.
I usually drive to work.
I'm going to a party later.

2 **Group work. Put your piece of paper on the table. Take another student's piece of paper. Report what they said. Because your report is immediately after the statement, you don't have to backshift, but try it for practice.**
e.g. *Maria said she'd met some friends on Saturday.*
She said she usually drove to work.
She said she was going to a party later.

D Complaints

1 **Listen to a travel agent describing the hotel to her clients, Jerry and Liz. Which things from the brochure does she mention?** (✳ 2.79)
What does she say? Choose the correct word.
- It's only 25 metres from the (sea / beach).
- (Great Ray / Your hotel) has empty sandy beaches.
- You can hire a (car / moped) and visit them all.
- It'll be (hot / dry).
- It's (always / very) quiet and peaceful.
- The hotel's got a fish (restaurant / shop).

2 **Three months later Jerry has just come back from the holiday. He's speaking to the travel agent.** (✳ 2.80)
What does Jerry say to the agent? Look at 1 and make sentences.
You said we could hire a car.

3 **What are Jerry's complaints? Make sentences.**
You said we could hire a car, but we couldn't. They only had mopeds.

E *She asked ...*

Reported questions
Direct questions:

*'**Are** you a stranger?'*	*She asked (me) if I **was** a stranger.*
*'**Do** you **speak** French?'*	*She asked (him) if he **spoke** French.*
*'**Have** you **seen** David?'*	*She asked (us) if we **had seen** David.*
*'**Can** you **remember** it?'*	*She asked (her) if she **could remember** it.*

***Wh-* questions**

*'Where **are** you **going**?'*	*He asked (them) where they **were going**.*
*'What **did** you **do**?'*	*He asked (her) what she **had done**.*
*'What **can** you **do**?'*	*He asked (me) what I **could do**.*

1 **Listen to this oral English interview. The teacher asks nine questions. Listen for them.** (✳ 2.81) **Can you remember the questions? List them.**
How long have you been studying In English Pre-intermediate?
Has your English improved?

2 **Enrique is reporting the interview to a friend. The friend wants to know because their interview is next! Report the questions. e.g.**
First she asked me how long I'd been studying this book.
Then she asked if my English had improved.

3 **Can you remember Enrique's answers? Listen again. Report Enrique's answers.**
He said / told her that he'd been studying it since January.

4 **Make a list of questions about this book for your partner.**
Can you remember one of the jokes?

Ask your partner the questions, then report back to the class.
I asked him if he could remember one of the jokes.
He said that he could, and he told me the joke about the hunters in the woods.

See **Extension 30** p.209

Grammar index
Extensions
Communication activities
Transcripts

GRAMMAR INDEX

You can find references to the units and to language boxes in the Student Book main pages and Extensions (ext) below.

EXTENSION 1

Relationships

1 Match the sentences with the meanings.

1 'This is my partner, Tom.'
2 'I'm a widow.'
3 'I'm a widower.'
4 'I'm divorced.'
5 'I'm separated.'
6 'I'm engaged. This is my fiancé.'
7 'I'm a single parent.'
8 'This is my flatmate, Tom.' (US: roommate)

A We're going to get married.
B My wife's dead.
C I was married, but not anymore.
D I don't live with my child's father / mother.
E We're in a relationship and we live together.
F We share accommodation, but we aren't in a relationship.
G My husband's dead.
H My husband / wife and I don't live together anymore.

2 Can you explain these relationships?

ex-wife, ex-husband, ex-girlfriend, ex-boyfriend, my 'ex',
stepson, stepdaughter, stepfather, stepmother, half-brother / stepbrother
great uncle, great aunt, great nephew, great niece

EXTENSION 2

on / off

Match the parts of the sentences and connect them with *on* or *off*.

1 Can I try this jacket		A at the hi-fi store tomorrow.
2 Come in. Take your coat		B for senior citizens.
3 What's		C because I can't hear!
4 *Star Wars III* is		D please?
5 There's 10%		E so don't eat it.
6 There's a sale	**on**	F and sit down.
7 It's upstairs		G the west coast of the USA.
8 This fish smells	**off**	H TV tonight?
9 I'm on the phone! Turn the radio		I the way home?
10 She's		J at the cinema this week.
11 Hey, ref! Send him		K the second floor.
12 Los Angeles is		L That was a foul!
13 Can you stop at the supermarket		M holiday this week.

KEEP OFF THE TRACKS

TURN ON LIGHTS

Simple or continuous?

1 Do these time words go with the present continuous or the present simple? Write *PC* or *PS* next to the words.

1 now
2 every day
3 usually
4 at the moment
5 twice a week
6 right now
7 on Tuesdays
8 often
9 once a month

2 Choose the best ending (A to J) for the sentences (1–10).

1 I'm doing
2 I do
3 I have
4 I read
5 I'm learning
6 I play
7 I hardly ever meet
8 I go
9 I'm reading
10 I don't eat

A a shower every day.
B tennis on Tuesdays.
C on holiday twice a year.
D a computer course at the moment.
E meat.
F English people.
G the washing-up every evening.
H for half an hour before I go to sleep.
I to drive.
J *Hamlet*. It's taking me a long time.

EXTENSION 4

Air travel

Find the traveller's route through (1) Departures (2) Arrivals.

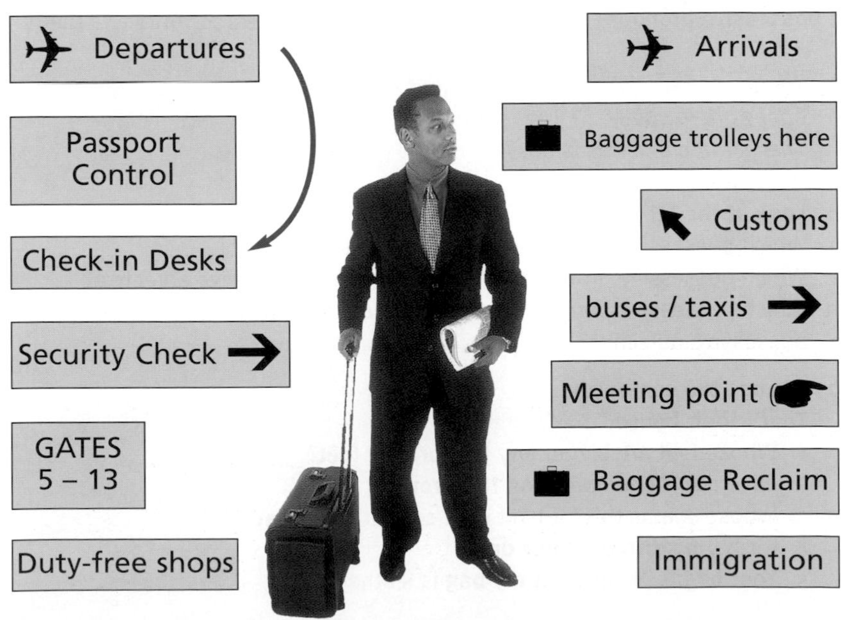

Possessive pronouns

possessive adjective	my	your	his	her	our	their
possessive pronoun	mine	yours	his	hers	ours	theirs

We use possessive pronouns without nouns. Compare:
These are my books. / These are mine.
This is our car. / This is ours.

1 Look at the table.

1 Which possessive pronouns are 'possessive adjective + s'?
2 Which possessive pronoun is the same as the possessive adjective?
3 Which possessive pronoun is most different from the possessive adjective?

2 Change the sentences.

That's **their house**. That's theirs.

1 Whose feet are bigger, **my feet** or **your feet**?
2 I like **our room** more than **their room**.
3 Whose coat is this? It isn't **your coat**, it's **his coat**.
4 It isn't **my drink**, it's **her drink**.
5 **Your bag** is plastic, but **my bag** is leather.

Schooldays

1 Find someone who did these things. Ask questions:

Did you have a crush on a teacher?
No, I didn't. / Yes, I had a crush on my biology teacher.

had a crush on their teacher	came top of their class in a school subject	can remember the names of three of their primary school teachers ....
got into trouble (and had to see the head teacher)	always passed their exams	studied art at school (i.e. painting and drawing) ....
learned to play a musical instrument at school	played in a school sports team	hated school ....

2 Discuss your answers.

Q: *Who* ***came*** *top of the class in a school subject?* **A:** *Anna* ***did****.*
Q: *Which subject* ***did*** *she* ***come*** *top in?* **A:** *Physics.*
Q: *Who* ***hated*** *school?* **A:** *Paul* ***did****.*
Q: *Why* ***did*** *he* ***hate*** *school?* **A:** *Because he always* ***failed*** *his exams.*

EXTENSION 7

Collocations

1 Match the sentence beginnings to a group of three endings. The beginning must match all of the endings in the group.

beginning	endings
I'd rather	the blue one best meeting people Japanese films
I'd like	any more tea, thank you to be late for the film another drink, thank you
I don't want	not take an exam go by train than by car have the blue one, please
I like	to ask her out another drink, please you to help me

2 Think of a short conversation (2 to 4 lines) with each of the sentences in it.

EXTENSION 8

yet, already, just, still

1 You are planning a wedding. There are ten things to do. You have just done four of them. Tick them. Then ask about your partner's list:

Have you (done this) yet?
No, I haven't (done that) yet. / Yes, I've already (done that).

Book St. Winifred's church for the wedding
Book Forest Hotel for the reception
Send out the invitations
Order the wedding cake
Order the flowers and the bride's bouquet
Book the wedding car (Rolls Royce?)
Arrange a fitting for the dress
Make the bridesmaids' dresses
Hire suits for the men
Book the plane tickets for the honeymoon

2 Imagine. It's the next day. Tick three more things. Ask about your partner's list again.

Have you done this yet?
Yes, I did that yesterday. / Yes, I've just done that. /
No, I still haven't done that.

EXTENSION 9

could / *couldn't* for ability; reasons

Match the beginnings and endings.

1 I couldn't breathe 2 I couldn't stay late 3 I could afford to buy it 4 I couldn't go swimming 5 I could understand her 6 I couldn't find the road 7 I could do the exercise 8 I couldn't hear her 9 I couldn't drink wine	**because**	A I didn't have a map. B it was very cheap. C the music was too loud. D of the air pollution. E she spoke slowly and clearly. F it was too cold. G I had to drive home afterwards. H I had to get up early the next day. I it wasn't very difficult.

***could* / *couldn't* for past ability**
Could *you do it?* *Yes, I* ***could****.* / *No, I* ***couldn't****.*
Often people are exaggerating:
I couldn't breathe! means it was difficult to breathe, not it was impossible.
Or they are 'boasting' (telling you how good something was)
My daughter could play chess when she was three!

EXTENSION 10

Prepositions

Complete the spaces with words from the box.

away into down beside over through
inside towards above on onto under

Frozen in time

In A.D. 79, a volcanic eruption destroyed the Roman city of Pompeii. First stones and hot ash fell .... the town, then there was a second eruption and poisonous gas rolled .... the side of the volcano and .... the streets of the town. Some people ran .... the sea, hoping to get .... from the stones and gas. They died .... the beach. Others ran .... buildings and hid .... beds or tables. One family went upstairs after five metres of ash filled the ground floor rooms. They died when more ash fell. Archaeologists found spaces .... the ash where it covered .... the bodies of the victims. They filled the spaces with concrete. The concrete is in the shape of the dead bodies. They found a man lying .... a woman in bed, and a mother holding her child .... the hot ash.

EXTENSION 11

Phone formulas

Replace the underlined words in the sentences with words from the box.

connect you answer I'm losing the signal connection louder call wait a moment disconnect hear soon

1 Sorry, I didn't catch that. Can you repeat it?
2 I'll try to put you through.
3 I need to check on the computer. Please bear with me.
4 Can you ring him back?
5 Please speak up. I can't hear you.
6 It's OK, I'll get the phone.
7 Sorry, it's a bad line.
8 I'm on my mobile. Sorry, it's breaking up.
9 I'll hang up and call you back.
10 Your call will be answered shortly.

EXTENSION 12

Quantity

Every person on Earth has an 'ecological footprint'. This measures the food and energy that you use, and how much land it takes to produce it. There are 2.2 hectares of biologically productive space per person in the world. If most of the sentences below are true for you, your ecological footprint is probably about
9 hectares a year.

- I throw away too much of the food that I buy.
- I don't buy enough fresh, locally-produced food.
- I use my car far too much. I often travel alone.
- I only recycle a little of my household waste.
- I spend more than five hours a year on planes.
- My home is more than 200 square metres.
- Only a few of the light bulbs in my home are low-energy.
- Very little of the electricity I use comes from renewable sources (wind, sun, hydro-electric power).

Make the sentences true for you.
(You can calculate your footprint on the Internet. Type 'ecological footprint' into a search engine. There are several websites with surveys.)

EXTENSION 13

Expressions with *'ll*

Put the expressions into the spaces.

I'll see / It won't last forever / We'll let you know / it'll do / It won't be long / I'll give you a ring / You'll never guess / It'll only take a minute

1 Cheer up! .... before you're back home again.
2 .... who I've just seen!
3 No, I agree. It's not perfect, but ....
4 Come on! Let's finish the job. ....
5 It's probably a good idea. I'm not sure. ....
6 Enjoy your honeymoon while you can. ....
7 We must meet for a coffee some time. ....
8 Thanks for coming to the interview.
We have a few more people to see. ....

EXTENSION 14

more, fewer, less

quantifier	comparative form	superlative form
a lot / much / many	more	most
a few / not many	fewer	fewest
a little / not much	less	least

more is used with countables and uncountables.
less is used with uncountables, *fewer* with countables.
Nowadays some people use *less* with both. Others think this is incorrect.

Make sentences with opposites of the words in bold.

She has **more** free time than me. *I have less free time than her.*
1 She gets **the most** phone calls in our office. I ....
2 She earns **more** money than me. I ....
3 At parties, she drinks **the most** wine. I ....
4 She spends **less** money than me. I ....
5 She does **the least** work in our office. I ....
6 She has **the fewest** qualifications in our company. I ....
7 She receives **more** e-mails than me. I ....
8 But she has **fewer** friends than me. I ....

EXTENSION 15

Complete the spaces in this 'In flight' announcement with words from the box. Some of the words are used more than once.

must not allowed do not must not should

Global Airlines welcome you to Flight 456 to Miami. Smoking is .... on this flight, and smoke detectors are fitted in all toilets. You .... fasten your seat belt whenever the 'Fasten Seat Belts' sign is on. We also advise that you .... keep your belt fastened at all other times. Please .... eat or drink while moving around the cabin, and you .... congregate in the aisles or near the toilets when we are in US airspace. Passengers .... complete a US landing card and a customs declaration before arrival. On arrival in Miami, all passengers .... go through US Immigration. Transit passengers .... then proceed immediately to the transfer desk. All passengers .... watch the safety video which will be shown in a few minutes. You .... do this even if you are a frequent traveller. Our flight attendants are now showing you the nearest emergency exits.

EXTENSION 16

Direct and indirect questions

1 **Choose the correct words.**

1 Can you tell me what time (☐ is it ☐ it is)?
2 Could you tell me how much (☐ do you earn ☐ you earn)?
3 How often (☐ you rent ☐ do you rent) DVDs?
4 Do you know if (☐ can I ☐ I can) smoke in here?
5 Could you tell me where (☐ did she go ☐ she went)?
6 What (☐ should I ☐ I should) wear to the party?
7 Do you know if (☐ has she ☐ she has) had her baby yet?
8 Do you know what (☐ would she ☐ she would) like for her birthday?
9 Why (☐ did you go ☐ you went) home early?
10 Did you know what (☐ was the answer ☐ the answer was)?
11 Can you tell me if (☐ he got ☐ did he get) the job?
12 Do you remember what time (☐ are we ☐ we are) meeting them?

2 **Which examples are direct questions? Which are indirect questions?**

3 **Give short negative answers to the indirect questions.** 1 *No, I can't.*

EXTENSION 17

Making past participles

Dictionaries show you past tenses and past participles:

speak /spiːk/ verb (pt spoke /spəʊk/; pp spoken /spəʊkən/)

1 **Add one letter and make these *past tenses* into past participles.**
spoke chose broke stole woke froze

2 **Add one letter and make these *present tenses* into past participles.**
take give know grow show draw see drive hear mean

3 **Add two letters and make these *present tenses* into past participles.**
be fall beat

4 **Change one letter and make these *past tenses* into past participles.**
began drank rang sang swam came ran send lend sit

5 **Take away one letter and make these *present tenses* into past participles.**
feed meet shoot

EXTENSION 18

Adverbs of manner: collocations

	well	hard	badly	fast	slowly	carefully
A good student always **tries**		✔				
Dangerous drivers **drive**						
My local football team **play**						
I always **work**						
I think English people **speak**						
A good driver always **drives**						
He had bad teeth so he **ate**						
You should **listen**						

Strong collocations
tries hard is a strong collocation. *try* and *hard* often go together.
It is the only strong collocation with *try* in the table.
drive has several strong collocations, some positive and some negative.

1 **Tick the strong collocations for each sentence in the table.**

2 **Which of the adverbs of manner are irregular?**

Passives

Complete the spaces with the words in blue.

were / was

The first **baseball caps** .... worn by a team in Brooklyn, New York, in 1860. The modern cap .... designed in the 1940s. Kids started wearing their baseball caps backwards in the late 80s.

wore / worn

T-shirts were originally .... by sailors in the United States Navy. They were made popular by Marlon Brando in the 1947 theatre play *A Streetcar Named Desire*. He also .... a white T-shirt in the film *The Wild Ones* (1954).

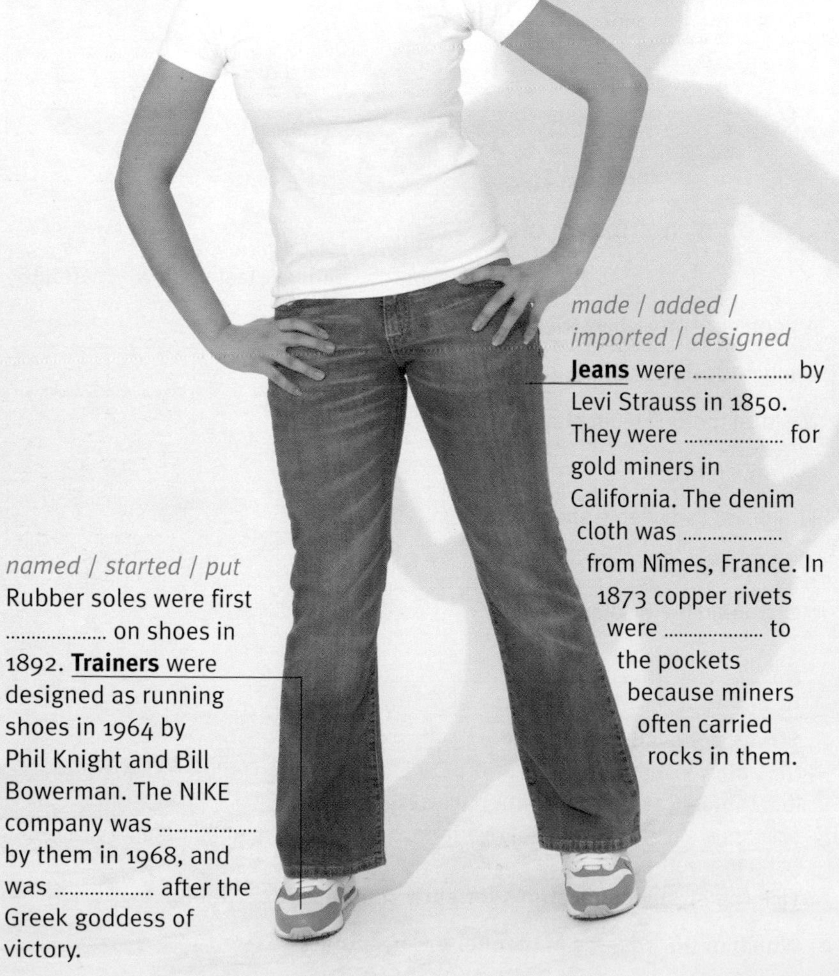

made / added / imported / designed

Jeans were .... by Levi Strauss in 1850. They were .... for gold miners in California. The denim cloth was .... from Nîmes, France. In 1873 copper rivets were .... to the pockets because miners often carried rocks in them.

named / started / put

Rubber soles were first .... on shoes in 1892. **Trainers** were designed as running shoes in 1964 by Phil Knight and Bill Bowerman. The NIKE company was .... by them in 1968, and was .... after the Greek goddess of victory.

EXTENSION 20

Conditionals

Complete the table with your ideas:

	optimist ☺	pessimist ☹
If I win the lottery ...		I'll lose all my friends.
If I lose my job ...		I won't find another one.
If I go out tonight ...	I might meet someone interesting.	
If the phone rings ...	it'll be one of my friends.	
If I stop eating chocolate ...		
If I go away on holiday ...		
If I have to work late ...		
If I change my hair colour ...		
If I stay at home tonight ...		

EXTENSION 21

Reflexive pronouns

myself / *yourself* are reflexive pronouns.
The reflexive pronouns are:
singular: *myself, yourself, himself, herself, itself*
plural: *ourselves, yourselves, themselves*

Complete the sentences with reflexive pronouns.

1 The salad's in the middle of the table. You can all help ....
2 The microwave's got an automatic timer, so it'll switch .... off when the food is cooked.
3 Jackie! Be careful with that knife, or you'll cut ....
4 'Who taught you to type?'
'No one. I taught ....'
5 Thank you for the party, we both really enjoyed ....
6 He fell down and hurt ....
7 It's a beautiful dress, and she made it ....
8 They couldn't afford a decorator, so they painted the house ....

People

1 What is important to you about a new friend or partner?

	very important	quite important	not important
appearance			
personality			
clothes			
education			
job			
money			
interests			
family			
religion			
politics			
sense of humour			

❤ LONELY HEARTS ❤

Professional man, mid-30s, well-dressed, friendly, seeks woman 20s-30s, attractive, sincere, well-educated, good sense of humour, non-smoker for friendship, trips to theatre. Apply Box # 4358

2 Read the advert. What is important for the advertiser?

He's looking for someone who | is …
has got …
likes …

3 What about you?

I like | people / men / women | who | are … / have got … / like …

My ideal partner must be | tall … / a non-smoker … / rich …

Approximation

That building is	about around approximately nearly	250 years old.
	more than less than at least	200 years old / 300 years old.
	between	200 and 300 years old.
It was built	in	the 18th century. / 1763.

Make sentences about:
- an old building in your town
- a modern building in your town
- the distance from your town to the next large city
- the distance from your home to the school
- the age of two or three famous people
- the height of a famous person
- the height of the tallest building in your town
- the amount of money in your purse / wallet

EXTENSION 24

Changes

1 **Make sentences with *used to* / *didn't use to*.**
Use your imagination, e.g.

He lives by himself now. He used to live with his parents.
He used to be married. He used to share a flat.

His life now ...	How it has changed ...
He lives by himself now.	
He doesn't smoke anymore.	
His hair is shorter now.	
He's lost weight.	
He hasn't got a beard anymore.	
He wears glasses now.	
He moved to London last year.	
He's got a Toyota Corolla now.	
He doesn't play football anymore.	
He's stopped gambling.	

2 **How did your partner answer? Compare.**

EXTENSION 25

Adjectives with *–ing* / *–ed*

Complete the survey for your partner.

WHAT KIND OF TOURIST ARE YOU?

1 What do you think of these places and things to do?
museums A educational **B** interesting **C** boring
beaches A fun **B** relaxing **C** boring
fast food restaurants A cool **B** convenient **C** disgusting
roller coasters A terrifying **B** thrilling **C** dangerous
mountain walks A exhausting **B** relaxing **C** boring

2 You are asked to sing in a karaoke bar. How do you feel?
A excited **B** embarrassed **C** terrified **D** relaxed (You'd be drunk!)

3 You walk onto a nudist beach by accident. How do you feel?
A shocked **B** embarrassed **C** interested **D** offended

4 What do you think of rude comic postcards? Are they ...?
A offensive **B** amusing **C** embarrassing **D** shocking

EXTENSION 26

Wishes

We use the past tense with unreal conditionals to show that it is an imaginary situation.
We also use the past tense with *wish* to show that it is unreal.
I haven't got many friends. I wish I ***had*** *more friends.*
I can't afford a new car. I wish I ***could*** *afford a new car.*
I've got a terrible cold. I wish I ***were*** *feeling better.*
(We say *If I were you ...* and also *I wish I were ...*)

Three men were on a desert island after their ship sank in the ocean. They found an old lamp on the beach. One man rubbed the lamp, there was a flash, and a genie came out of the lamp. 'Thank you for rescuing me,' said the genie, 'I'm going to give you each a wish. You can wish for anything you want.'

The first man said, 'I wish I were back home.' There was a flash, and he disappeared.

The second man said, 'I wish somebody would rescue me.' A helicopter appeared on the beach. The second man got in and it flew away.

The third man looked around the empty beach, 'It's so lonely here now,' he said to himself, 'I wish the others were here!' There was a flash and the other two men appeared on the beach.

Imagine. You can have three wishes. What would they be? Compare with other students.

EXTENSION 27

Quantifiers / adjective + infinitive

Make conversations. The doctor uses the appropriate response.

Doctor Good morning. How are you today?

Patient

I'm feeling	very much much a lot a bit a little slightly	better, worse,	thank you. I'm afraid.

Doctor

I'm	– so very	glad pleased sorry	to hear that.

feel is usually a simple present verb, like *look, sound, seem*
In this example, *I'm feeling* ... is more frequent.

EXTENSION 28

Past perfect continuous

The past perfect has a continuous form:
How long had you been waiting?
I had been waiting for an hour (when he arrived.)
Compare with the present perfect continuous.

Read the newspaper article.
How long had they been drifting when she sent the message?
How long had she been speaking to the coastguard when her batteries ran out?
How long had they been waiting when the rescue boat arrived?

23,000 mile rescue

19-year-old British tourist Rebecca Fyfe was saved by a text message. She was on a tourist catamaran when its engines stopped in a storm, just a few miles from the Indonesian island of Bali. She didn't speak the local language, and knew no local phone numbers. They had already been drifting for several hours when she sent a text message to her boyfriend in England. He phoned the British coastguards who phoned her back, but her phone batteries ran out after three minutes. They then phoned the Australian coastguards, who contacted the Indonesian navy and a rescue boat was sent. They had been waiting for 48 hours by the time the boat arrived.

EXTENSION 29

Passives

Highlight the passives in these computer screens. Can you make the sentences active? (e.g. *The program / computer has found no errors.*)

The passive sounds better than the active in all these examples.

DISK CHECKER
Checking complete
No errors have been found

Progress
Your message is being sent

☑ Entourage ☑ Explorer
☐ MS Word ☐ MS Excel
☑ Photoshop ☐ In Design
The selected items will be opened at system startup time

This program must be registered before use.
● Register now ● Cancel

Your password can be changed.
Key in your new password (6 letters)
☐☐☐☐☐☐

Your disk has been checked.
✖ A major error was found in the directory record in the catalog B-tree

Super Search: 0 items
No items containing the name:
'Bob Dylan'
have been found on Mac HD

☐ Select the files and folders to be copied. No items have been selected.

EXTENSION 30

Now that you've finished ...

1 What do you think of the book?

I think	all some a few none	of the units	were	quite really very	easy. difficult. interesting. boring. useful.

2 What are your strengths and weaknesses?

I'm	good OK quite good not very good	at	listening. speaking. reading. writing.

3 What will you do next?

I'd like to ... I don't think I'll ... I plan to ...
It depends on ... I'll definitely ... I don't know.

Ask your partner. Report your partner's answers to someone else.

ACTIVITY ONE

Unit eight. Student A

Canada's favourite joke:
When NASA started sending American astronauts into space, they discovered that ballpoint pens didn't work in zero gravity. So NASA scientists spent ten years and twelve billion dollars, and they made a pen that works in space. The Russians used a pencil.

ACTIVITY TWO

Unit seven. Student A

Here are examples of the word *do* in use.
Read them and correct your partner.

I always	do	aerobics on Mondays and Fridays.
My daughter	does	her homework in front of the TV.
Why do I always have to	do	the washing-up? It's not fair.
Someone always phones while I'm	doing	the cooking.
When I was at school, we	did	exams every term.
I get really bored	doing	the same things all the time.
I've	done	yoga for three or four years now.
I'm not ready yet. I've got to	do	my hair before we go out.
I'd like to	do	a more interesting job.

ACTIVITY THREE

Unit fifteen. Student A

- You must wear a seat belt in cars.
  This is the law in the United Kingdom.
- You should take off your shoes when you enter someone's home.
  This is true in most of Asia.
- You shouldn't give people things with your left hand.
  This is true in Muslim countries.
- You mustn't drink and drive.
  This is true in most countries.
- You must not carry an open bottle of alcohol in the street or in a car.
  This is the law in most American states.
- You should never touch people on the head.
  This is true in Thailand and other Buddhist countries.

ACTIVITY FOUR

Unit eleven. Student A

You flew to London yesterday on Super Jet. Your bag didn't arrive. You are phoning Lost Property at Super Jet (Student B) to ask about your bag. Look at the three documents:

THE DOVER HOTEL
350 Canford Road,
London SW1 5WV
Tel: 020 765 8139

Welcome

Guest name: (your name)
No. of nights: 5
Room number: 713
Departure date: 20th May

CHECK-OUT TIME IS 11 A.M.

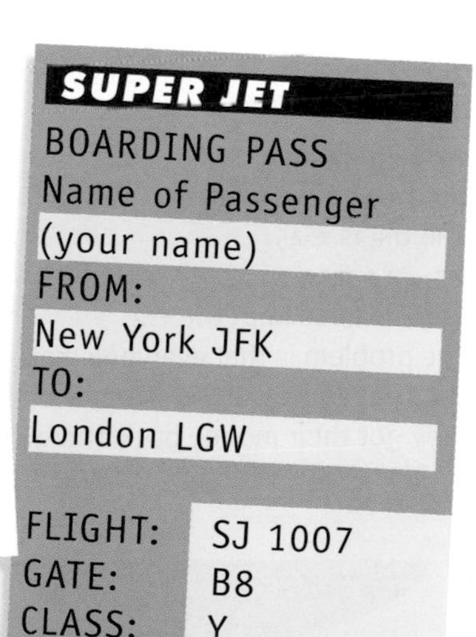
SUPER JET
BOARDING PASS
Name of Passenger
(your name)
FROM:
New York JFK
TO:
London LGW
FLIGHT: SJ 1007
GATE: B8
CLASS: Y
DATE: 14 May

SUPER JET
Baggage identification tag
SJ 17048365
JFK NEW YORK

ACTIVITY FIVE

Unit fourteen. Student A

A survey in the United Kingdom found this:

The most popular topics of conversation for men were:

1 work
2 sport
3 jokes
4 women

Student B has a list of the most popular topics for women.

ACTIVITY SIX

Unit twenty-three. The missing Euro

Solution: The missing euro
There is no missing euro.
They paid €30, and got one euro back each.
30 – 3 = 27
27 divided by 3 is 9
So they paid €9 each.
The bill is €25.
27 – 2 = 25
The waitress kept the €2.
The problem is that everyone makes an illogical deduction: 27 + 2 = 29 (not 30)
But the real calculation is 27 – 2 = 25. The number 30 is irrelevant because they got their money back and only paid €27 each.
27 is the total, not 30. Because 30 is at the beginning it confuses you.

ACTIVITY SEVEN

Unit nineteen. Section A

A tablets (e.g. Vitamins)
B a video cassette
C a bottle of wine
D orange juice
E a battery
F a dress, or shirt
G an electrical item
H eggs
I a DVD
J a bottle of whisky
K a woollen sweater
L a T-shirt

ACTIVITY EIGHT

Unit eight. Student B

Australia's favourite joke:
A woman runs into the doctor's surgery. She says, 'Doctor ... take a look at me. When I woke up this morning I looked at myself in the mirror. My hair was grey, my face looked old and wrinkled, and my eyes were red. What's happened? What's *wrong* with me, Doctor?' The doctor looks at her, and replies, 'Well, there's nothing wrong with your eyesight.'

ACTIVITY NINE

Unit seven. Student B

Here are examples of the word *make* in use.
Read them and correct your partner.

It's difficult to	make	friends in a new town.
Jaguar cars are	made	in Coventry.
I'm very sorry. It's not my fault. I	made	a mistake, that's all.
Don't forget!	Make	your bed before you go out, please.
	Make	love, not war.
What are you doing? I'm	making	a chocolate cake.
Shh! Don't	make	any noise. The baby's sleeping.
Women don't	make	their own dresses anymore.
If you can't pay the full price,	make	me an offer.

ACTIVITY TEN

Unit twenty-two. Student A

You have information about three pictures. Your partner has information about the other three pictures.

The men who are wearing sunglasses.
The man at the front is John Prescott. When the picture was taken, he was Deputy Prime Minister of the United Kingdom. So he's a politician. The other man is an assistant.

The woman who's wearing a low-cut dress
She's an Olympic gold-medal winner. She's British and her name is Denise Lewis. She won a gold medal for the heptathalon. She had to compete in seven different events. So she's an athlete. She's also very glamorous, and is a mother.

The four people who are sitting down, wearing formal suits.
These people are members of the British rock group, Dexy's Midnight Runners. This photograph is from their album 'Don't Stand Me Down'. They're professional musicians.

ACTIVITY ELEVEN

Unit twenty-seven. Student A

Ask your partner these questions:

1 What's eighty-four divided by seven?
2 What's the capital of the Republic of Ireland?
3 What's the meaning of 'hangover'?
4 Do you prefer classical music or rock music?
5 Are you better at reading English or listening to English?
6 What would you do if you lost your credit card?

Can you add four more questions?

Possible replies are:

1 twelve
2 Dublin
3 The bad feeling the day after drinking too much alcohol.
4 Generally I prefer (....................) but sometimes I prefer (....................)
5 I'm better at ...
6 I'd (phone ... / cancel it immediately ...)

Then your partner is going to ask you questions. Try to get thinking time before you reply. You should use all of the techniques in Section D, and you can use more than one at the same time.

Unit two. Both students

Role play:
Student A is a souvenir trader in a market in your country, and is the **seller** in this situation.
Student B is a foreign tourist, and is the **buyer** in this situation.

Before you start ...

Decide which souvenirs the seller has got on his market stall. List four.

1 .... 3 ....
2 .... 4 ....

SELLER:	BUYER:
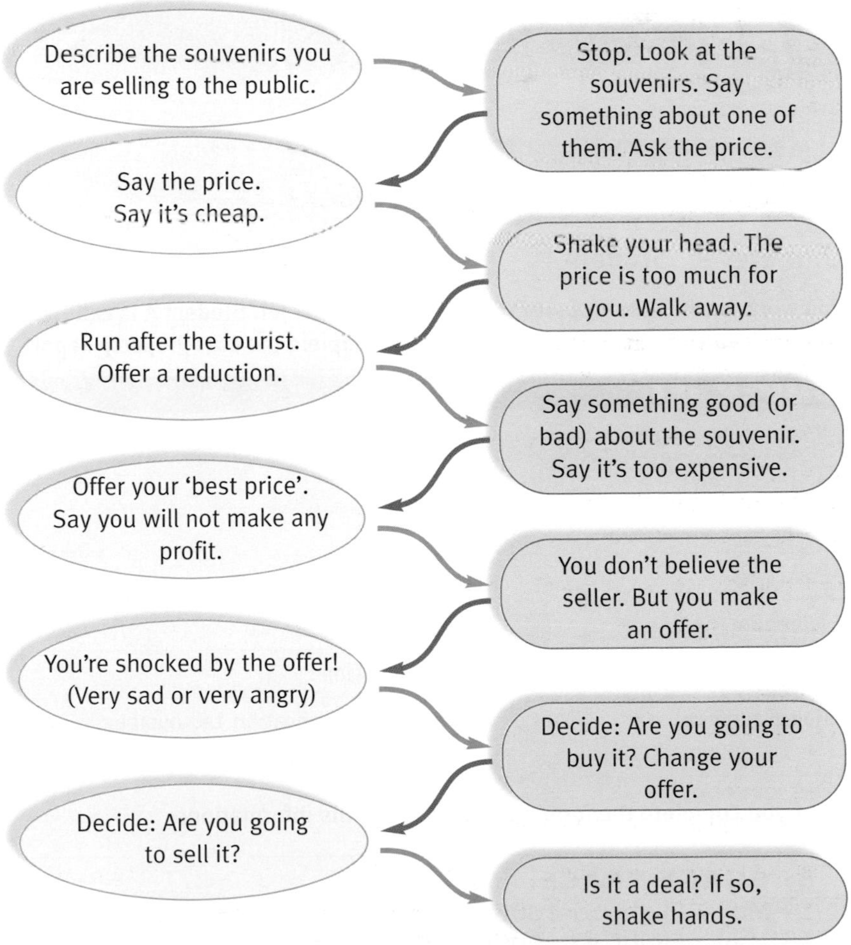 Describe the souvenirs you are selling to the public.	Stop. Look at the souvenirs. Say something about one of them. Ask the price.
Say the price. Say it's cheap.	Shake your head. The price is too much for you. Walk away.
Run after the tourist. Offer a reduction.	Say something good (or bad) about the souvenir. Say it's too expensive.
Offer your 'best price'. Say you will not make any profit.	You don't believe the seller. But you make an offer.
You're shocked by the offer! (Very sad or very angry)	Decide: Are you going to buy it? Change your offer.
Decide: Are you going to sell it?	Is it a deal? If so, shake hands.

ACTIVITY THIRTEEN

Unit eight. Student C

Scotland's favourite joke:
I want to die peacefully in my sleep, like my grandfather.
Not screaming in terror like his passengers.

ACTIVITY FOURTEEN

Unit eleven. Student B

You work for the Lost Property Department at Super Jet. Student A is calling to ask about a lost bag. Ask questions and complete the Lost Property Report.

SUPER JET LOST PROPERTY REPORT	
Name of passenger:	Flight number:
Address (now):	From:
	To:
Postcode:	Seat number:
Telephone no:	Date:
Mobile phone no:	Boarding Time:
Home address:	Baggage identification tag number:

After you complete the form, give Student A this information:

BAGGAGE TRACE:

14 May	Flight SJ 1008	New York	–	Manchester
15 May	Flight SJ 1009	Manchester	–	New York

ACTIVITY FIFTEEN

Unit fourteen. Student B

For the same percentage of conversation, women discussed twelve topics, and men discussed only four. The most popular topics for women were:

1. sex, marriage, men
2. family and friends
3. relationships
4. children and education
5. clothes, hair and cosmetics
6. shopping
7. health
8. films and TV
9. celebrities
10. food
11. holidays and travel
12. sport

Student A has a list of the most popular topics for men.

ACTIVITY SIXTEEN

Unit fifteen. Student B

- You should use two hands when you pass something to someone.
  This is true in Korea.
- On trains, you must give your seat to people who were injured in wars.
  This is true in France.
- You can cross a red traffic light if you are turning right.
  This is true in most American states.
- You must display your insurance certificate on your car.
  This is true in several European countries (but not the UK).
- You mustn't chew gum in the street.
  This is the law in Singapore.
- You must not smoke in restaurants.
  This is true in California.

ACTIVITY SEVENTEEN

Unit twenty-three. E Facts and figures

1 Four-fifths (80%) of an iceberg is under water.
2 Twelve inches (one foot) is approximately thirty-centimetres.
3 A Gigabyte is one million bytes.
4 100° Celsius is 212° Fahrenheit. Water freezes at 0° Celsius, which is 32° Fahrenheit.
5 48.7% of babies born in the United Kingdom are girls. The figures are similar in the USA. More boys are born than girls.
6 87.8% of Americans travelled to work by car in 2001.
7 33 1/3
8 A3 paper is twice as big as A4. A5 paper is half as big as A4.

ACTIVITY EIGHTEEN

Unit twenty-two. Student B

You have information about three pictures. Your partner has information about the other three pictures.

The woman who's wearing boots (and pushing a shopping trolley).
This is Helena Bonham-Carter, who's British. She's an actor, and a major film star. In most of her films she's very glamorous. This photo was taken on a Saturday morning.

The man who's wearing a wig.
This is Steve Van Zandt, who's American. The photo is from the TV series, *The Sopranos*. In the series, he plays Silvio Dante who is a Mafia gangster in New Jersey. Steve Van Zandt is also the guitarist in Bruce Springsteen's E-Street Band, and he has made solo records as Little Steven. He also has a radio programme. He's an actor, a guitarist, a singer, and a disc jockey.

The man who's playing guitar.
This is Paul Allen, who's one of the richest men in America. He started MicroSoft with Bill Gates, and is a billionaire. He has a rock group, the Paul Allen Band, and in the photo he was playing with his band.

ACTIVITY NINETEEN

Unit eight. Student D

The USA's favourite joke:
A man and his friend are playing golf. One of the guys is just going to hit the ball, when he sees a funeral procession going along the road. He stops, takes off his golf cap, closes his eyes, looks down and says a prayer. His friend says, 'Well, that's the nicest thing I've ever seen. You're a very kind man.' The man replies, 'Well, we were married for 35 years.'

ACTIVITY TWENTY

Unit sixteen. Section A Scores

Scores:

1 A 2 B 1 C 0
2 A 2 B 0 C 1
3 A 0 B 1 C 2
4 A 2 B 1 C 0
5 A 0 B 1 C 2
6 A 2 B 1 C 0

Scores 9–12 You are an extrovert. You like meeting people.
Scores 5–8 You are about average. Sometimes you're an extrovert and sometimes you're an introvert.
Scores 0–4 You are an introvert.

ACTIVITY TWENTY-ONE

Unit twenty-seven. Student B

Your partner is going to ask you questions. Try to get thinking time before you reply. You should use all of the techniques in Section D, and you can use more than one at the same time.

Then ask your partner these questions:

1 What's fifteen multiplied by three?
2 What's the biggest city in the USA?
3 What's the meaning of 'happy hour'?
4 Do you prefer espresso or cappuccino?
5 Are you better at speaking English or writing English?
6 What would you do if you had a headache?

Can you add four more questions?

Possible replies are:

1 forty-five
2 New York
3 A time of day when drinks are cheaper than normal.
4 Generally I prefer (....................), but sometimes I prefer (....................)
5 I'm better at ...
6 I'd probably take (an aspirin).

ACTIVITY TWENTY-TWO

Unit four. Student B

You're flying from London to Mexico. Ask the travel agent for advice.

- You really want to travel on Sunday because you've only got one week's holiday.
- You don't like getting up early, and you're staying two hours from Heathrow Airport in London.
- Monday is possible, but then you're only going to have 6 days in Mexico.
- Last time you were in the USA, the transit time was nearly three hours and you missed your connecting flight.

unit one

1.02

A Question one. What does he do?
B I dunno ... I ... I think he's ... um ... no, I don't know.
A Well, I think he is a teacher.
B No! He is not a teacher.
A OK, what do you think, then?
B I think he ... he works in a ... bank.
A Sorry, I don't agree. Anyway, let's try the second question. How old is he?
B Um... in his fifties?
A Yeah, I think so too. He looks about fifty-five. Is he married?
B Mmm, maybe.
A Yes, or no?
B Uh ... OK, yeah. Married.
A Right, me too. So ... how many children has he got?
B No idea. Really, I've got no idea.
A I think he's got ... um ... seven children. Four girls and three boys.
B You're joking! Two, maybe.
A OK, two.

1.03

Donna My name's Donna and I'm a hairdresser. I work for a TV company in Manchester. It's very interesting because I meet a lot of famous people. I'm not telling you my exact age ... but I'm in my twenties. I'm single, and I haven't got any children. And I'm not in a relationship ... at the moment. In my free time I like dancing ... and going to concerts ... I love classical music.

1.07

Assistant I'm sorry, madam. Your credit card company wants to check some information.
Trisha Why? What's wrong?
Assistant Nothing's wrong. It's just a security check. They want to speak to you. Here's the phone.
Trisha Right ... thank you. Trisha Hudson speaking. What's the problem?
Operator No problem, Mrs Hudson. This is a security check. You're talking to Philip. May I ask you a few questions?
Trisha Yes... all right. But I'm in a hurry.
Operator Can you confirm your middle initial?
Trisha N.
Operator Is that M?
Trisha No, N. For Nancy.
Operator And your mother's maiden name?
Trisha My maiden name's Grant.
Operator No, Mrs Hudson. What's your mother's maiden name.
Trisha Sorry. Yes. Her maiden name was Wallace.
Operator Can you spell that?
Trisha Huh? Yes. W-A-double L-A-C-E. Wallace.
Operator Thank you. And what's your place of birth?
Trisha I was born in Oxford.
Operator And your date of birth?
Trisha I was born on ... Um, is this really necessary?
Operator Sorry, but the security check is for your protection.
Trisha But there ... there are people listening. This is embarrassing. Um, do I have to say the year?
Operator I'm sorry. OK, when's your next birthday?
Trisha November the 12th.
Operator That's fine, Mrs Hudson. Sorry for the trouble. May I speak to the shop assistant?
Trisha Yes, all right. It's for you.
Assistant Yes? Hadley's Department Store?
Operator That's fine. I have a confirmation number for you. It's 195743YZ.
Assistant 195743YZ?
Operator That's correct.

unit two

1.15

1 I'd like tea. **2** I like this one!
3 I'll pay by credit card. **4** I usually pay cash. **5** I'm a size 12. **6** I want a size 12.

1.16

Market trader Oriental carpets! Best prices! Genuine Oriental carpets ... top quality ... How about you, madam?
Tourist Yeah. Nice carpets. How much is this one?
Trader Ah, very nice, this one. It normally costs two hundred in the shops. I get them direct from the factory at a very special price.
Tourist Oh, yeah? How much is it then?
Trader You can have it for a hundred and fifty.
Tourist Oh. That's too much. Sorry.
Trader Wait a minute ... for you, special price. A hundred and thirty.
Tourist Oh, I don't know.

Trader That's my best price.
Tourist Mm. I like it. I like the colours, but ...
Trader Where are you from?
Tourist Chicago, Illinois.
Trader Ah, I've got a brother in Chicago. Great place.
Tourist Yeah.
Trader Look. Just for you. A hundred and twenty-five.
Tourist No ... it's still too much for me.
Trader Make me an offer ...
Tourist A hundred?
Trader You're joking! It cost me a hundred.
Tourist You paid a hundred for it?
Trader Yes! This is top quality.
Tourist Oh. A hundred and ten?
Trader A hundred and fifteen for cash. That's my final price. It's a bargain!
Tourist OK, OK, it's a deal. A hundred and fifteen.

1.17
Tanya Look, Dave, there's a sale on. Let's go and have a look.
Dave But Tanya, I want a coffee ...
Tanya You need a new sweater. Come on ...
Dave Five minutes then, OK?

Tanya This is nice ... and it's twenty per cent off.
Dave Mmm.
Tanya What size are you?
Dave Oh, I don't know. Large ... or extra-large maybe.
Tanya This one's a large. Try it on.
Dave No, I don't like it.
Tanya Oh, go on ... it's a bargain.
Dave I really don't like it.
Tanya Well, what about this one?
Dave No, I don't like the colour.
Tanya I love the colour. It looks really expensive. Why don't you try it on?
Dave What ... here?
Tanya No, in the changing room.
Dave All right then.

Dave What do you think?
Tanya I think it's great. I really like it.
Dave I'm not sure about the colour.
Tanya What's wrong with the colour? You look good in it.
Dave Do you think so?
Tanya Yes, I do.
Dave Oh, all right, then. How much is it?
Tanya A hundred and forty pounds.
Dave What? You're joking! I'm not paying that much. Let's go and have a coffee ...

Tanya Dave ...
Dave Yeah?
Tanya Take the sweater off first.

Tanya Well, what about *this* one? / I *love* the colour / I *really* like it / You look *good* in it.
Dave I *really* don't like it. / I'm not paying *that* much.

unit three

1.19
Jean Hello, Margaret. Are you enjoying the party?
Margaret Oh, yes. It's very kind of Colin and Linda to invite me every year. They're such a lovely couple.
Jean Oh, well, don't you know?
Margaret Know what? I don't know anything.
Jean Linda's upstairs. She's crying her eyes out.
Margaret Oh, dear. What's the matter?
Jean I'm not sure ... You know me, I don't like to gossip.
Margaret You can tell me, Jean. I won't tell anyone.
Jean Well ... Colin hasn't got a job at the moment, so Linda's working for Max at the video shop, because they need the money. She often works very late in the evening, and Colin's ... well ... Colin thinks that Linda ... and Max ... are ...

1.20
Lulu Ouch! Robbie! What are you doing? That's cold!
Robbie It's suntan lotion ... your back's going red. You know, the sun is too hot at this time of the day. It's bad for your skin, Lulu. You need this, it's Factor 30.
Lulu OK, OK. Mmm. Are the hamburgers ready?
Robbie Nearly. Dad's cooking them now.
Lulu Great. Where's your mum?
Robbie She's having a rest, I think. She's really busy at the moment, what with her new job, and the party and everything.
Lulu Yes, she works late every night, doesn't she?
Robbie Yeah. I don't see her very often.
Lulu Does your dad miss his job?
Robbie I don't know. But he isn't very happy, I know that ...

1.21

Max Hi, Colin. That smells good.
Colin What are you doing here?
Max Uh, Linda invited me. Is anything wrong?
Colin Wrong? You tell me, Max!
Max I don't understand. What do you mean?
Colin Do you think I'm stupid? I know what's going on.
Max Put that fork down, Colin.
Colin I know about you and Linda ... You're having an affair with my wife!
Linda Colin! Put the fork down. Max and I are ...

unit four

1.24

Agent Which day of the week do you want to fly?
Woman Sunday. I'm meeting some people in Mexico City on Monday.
Agent That's a pity. There aren't any direct flights on Sundays. Can you change the meeting to Tuesday? Then you can take the non-stop Monday flight.
Woman No, people are coming from Australia and Japan ... so what flights are there on Sundays?
Agent There are two possibilities really. Either you can change planes in Europe, in Paris or Madrid for example, or you can change planes in the USA.
Woman What's best?
Agent Well, the flights via Europe leave very early in the morning. The American ones leave later.
Woman I don't live near the airport. Later, I think.
Agent OK. How about this one. Delta Airlines. It leaves London at 11.25 and it goes via Atlanta. It arrives in Atlanta at 15.40 ...
Woman That's quick ...
Agent Not really, Atlanta's six hours behind London!
Woman So I arrive in Atlanta at 15.40 ...
Agent Right. Then you take the AeroMexico flight at 17.30 direct to Mexico City. It arrives at 20.10. There's no time difference between Atlanta and Mexico City.
Woman Is there enough time to transfer to the Mexico flight?
Agent About two hours. I think it's OK. But there are sometimes long lines at US immigration.
Woman Do I have to go through immigration?
Agent Yes, you do. Then there's a security check before the flight to Mexico.
Woman Two hours ... what happens if I miss the Mexico flight?
Agent Don't worry. They can put you on the next flight with a different airline.
Woman But is there another flight that evening?
Agent Well, yes ... but they aren't direct. You change in Dallas or Miami and then arrive in Mexico around midnight ...

1.25

Gran Aren't you leaving university this summer, Tony?
Tony Yes, I am, Gran.
Gran Are you looking for a job?
Tony I've got one.
Gran Have you? What are you going to do?
Tony I'm going to work for a travel company.
Gran Are you? Doing what?
Tony I'm going to be a tour guide.
Gran Really? What does a tour guide do?
Tony Lots of things. I'm going to work in Bermuda.
Gran Bermuda? Can you speak the language?
Tony Yes, Gran.
Gran Can you?
Tony Of course I can. They speak English.
Gran Oh. When are you going to start?
Tony As soon as possible. But I'm going to have a holiday first.
Gran Are you? Where are you going?
Tony Australia.
Gran Hmm. That's a long way.
Tony I like travelling.
Gran Do you? I like travelling too, but I can't afford it now.
Tony Don't they do cheap foreign holidays for senior citizens, Gran?
Gran Yes, but only in January when it's cold and miserable. Anyway, who's going to look after the cat?

1.26

1 (1) 2 (2) 3 (3) 4 (3) 5 (1) 6 (2)

1.27

1 I don't want to watch TV. I'm going to have an early night. I'm really tired.
2 There are only five minutes left. England are going to lose! The score's 3-0 to France.
3 Sorry, he can't see you then. He's having lunch with a client at 12.30. How about 3 o'clock?

4 I feel terrible! I'm going to be sick! I want to get off!
5 Hurry up! The taxi's coming in five minutes. We don't want to miss the plane.
6 Oh, no. Look at those clouds! It's going to rain. Did you bring an umbrella?

unit five

(1.30)
Ellie I'm really hungry. How about you?
Carl Yeah ... what would you like?
Ellie Mmm, I don't know ... The vegetarian sounds nice ... but it's got mushrooms, and I don't like mushrooms.
Carl You can have it without mushrooms. Just ask.
Ellie Mmm, what are you going to have?
Carl I always have the same. Hot American.
Ellie Eugh ... that's too hot for me. Oh, I can't decide ... I like anchovies ...
Carl Well, would you like the seafood pizza? That's got anchovies.
Ellie Oh, yes ... Oh, no! It's got prawns.
Carl You don't like prawns?
Ellie No.
Carl Why don't you try the Napoletana?
Ellie Yeah, OK, but without olives.
Carl Don't you like olives either?
Ellie Not much. And I'd like a green salad with it.
Carl What about garlic bread?
Ellie Eugh, no. I hate the smell of garlic!
Carl Would you like anything to drink?
Ellie No, water's fine for me.
Carl Wouldn't you like some wine?
Ellie Definitely not. No alcohol for me. I'm driving.
Carl OK.

(1.33)
Carl Phew! That was hot! I'm really thirsty.
Ellie Here, have some of my water ...
Carl Thanks. Excuse me! Could I have the bill, please?
Waiter Was everything OK?
Ellie Yes, very nice, thank you.
Waiter You're welcome.
Carl Do you take American Express?
Waiter Yes, we do.
Carl Is service included?
Waiter No, it isn't.
Ellie Wait, Carl ... let me pay half.
Carl No, this is on me.
Ellie No. Let's split the bill.
Carl If you're sure ...
Ellie I'm sure. How much is it?
Carl Um ... thirty seven thirty five. But I had two beers ...
Ellie Well, that's about forty with a tip. Here's twenty.
Carl Right ... here's my card.
Waiter Thank you very much.

unit six

(1.35)
Alan What are you doing?
Amy I'm looking at the Old Friends website ...
Alan Which school?
Amy My middle-school. There are five people from my old class.
Alan Really? Are you on there?
Amy Not yet ... I'm going to register in a minute.
Alan Do you remember any of them?
Amy Not all of them. I can't remember Harry Trotter at all. But I remember the others. Especially Sarah. She was my best friend. I sat next to her. We left in 1989 and she went to a different school. I never saw her again. I don't know what happened to her ... I remember Claire. We were both at the same secondary school. She got married when she was eighteen. And William Brown! I remember him! He was always in trouble with the teachers. And Lisa ... I never liked her. She was so clever ... she was always top of the class.
Alan Ah, that's why you didn't like her.
Amy No! She was horrible to me. She's probably got an amazing job now.
Alan Well, find out ...
Amy OK, I will.

(1.36)
She started at Blyton Middle School in 1985 and she left in 1989. She moved to Northchester with her mother. She went to Northchester Comprehensive. She passed all her exams with A grades. She left in 1996, then she went to university. She studied Anglo-Saxon and Latin. She dropped out in her second year. She travelled to Australia with friends in 1998. She had several temporary jobs. Then she became an artist. She became an Australian citizen in 2003. She is now living in Queensland. You can buy her paintings from her website.

(1.37)
Listen to the verbs in the exercise:
/t/ faxed
/d/ e-mailed, /d/ videoed
/ɪd/ texted, /ɪd/ downloaded, /ɪd/ posted

/t/ dropped, helped, liked, passed, stopped
/d/ believed, happened, moved, studied, travelled
/ɪd/ emigrated, hated, shouted, started, wanted

unit seven

(1.38)
I've had a great career ... fantastic, really. I did everything I ever wanted to, you know, I played for England, I won the European Cup. But now I'm thirty-seven, and I'm retired. That's right, that's the end of it. I don't need to work again, I've got plenty of money, but you can't sit around the house all day, can you? I mean, football was my whole life. I'm not interested in doing anything else. I really miss it. I loved the travelling, and being with the other players. Now I'm bored all day. I don't like having nothing to do and I don't like being on my own.

(1.39)
So, I'm going to start college next September. I'm taking a degree in Sports Science, because I want to get a coaching certificate. I hope to be a football manager one day. I'd like to do some television work too, if possible. I was on several sports programmes last year, and I enjoyed it. I think I'm good at it, too. But I'd rather be a manager. That's my ambition now.

unit eight

(1.48)
Gina Is it switched on?
Sam Yes, I think so.
Gina All right, I'm going to call it from my phone.
Sam Why didn't I think of that?
Gina Just listen.
Sam I can hear it. Oh, no ... it's in my jacket pocket. It's been there all the time! Thanks, Gina.

unit nine

(1.51)
FA Cup Fifth Round

Home	Away	Result
Manchester Utd. 3	Manchester City 0	1
Arsenal 1	Swindon 2	2
Liverpool 2	Newcastle 2	X
Cambridge 0	Oxford 7	2
Bournemouth 1	Brighton 0	1
Tottenham 4	Birmingham 4	X
Southampton 2	Northampton 1	1
Leeds United 3	Bristol City 4	2

(1.52)
'I didn't enjoy sport at school. We had to play football in the winter. When it was too cold and wet to play football, we had to do cross-country running, and I was always last. In the summer we had to play cricket, and I was never any good at it because I couldn't hit the ball. I watched a lot of Jackie Chan movies when I was a kid, and I started doing martial arts when I was fifteen. Last summer I went to one of the kung-fu schools at the Shaolin Temple in China. There were thousands of students at the schools but there were only a few Westerners. We had to get up at 5 a.m. every morning and go for a run. Then we trained until midday. We couldn't train in the afternoon because it was too hot. We couldn't speak Chinese, but it didn't matter. We understood the instructions. It was hard work but I really enjoyed it. I don't know why they don't teach martial arts in British schools.'

(1.54)
Steve What do you want to watch, Tina?
Tina There's ice dancing on in five minutes. I'd like to watch that.
Steve Yeah, OK. You watch that and I'll go on the Internet for half an hour.
Tina You're not interested in ice dancing, then?
Steve No. I don't know why it's on the sports channel. It's not really a sport, is it? It's entertainment.
Tina What do you mean, 'not a sport'? It's in the Olympic Games.
Steve Is it?
Tina Yeah. Has been for ages.
Steve Hmm. Didn't know that. So what about ballroom dancing ... is that a sport nowadays?
Tina No.

Steve Why not? They're the same thing ... except for the ice. I don't get it.
Tina Well, maybe it should be. Ballroom dancing's very popular, you know ... they have international competitions and everything.
Steve Yeah, but it's dancing! It's not like football ... or running ... or...
Tina Come on, Steve. What about the samba? You have to be really fit to do that.
Steve But it's not a game, is it? There aren't any winners or losers.
Tina Yes, there are. They have judges, and they give them marks out of ten.
Steve But they don't have to train like a footballer or ...
Tina Yes, they do. And anyway, snooker players and darts players don't have to be fit at all! And you call them sports.

(1.55)
Tina And what about boxing? That's disgusting. Boxers get brain-damage. I think they should ban it.
Steve Yeah, well, professional boxing's dangerous ... but amateur boxing isn't. They have to wear a helmet.
Tina And what about horse-racing? That's not a sport at all in my opinion. It's cruel as well.
Steve Of course it isn't cruel! Horses like running. And the jockeys have to be good. There's a lot of skill in it.
Tina OK, greyhound racing, then. Where's the skill in that? It's just gambling.
Steve Ah, I get your point. I don't think that's a sport either.
Tina So why is it on the sports channel?
Steve I don't know. Isn't it time for the ice dancing?

unit ten

(1.58)
It was a lovely summer day. The sun was shining, the sea was warm, and the beach was crowded. People were sunbathing. Some of them were swimming, someone was fishing, and children were playing on the beach. A lifeguard was watching the sea. Suddenly, the lifeguard shouted 'Shark!' The fisherman saw the shark's fin, and stood up. The boat turned over and the fisherman fell into the sea. Everybody ran out of the sea. Everybody on the beach ran away from the sea. But it wasn't a shark. It was only a surfer. 'Where's everybody gone?' he said.

unit eleven

(1.61)
Hello, Mike? This is David. Excuse me, I'm just having my lunch ... I wanted to ask you about ...

(1.62)
Tell me more about (*ring*) oh, sorry, that's my phone ... Hi, Dan. I'm with Lisa. I'll call you back ... Sorry, Lisa, what were you saying? (*ring*) Uh, oh! My phone again ... Oh, hi, Sally. How are you?

(1.63)
Good evening. I represent Sunlight Insurance. Have you thought about dying? We're offering a discount on life insurance ...

(1.64)
Hello, Paul. I'm not interrupting your dinner, am I? ...
Oh, sorry, but this won't take long ...

(1.65)
This is a recorded message, Your call is important to us. Please hold for an operator (loud music). This is a recorded message. Your call is important to us. Please hold for an operator ...

(1.66)
Yeah, it's me! I'm calling from the train. ... We've just left London ...
Yeah, it's full. Loads of people on the train ...
Yeah, I've got a seat ...
Yeah, lots of people standing ...
I'm sending you a video message. Can you see me? ...
Yes, I love you, too ...

(1.68)
B Good afternoon, Mrs Graham. My name's Colin, and I'm calling from Edinburgh Mail Order. You ordered a catalogue from us ...
A Sorry. I didn't catch that. Could you speak up a bit?
B Of course. This is Colin from Edinburgh Mail ...
A Sorry, Colin. Could you speak more slowly?
B Sorry, Mrs Graham, I'll start again. I'm calling from Edinburgh Mail Order ...
A Could you repeat that?
B Edinburgh Mail Order.
A Sorry ... the reception isn't very good.... Could you spell that?
B Edinburgh ... E for echo, D for delta, I for India, N for November, B for bravo, U for uniform, R for Romeo, G for golf, H for hotel.

A Oh, yes! Edinburgh Mail Order. Your catalogue arrived this morning.
B Oh, good. I was just checking. Have you looked at it yet?
A Sorry, you're breaking up ...
B I'll hang up and call you back.
A Hello? Hello?

(1.70)
Thank you for calling Super Jet.
You can book online at www.superjet.co.uk, or please choose from one of the following options. For flight reservations, please press one.
For schedule information, please press two.
If you wish to join ClubSuper Jet, our frequent flyer programme, please press three.
For all other enquiries please press four.
Please hold while we transfer you to a customer services representative.
All our operators are busy with other customers. Your call is important to us. Please hold, your call will be answered shortly ...

(1.71)
A Thank you for calling Super Jet. Fiona speaking.
B Good afternoon, I want ...
A Are you a member of Club Super Jet?
B Yes, I'm phoning to ...
A May I have your membership number?
B Right. It's 213 968 5400 1740. I'd like to ...
A Please bear with me while I access your file.
B OK, but I ...
A Mr Lawrence?
B That's right.
A Could you please confirm your postcode, Mr Lawrence?
B Right. BR7 9FL. I'm phoning to ...
A And may I have the first line of your address?
B 36 Pine Avenue.
A And as a security check, may I have your date of birth?
B Er, yes ... it's 12.8.79
A Thank you, Mr Lawrence. And how can I help you today?
B I'm phoning to enquire about lost property. I left some documents on Flight 357 from Prague yesterday and ...
A Can I just stop you there, Mr Lawrence?
B Uh, yes ...
A You need to call our lost property office on 0845 320 320.
B Can't you put me through?
A I'm sorry, Mr Lawrence. I'm afraid I can't. We're very busy and there's usually a long wait-time on that number.
B Oh. Can you give me the number again?
A Yes. 0845 320 320. Thank you for calling Super Jet, Mr Lawrence.

(1.72)
Welcome to Super Jet General Office.
If you wish to make a flight reservation or to enquire about schedule information, please call Super Jet Customer Services on 0845 300 300.
If you know the extension number you require, you may dial it now. Please press star followed by the extension number.
For all other enquiries please hold for an operator.

C Super Jet. Angus speaking.
B I'd like to speak to Lost Property, please.
C Trying to connect you.

This is Super Jet Lost Property. If you are enquiring about lost or misdirected luggage, please press one of the following numbers.
For flights to Gatwick Airport, press one.
For flights to Stansted Airport, press two.
For flights to Manchester Airport, press three.
For all other lost property enquiries, please press four.

You are through to the Lost Property Office. All our operators are busy. Your call is being held in a queue.

D Tracy speaking. How may I help you?
B Hello, I left some documents on Flight 357 yesterday, and ...
D Flight 397?
B No, 357. From Prague to London Stansted.
D That was the 11.15 flight?
B Yes. I put the documents in the seat pocket in front of me, and I forgot they were there.
D Do you remember your seat number?
B No, I'm afraid I don't. It was a window seat near the back.
D Bear with me while I check our lost property records. No ... I'm afraid there's no record on the system.
B Oh, no! They were very important.
D That aircraft flew back to Prague last night. Why don't you phone our office at Prague Airport? I'll just find you the number.

unit twelve

(1.73)

Helen We moved out of the city a year ago. We have two young children and we wanted to live in the country. There were too many problems with city life. You know, too much crime, and not enough policemen on the streets. We lived on a busy road, and there was far too much traffic ... too much pollution. The children didn't get enough fresh air. We wanted peace and quiet. We were so happy when we found this cottage.

(1.74)

Our neighbour's a farmer, and we dreamed about little lambs in the spring, and fields of wheat in the summer. Perfect for our children. But it's not like that at all! First there's the noise. The farmer keeps chickens and the cockerel starts crowing at five in the morning and wakes us up. We can't go back to sleep because the farmer starts his tractor at 5.30. There is a field of wheat at the end of our garden. But the farmer sprays pesticide on it frequently during the summer, so the children can't play outside while he's doing it. In the autumn he has fires which continue for days. Our cottage is full of smoke. Then there's the smell. Pig manure on the fields. It's disgusting. You can't breathe! You can't walk across the fields because the cows chase you. They're very frightening. We've had enough! We want to move back to the city.

(1.75)

The farmer Well, I don't know, I really don't. People move here from the city, and they don't know anything about the country. They don't! I've had a lot of complaints from them, I can tell you. I mean, they complained about a little bit of manure. Manure does smell. Of course it does. You have to expect that. It's a nice, natural smell. I don't mind it. But I've lived on this farm, man and boy, for fifty-five years and I can't smell it myself. She doesn't like the spraying. But I have to spray my wheat. All farmers do. I don't use much pesticide because it's expensive ... and it's safe – well, I don't mind it anyway. My kids grew up on the farm, and there's nothing wrong with them. And animals are noisy ... Get down, Shep ... down, boy! ... What would you rather have? An alarm-clock or a nice cock-crow? We all get up early in the country. The cows won't wait for milking. And talking of cows, she's ... she's frightened of a few cows in a field! Well, the cows were here before she was. I'm sorry, but I've had enough of her complaints. If they don't like it, they can go back to the city!

unit thirteen

(1.76)

Kevin This job is really boring. I won't stay here long. I'm having an interview tomorrow, actually. For a job as a sales rep for a pesticide company. You know, driving round the farms. I'll get a car! Everyone here knows I'm having the interview, but they don't mind. Nobody stays here long. I'm meeting my friends tonight. We're going to watch the football match down the pub. They've got a massive TV screen. We'll probably have a few drinks! We usually do!

(1.77)

Zoe This is just a summer job. I've just done my exams, and I've had enough of studying, so I'm going to have a gap year. Then I'm starting university in October next year. I'm quite enjoying this job, because I finish at three o'clock. Then I'm free! This afternoon I'm going shopping. I haven't got any plans for this evening yet. But I think I'll go to the pub and see my friends. Then we'll go on somewhere. Maybe a club. It depends.

(1.78)

Debbie I won't finish until six-thirty tonight. I've got to work late. My sister is looking after the kids ... I've got two. I'll go straight to her house after work and pick the kids up. Then we'll go home and have dinner. I'm tired out at weekends. And the kids are always saying, 'What shall we do this weekend, Mum? Where shall we go? Will you take us to McDonalds?' Kids have so much energy! But I have to do all the housework.

(1.79)

Brian I'm looking forward to my retirement next year. We're planning on moving to the country. We'd like a bit of peace and quiet. I'm going to play golf everyday! I shall have the time at last. I certainly shan't miss this office. The insurance business has changed, you see. You don't meet people anymore. Everything's done on the computer and by telephone. I've had enough of it, I can tell you. After work tonight I'm going to visit my wife in hospital. She's just had an operation. But she'll be home by the weekend.

(1.84)

1 I'll do it later.
2 What do you do?
3 It'll be here soon.
4 We see them in the morning.
5 Shall I help you?
6 You'll be late.
7 They live near us.
8 Who'll be at the party?

unit fourteen

A ... no, honestly, I've got to tell you, Kevin ... she's absolutely gorgeous.
B Yeah?
A Really beautiful ... here's a photo.
B Oh, yeah – lovely. How old is she there, then?
A Three hours. She looks just like Caroline ... see that funny little nose?
B Mmm, sweet.
A And she's really good. She only wakes once in the night ...

(1.88)

A Turn round ... let me see the back ...
B Does it make me look fat?
A No. Not at all, you're not fat anyway.
B What about the colour? Does it suit me?
A Yeah, you always look good in turquoise. I like it.
B Hmm, I'm not so sure. It's a bit expensive. I don't know.

(1.89)

A I've been meaning to say this for a while ... the thing is Dave, I think things are moving too fast.
B I don't know what you mean.
A Look, I really like you as a friend, but ... I don't know how to say this ...
B You don't fancy me, do you?
A Uh, can't we just stay friends? ... Don't be upset ...
B I wasn't expecting this. It's come as a bit of a shock.

(1.90)

A Oh, wow! Let's have a look at it. It's really tiny.
B That's why I bought it ... I'm really pleased with it.
A What sort of card does it take?
B One megabyte. You can get hundreds of pictures on, if you use lo-res.
A What about printing?
B I don't bother with that anymore, I just keep them on CD. It hardly seems worth it but I'm going to print my own Christmas cards this year.

(1.91)

A I thought it was obvious. It stands to reason. You've got to red card him.
B Yeah but it wasn't deliberate ...
A You say that, but the end result is he's lying there with a broken leg ... what else are you going to do?
B He gave him a yellow card, didn't he?
A They get away with murder these days ... it's killing the game.
B Yeah, yeah, but he's got two yellows now, so he's out of the semi-final. And that's going to hurt the team. I mean, he's the only player ...

unit fifteen

(1.93)

Liz Tut, tut, tut. You've been a naughty boy, Damian.
Damian Yeah, well, I guess so.
Liz Look at these bank statements. Look at these credit card statements. What do they tell you?
Damian I'm spending too much?
Liz Yes, Damian. You've got two choices. You can earn more ... or you can spend less. Which one is it going to be?
Damian Well, I can't earn more because ...
Liz What about taking a second job?
Damian You must be joking! I don't have enough free time now.
Liz OK, then. So you must spend less. You must cut down your spending. You must give up some of these expensive habits.
Damian Well, I work hard ... and I like to have fun.
Liz But you can't afford it. You owe too much on your credit card. Your main problem is the monthly payments. You haven't paid them for three months. And the interest rates on these are massive.
Damian I know, I know ...

(1.94)

Liz How do you travel to work?
Damian By car.
Liz How far is it?
Damian About three miles.
Liz Do you have to pay to park?

Damian Yes ...
Liz Right. I see you're a member of the Lifestyle gym. It's very expensive.
Damian Yes, it is, but I've got to keep fit ...
Liz And you can. You should stop driving to work, and you should get a bike and cycle. Then you won't need the gym. And you save on petrol and car parks.
Damian Oh, I don't know ...
Liz I don't think you have a choice, Damian.

(1.95)
Liz You buy a lot of DVDs.
Damian Yeah, I usually buy a couple of DVDs a week.
Liz How often do you watch them?
Damian Once or twice.
Liz You should rent them. You can rent five times for the price of one DVD.
Damian I like collecting old films.
Liz You can't afford it.

(1.96)
Liz Wow. Do you know how much you spent on food last month?
Damian No ...
Liz I've added it up. It's far too much ... Supermarket bills, take-aways, and restaurants. And I've looked in your fridge. You only have ready-made meals. Do you ever cook anything?
Damian No, I'm too tired when I come home. I microwave stuff. Or I phone for a pizza.
Liz Fresh food is cheaper than ready-made.
Damian But I can't cook.
Liz Then you should learn to cook!
Damian Oh, no.
Liz And you must cut down on these restaurant bills.
Damian This week was special ... it was Valentine's Day. I took my girlfriend out for dinner ...
Liz And you bought twelve red roses? How much did they cost?
Damian A lot ... but it's only once a year.
Liz Right, next year you should cook a meal for her. You know, candlelight, one red rose, a nice bottle of wine ... not champagne ... very romantic. And you won't need a taxi.

(1.97)
Liz What are these?
Damian Lottery tickets.
Liz Why do people buy them? I don't know. You're not going to win.
Damian Well, it's possible ...
Liz Damian, you are not going to win. You mustn't buy them. And sorry, but your credit card has got to go. You must cut it up.
Damian I know I should ...
Liz I didn't say 'You should.' I said 'You must.'
Damian I can't ...
Liz Give it to me. I'll do it.

unit sixteen

(2.03)
- Excuse me, Do you know where Gate 37 is?
- Where's Gate 37?

- Do you know what time it is?
- What time is it?

- Do you know how old it is?
- How old is it?

- Could you tell me when it opens?
- When does it open?

- Do you know if we'll see any lions today?
- Will we see any lions today?

- Could you tell me where the nearest toilets are, please?
- Where are the nearest toilets, please?

- Can you tell me if this train goes to Tokyo?
- Does this train go to Tokyo?

- Can you remember where you left it?
- Where did you leave it?

(2.05)
1 It's a nice day, isn't it?
Yes, it is. Very nice.
2 It was a cold morning, wasn't it?
Yes, it was. Freezing!
3 It won't rain this afternoon, will it?
No, I don't think so. I hope not.
4 It isn't very warm today, is it?
No. Brrr.
5 That wasn't thunder, was it?
No ... it wasn't ... I don't think so.
6 It rained all day yesterday, didn't it?
Yes, it certainly did.
7 The weather's been lovely, hasn't it?
Yes, it has. Really lovely.
8 It'll be hot again tomorrow, won't it?
Yes, I hope it will.

unit eighteen

(2.13)
Mrs Cook Hello. Belinda Cook speaking.
Simon Hello, Mrs Cook. Can I speak to Mandy, please?
Mrs Cook I'm afraid she's out.
Simon Oh, dear. When will she be back?
Mrs Cook I don't know. She didn't tell me.
Simon Could you give me her mobile number?
Mrs Cook Uh, well ... who's speaking?
Simon Sorry. I'm Simon Nolan, a friend from college.
Mrs Cook Ah, yes. Simon. It's 07973 081254.
Simon Thank you very much, Mrs Cook. Goodbye.
Mrs Cook Goodbye.

(2.15)
called / shouted / hissed /whispered / replied / suggested / complained / added / said / answered / begged / promised / told / warned

unit nineteen

(2.16)
made / built / employed / given
rescued / taken / dressed
completed / built

(2.17)
Anne You've just won five hundred pounds! Do you want to try for a thousand?
Ron Yes, please, Anne.
Anne Very well. The next question is for one thousand pounds. When was the film *Grease* made? Was it A 1958, B 1968, C 1978, or D 1988?
Ron When was *Grease* made? I've seen that film ... John Travolta was in it ... er, and I remember the clothes ... they ... they were definitely 1950s clothes ... it's a rock 'n' roll film. Yes. I'll guess 1958 ...
Anne Are you sure?
Ron Yes, I'll go for 1958.
Anne Final answer?
Ron No! Most of the time I'm wrong when I guess ... I don't think it's 1978 ...
But it may be. Let me think ... John Travolta isn't that old, so not 1958 ... Sorry, I'm talking to myself ... yes, maybe the film was later ... 1978? Or maybe 1988 ... So ... is it 1958, or 1968 or 1978 or 1988? Yes, it was made in 1978.
Anne Sure?
Ron Yes, I'm going to choose 1978.
Anne Final answer?
Ron Yes, Anne. That's my final answer. 1978.
Anne And 1978 is ... the correct answer! You have just won one thousand pounds!
Ron Phew. Great.
Anne Are you going to try for two thousand pounds?
Ron Yes ... OK ... let's go for it.

unit twenty

(2.18)
Woman As soon as I get home, I'll have a long hot bath. I'll wash my hair and I'll put on some clean clothes.

(2.19)
Man When we get to Florida, we'll get a taxi to our hotel, then we'll go straight to DisneyWorld. We won't have a shower or anything to eat. We'll just go straight to the park!
Woman No. We'll have a shower first ...
Man There won't be enough time

(2.20)
Man If it lands on twenty-one ... please! ... if it lands on twenty-one, I'll win thousands! If I win, I won't put any more money on the table. I'll leave the casino immediately and ...
Croupier Thirty-two! Place your bets ... place your bets ...
Man Right. Twenty-one again. If it lands on twenty-one ...

(2.21)
Woman While I'm watching TV tonight, I'll eat ... no, I won't. I definitely won't eat any chocolates ... well, I might eat one or two ...

(2.22)
Man After this dance, I'll ask her for a drink. She'll say yes, then I'll ask her out, and then ...
Woman After this dance, I think I'll go home. There's nobody I like here tonight. This place is full of creeps. I don't think I'll come here again.

(2.23)
Man Before I get a job and settle down, I'm going to travel. I'll go round the world. I might go to Australia first ... or America. It depends, really.

2.24

If I go to university, I'll get a degree. If I get a degree, I'll get a good job. If I get a good job, I'll earn a lot of money. If I earn a lot of money, I'll retire early. If I retire early, I'll have lots of holidays. If I have lots of holidays, I'll spend all my money. If I spend all my money ...

2.25

Guide Right, before we go into the bush, there are a few basic rules. The first thing is, the most dangerous animal out there is ... the human being. And that means you guys. But if you follow my instructions, and stay close to me, you'll be safe. We're hoping to see some lionesses today. That's why we're leaving early while they're still awake. Now I'm carrying a rifle. But you won't see me use the rifle unless I really have to. A lioness can run 25 metres in three seconds. She'll keep her head low and she'll move from side to side. Even if I have time to fire, I'll probably miss. And the last thing I want to do is kill a lioness. Because lions are our business here. If we don't have lions, we don't have tourists. Right? So what do you do if a lioness attacks? First, you'll get one warning. She'll give a single warning growl. If you move away slowly, and you don't run, and you don't turn your back on her, then ninety per cent of the time, she'll walk away. Get one thing clear, she isn't just trying to frighten you away. She doesn't know if she's going to attack until she sees your reaction. If you panic, you're in trouble. Dead trouble. If she does attack ... and believe me, she won't ... you'll be fine. I'll be the nearest person to her, and I'll try to shoot her. You don't fire warning shots in that situation, you shoot to kill. If I do miss, she'll get me first. Then she'll be too busy with me to worry about you guys. So is that OK? Any questions?

Tourist 1 I read somewhere that lionesses are only dangerous when they've got young cubs.

Guide They always have young cubs.

Tourist 2 What about the male lions?

Guide The old male lion will be asleep somewhere in the long grass. You only need to worry about him if you step on him by accident. And if you do that he will be ... annoyed. Any more?

Tourist 3 Yeah. What about leopards?

Guide Leopards run so fast that you'll never see them! If a leopard decides to attack, you'll be dead before you know it. No, sorry, sorry, only joking. Yeah, same rules apply to leopards.

unit twenty-one

2.26

1 I've got sore feet and my knee hurts. I've just run a marathon.

2 Ouch! I've burnt myself. I was cooking sausages and I touched the grill.

3 I've cut myself. Get me a plaster! I was cutting flowers and I was careless.

4 I've got stomach-ache, and I feel sick. I've had too much to drink.

5 Ow. My back aches. I've been carrying heavy boxes all day.

6 I've got toothache. I've just bitten into a hard apple.

7 I've got a temperature. I think I'm getting a cold. I got very cold and wet yesterday.

8 My arm hurts and I've got a pain in my shoulder. I've been painting all day.

2.31

Doctor What seems to be the problem?

Patient I've got a sore throat. I've had it for two weeks, and it's not getting any better.

Doctor Have you been taking anything for it?

Patient Just aspirins, and some throat spray from the chemist's.

Doctor Let's have a look, then ... open your mouth ... say 'Ah'.

Patient Ahh.

Doctor Yes, it's very red. Have you got swollen glands?

Patient My neck feels a bit sore, and swollen.

Doctor I'm just going to feel the glands in your neck. Yes, they are swollen. Have you got any other symptoms?

Patient Not really. I had a temperature when it started.

Doctor Runny nose? Cough? Aches and pains?

Patient No. Just the sore throat.

Doctor You haven't been shouting, or singing loudly?

Patient No.

Doctor Do you smoke?

Patient No. I just need some antibiotics, I think.

Doctor Well, if it's a virus, antibiotics won't help. But you've had it for two weeks, so it isn't a cold. Have you ever had

mononucleosis?
Patient What's that?
Doctor Glandular fever.
Patient No, never.
Doctor Hmm. I'm going to send you for a blood test, just to check. Take this form to the hospital, anytime between eight and four-thirty. We'll get the results in three days.
Patient Do you think it's glandular fever?
Doctor It might be. But it's probably just a bacterial infection. Have you had antibiotics before?
Patient Yes.
Doctor Are you allergic to them?
Patient No, I don't think so.
Doctor Take this prescription to the pharmacy. It's a five day course. One tablet three times a day. Now, you must finish the course. Even if your throat feels better, you must take the tablets for five days. That's important.
Patient OK. Um, can I drink alcohol?
Doctor No, you shouldn't drink while you're taking them.
Patient Right. Thank you, doctor.

unit twenty-two

(2.32)
A Look at her. What do you think she does?
B Well, she looks very glamorous. She looks like a model, or she might be a film star.
A Do you recognize her?
B No, I've never seen her before.
A Well, she isn't a model or a film star.
B What does she do then?
A She's actually a celebrity chef. She's got a British TV programme about cooking, and she's an author, too. She's written some cookery books.
B What's her name?
A Nigella Lawson.

(2.33)
man / runner / girl / children / whales / men / trees / parents

unit twenty-three

(2.35)
American The check, please.
Woman Here you are, sir.
American What sort of tip do you leave here in England?
Briton We usually leave ten to twelve per cent.
American Wow, that's not bad. In California it's fifteen to twenty.
Briton Too much for us.
American Let me see – eighty-eight pounds twelve, so I tip about ten per cent of eighty-eight – say nine pounds?
Briton That's generous. You see, the bill for the meal and drinks was seventy-five pounds, plus thirteen pounds twelve VAT – that's tax. The tax rate is seventeen point five per cent. You shouldn't tip on the tax. So seven-fifty or eight is fine.
American OK, Eight. Ninety-six pounds, twelve.

(2.36)
Ed Hello, Bella?
Bella Ed. Hi.
Ed Have you got your phone?
Bella Yeah, why?
Ed I want to get the lottery results. Can you check them for me?
Bella Yeah, OK. Why?
Ed I don't know. I just feel lucky, that's all.
Bella You know your chance of winning is only about one in fourteen million!
Ed It'll only take you a minute. Please.
Bella OK ... it's connecting ... right ... they're four, nine, twenty-six, thirty, thirty-one, and forty-nine ... what's the matter?
Ed I've won ...
Bella No! Are you sure?
Ed Yeah ... look at my ticket. Four, nine, twenty-six, thirteen, thirty-one, forty-nine.
Bella No, Ed ... the numbers are in order. Thirty, not thirteen.
Ed Oh. But that still means I've got five numbers! What's the prize for five numbers?
Bella Um ... two hundred and eighty seven thousand one hundred ...
Ed What! Great! I can buy a house, a car and ... oh, I'll give you a thousand ... and ... um ...
Bella Ed ... stop a minute. Sorry. I've made a mistake. The screen's very small – that's a comma then a full stop ... it's actually two thousand eight hundred and seventy one ... that's all.
Ed Oh ...
Bella Can I still have one thousand?

unit twenty-four

(2.37)
Alison Thank you ... can I have your attention, please? Shh! I just want to say a few words. As you all know Graham has been working for Acme Insurance for fifty years. He joined the company as a post boy when he was only fifteen, worked his way up to become first an area manager and finally assistant-director of this department. When Graham started at Acme, fifty years ago, there were only twenty employees ... all men ... and he has watched it grow into our present enormous organization. We shall all miss you, Graham ... and we shall miss all your stories about the past. Now, it's my great honour to present you with this gift. We hope that you will spend many happy hours on the golf-course.
All Speech! Speech!

(2.38)
Graham Thank you ... thank you for this splendid set of golf clubs. I hope to spend a lot of my time on the golf course ... if my wife lets me. As Alison said, I started work here when I was just a lad of fifteen. We could leave school at fifteen in those days. It was only a small office then, and I remember the annual Christmas party. The Managing Director used to come to the party every year ... it was the only time we ever saw him ... and he used to pay for all the food and drink. It wasn't like office parties nowadays, I can tell you. We used to call him 'sir' at all times, and the drink was one small glass of wine each.

(2.39)
Graham A lot of things have changed. I remember our first computer department. In those days computers used to be huge and slow. They needed a whole floor of the company offices. We had to employ fourteen people to look after them, but they were less powerful than one modern laptop.

(2.40)
Graham Of course all the office equipment was much bigger then. We used to have a special room for the photocopier ... we only had one ... and a girl who was employed just to do photocopying. And there were no fax machines either. I used to carry the messages from office to office when started. Nowadays we send e-mails, so there are no post boys anymore.

(2.41)
Graham And in my day, all the managers were men, and we never used to do our own typing. Most of us couldn't type. We had secretaries and typists, and they were all women. We used to dictate letters, and the secretaries used to take notes in shorthand and then type them afterwards. Half our managers are women now, and that's a positive thing.

(2.42)
Graham We used to dress smartly for work. Men had to wear a suit and tie to work at all times. I used to wear a three piece suit ... and women weren't allowed to wear trousers. We used to work regular hours, nine to five-thirty with an hour for lunch in the canteen. Nowadays people can choose their working hours, and very often lunch is just a sandwich. I think that's a bad thing, actually.

(2.43)
Graham But a lot of changes are for the better. One great change that I welcome is the ban on smoking. Nearly everyone used to smoke in those days. I used to smoke twenty a day myself, but I stopped many years ago and I'm very glad I did. We didn't know about the dangers, particularly the dangers of passive smoking, and the office was a very smoky environment. Now employees have to go downstairs and stand outside if they want a quick cigarette. Yes, times have changed.

unit twenty-five

(2.44)
We took the kids to Florida last year. We did all the theme parks. I didn't want to go on the roller-coaster, because I'm terrified of heights. But the kids wanted to go on the ride, so I had to ... and it was really thrilling! I loved it. They take your photo at the top of the ride. We went on five times and we bought a photo every time!

(2.45)
We went to St Martin in the Caribbean. Well, we were really tired when we arrived – it was a long exhausting flight. But the hotel was only a few minutes from the airport, which was great! We were pleased to get in and

have a hot shower so quickly. The next day we went to the beach. It was very relaxing. Then there was this tremendous noise above us – we were really shocked! This huge Jet flew right over our heads and landed at the airport. Actually, it was rather exciting! After that, we waited for the flights. A plane would come in, then it would take off two hours later. We'd all watch it.

2.46

I like short breaks. I get bored on the beach, so I prefer to go to a city. Recently I've been to London, Paris, and Boston. Last year I went to Vienna just before Christmas. They have these really interesting Christmas markets, and there's always somewhere to go and something to see. I'm interested in museums and art galleries, and it was good for shopping too. It was freezing cold, and there was snow on the ground, but the skies were blue.

2.47

I hate staying in one place, so I tend to go for Fly Drive holidays. The most recent one was in Nevada and California. We flew into Las Vegas, rented a car, and headed for Death Valley first. It's one of the hottest places on Earth. The desert scenery's fantastic, but you can't get out of the car for long. It's too hot to walk very far. I was a bit worried about the car – I kept looking at the water temperature dial, but it was fine. We drove two thousand miles in seven days, but the roads were empty so it was a relaxing drive.

unit twenty-six

2.54

Stewart This is Stewart Cogan. It's ten o'clock and it's time for problem hour, and now we have Josie on the line. Hello, Josie.
Josie Hello, Stewart. It's my son ...
Stewart Yes, what about your son?
Josie Well, I'm a single parent and I work full-time and Gary lives at home.
Stewart How old is Gary?
Josie Nineteen.
Stewart And what does he do?
Josie He's at college. He's studying.
Stewart So what's the problem?
Josie Well ... er ... he doesn't do anything to help me. When I come home from work, I have to do all the cleaning, the washing, and the cooking. His room's a mess. He just drops all his clothes on the floor.
Stewart Sounds pretty normal.
Josie Well, I've had enough. He has his friends round and plays loud music all night. It keeps me awake. And if I say anything, he says he's sorry and he might buy me a box of chocolates ... but I'm fed up with him! I feel ...
Stewart OK, I think we get the picture. Has anyone got any advice for Gary's mum? What should Josie do? Our phone lines are open. Call 0209 123 123 ... we're waiting for your calls ... Are you still there, Josie?
Josie Yes, I'm here, Stewart.

2.55

Caller Hello, Stewart. My name's Margaret, and I'm calling about Josie's problem ...
Stewart Go on, Margaret. What have you got to say?
Caller Well, I'm a grandmother, and I never see my grandchildren. I'd love to have one of them live with me. If I were you, I'd stop complaining, Josie. Make the most of it while you can. He'll leave home soon enough, and then you'll be all on your own ... like me.
Stewart Thank you, Margaret. We haven't got time for your problems as well. How do you feel about that, Josie?
Josie Well, it's made me think. She's right ... I would hate to be alone ...

2.56

Stewart And the next caller ...
Caller Hi. Alex, here.
Stewart How are you doing, Alex?
Caller Fine, Stewart. I've got some advice for you, Josie. I used to be just like your son. My mum did everything for me. Then I got a girlfriend ...
Stewart And now she does everything for you?
Caller No ... not at all. She won't do anything! And I realize how selfish I used to be. And I really appreciate my mum now. So I wouldn't worry about it. He'll change.
Josie Oh, that's nice. That's made me feel better.

2.57

Stewart Who's next?
Caller Hello, Stewart. My name's Annabel.
Stewart Have you got any children, Annabel?
Caller I've got a daughter, she's the same age as Gary.
Stewart Uh-huh.
Caller She's just as bad. She used to leave

her clothes on the floor. One day I put them all in a plastic bag and put them in the dustbin. She was shocked. She's been much better since then. So if I were you, Josie, I'd stop doing his washing and his meals. Don't buy any food, and go out for your meals. After a few days, he'll get hungry. Then tell him the rules for living at home.
Stewart Maybe your daughter should meet Gary. She could tell him.
Josie That's a good idea ...
Stewart Thank you for those wise words, Annabel.

(2.58)
Stewart And our next caller ...
Caller Hello? Stewart?
Stewart Who's that?
Caller My name's Derek. I'm a taxi driver.
Stewart What advice do you have for Josie? Are you listening, Josie?
Josie Yes ...
Caller Well, if he were a son of mine, he'd be right out on the street! Young people today have it too easy. I was in the army when I was his age. If I were you, Josie, I'd throw him out. He's old enough.
Stewart Strong advice there, Josie. What do you think?
Josie I couldn't do that. No ... that's awful.

unit twenty-seven

(2.60)
Interviewer OK, Judy ... what are your strengths and weaknesses?
Judy Well ... Basically I'm good at following instructions. I like working with other people so personally I think I'm a pretty good team member. I don't mind working late. Obviously if a job needs finishing, I'll stay until it's done. Weaknesses? Let me see ... Actually I don't make terribly quick decisions. Unfortunately, I have to think about things carefully first. At the end of the day, I think I want people to like me, so I'm far 'too nice'.

(2.61)
Interviewer What are your strengths and weaknesses, Terry?
Terry I'm good at following instructions and I like working with other people and I'm a good (breath) team member and I don't mind working late if a job needs finishing I'll stay until it's done (breath) I don't make quick decisions I have to think about things carefully first I want people to (breath) like me so I'm too nice.

(2.62)
Interviewer Marcia, what do you think your strengths and weaknesses are?
Marcia Strengths and weaknesses? Um, I'm good at ... um, you know, following instructions. I like ... um, sort of ... working with other people, you know, and, I mean ... I'm good at ... I'm a good team member. I don't mind ... you know, like ... working late? If a job needs finishing, I'll, like stay right until it's done? Weaknesses? ... um ... well, it depends, really ... I don't kind of ... make, um ... quick decisions, you know. I have to think about things ... um ... quite carefully first. I suppose I ... I sort of ... want people to like me, you know what I mean, so I'm like, a bit 'too nice'.

(2.63)
Interviewer What would you say your strengths and weaknesses are, Alvin?
Alvin I'm very good at following instructions. I like working with other people and I'm a really excellent team member. I don't mind at all working late. If a job needs doing, I'll stay until it's completely finished. I'm afraid to say I don't make particularly quick decisions, though (laugh). I have to think about things rather carefully first. I'm afraid I want people to like me, so I'm almost 'too nice'.

(2.64)
A
Madonna is a very popular singer. Personally, I don't like her music.
Madonna is a very popular singer. Speaking for myself, I don't like her music.
B
I know you like those shoes, but they're expensive. Basically, you're only a student and you can't afford them.
I know you like those shoes, but they're expensive. The important thing is that you're only a student and you can't afford them.
C
They've been living together for twenty years. Actually, they're not married.
They've been living together for twenty years. This might surprise you, but the truth is they're not married.
D
I missed the bus. Fortunately there was another one five minutes later.
I missed the bus. It was good that there was another one five minutes later.

E
I missed the bus. Unfortunately it was the last bus of the day.
I missed the bus. It was bad that it was the last bus of the day.
F
Honestly, I didn't see who did it. If I knew I'd tell you.
What I'm saying is true. I didn't see who did it. If I knew I'd tell you.
G
Obviously, there's a mistake in the price ticket. The price of a frozen pizza must be 4.99, not 499.
As you can see there's a mistake in the price ticket. The price of a frozen pizza must be 4.99, not 499.
H
Hopefully, our team will win the match.
If the best thing happens, our team will win the match.

2.65
Dear Anna comma David and Sarah comma
Thanks for your postcard full stop It was really great to hear from you again exclamation I've just bought a new computer comma printer comma scanner and CD burner full stop Now you'll be able to e-mail me full stop My new e-mail address is colon, new line, richard slash johnson dot family@btnet dot co dot uk By the way comma I found a new website for family history full stop The address is colon new line http colon slash slash family dash history dash north dot uk dot com backslash johnson backslash 8975
You should try it exclamation Do you know what I found out question mark Our family came from Sweden about two hundred years ago full stop
Very best wishes comma
Uncle Richard

unit twenty-eight

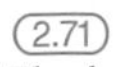

The legend
Jesse and Frank James were the most famous outlaws in the Wild West. The James Gang robbed banks and trains, and like Robin Hood, they stole from the rich and gave to the poor. By 1881, Frank had had enough of crime and left the gang. His wife had just had a baby and Frank wanted to become a farmer. Jesse decided to quit too. In 1882 Bob Ford came to visit him. When Jesse turned to get him a drink, Ford shot him in the back. The gun that he used had been a gift from Jesse. Ford collected the $10,000 reward for killing Jesse. But was that the end of the story?

2.72
The real story?
In 1948 newspapers found a 102-year-old man in Oklahoma called J. Frank Dalton. He told reporters that he was Jesse James. Dalton had exactly the same scars on his body that Jesse had had. Apparently, Bob Ford had killed another man, Charlie Bigelow, who had looked just like Jesse. Jesse had then sung at his own funeral, before leaving for South America. He had decided to keep the secret until his 100th birthday. Dalton died peacefully in 1951 at the age of 104.

Frank James spent the rest of his life looking for one million dollars worth of gold that he and Jesse had buried in Oklahoma. He had forgotten the exact location. Strangely, Frank never tried to kill his brother's murderer, and in fact a few years later he gave Bob Ford money to open a saloon. It seems that Ford was their first cousin, and, Frank James said, 'If Bob Ford had really shot Jesse James, he wouldn't have lived until sundown.'

unit twenty-nine

2.73
This is a newsflash. London is in chaos following a massive power failure at six-twenty this evening. Five hundred tube trains have been halted by the cut, and another four hundred main line trains have been halted above ground. Tens of thousands of passengers are stranded in tube trains deep underground and many people are trapped in lifts. A spokesperson for London Underground says, 'Stations are being cleared, and passengers are being taken to safety by underground staff. The trains which are at a standstill in the tunnels will be evacuated. Emergency power supplies cannot be switched on yet because passengers are walking along the lines.' More than 270 traffic lights have also failed, bringing chaos to streets which are jammed with rush-hour traffic. Thousands of homes have been left without electricity. Police are asking people to remain calm while they are waiting for power to be restored.

(2.74)
Good evening and welcome to the news from TV Wessex. There was a major accident today on the M27 when a truck crashed into a bus in thick fog. Passengers on the bus were trapped for three hours and had to be rescued by firefighters. The driver of the bus was killed, and ten passengers were badly injured and taken to hospital. Fifteen others were slightly hurt. The motorway has been closed since the accident causing massive traffic jams in the area. The motorway will not be re-opened until tomorrow morning. The driver of the truck has been arrested and charged with dangerous driving.

(2.75)
A 75-year-old woman was arrested and charged with murder early this morning after a 22-year-old man was shot and killed in her house. She has not been named by the police. Her house had been burgled several times in the the last year and she had bought a gun for self-defence. The dead man was known to the police and had been jailed three times for burglary.

(2.76)
A painting worth millions of pounds has been found in a phone box in Dorset. 'The Marooned Sailor' by Gustav Van Dorp was discovered this morning in a blue laundry bag inside the phone box. The picture was stolen from the Carter Museum two years ago. Following the theft two men were accused of stealing the painting but were later released. The painting was so famous that it could not be sold. A large reward had been offered for the return of the painting.

unit thirty

(2.77)
is / moves / have discovered / will / cannot / will

(2.78)
read / thought / told / heard / saw / asked

(2.79)
Agent How about this one? Do you know Great Ray Island?
Jerry No, I've never heard of it.
Agent It's a tiny island in the Caribbean. The Marine Hotel is right on the waterfront. It's only twenty-five metres from the sea.
Jerry That sounds good. We're looking for a beach holiday.
Agent Then this is just the place. Great Ray has lots of empty sandy beaches. You can hire a car and visit them all.
Jerry What's the weather like?
Agent When are you thinking of going?
Jerry August.
Agent It'll be hot.
Jerry That suits us.
Agent It's very quiet and peaceful. No all night discos.
Jerry There is somewhere to go in the evenings, I hope.
Agent Oh, yes. The hotel's got a fish restaurant and a bar.
Jerry OK, sounds great ...
Agent Are you going for seven days?
Jerry No, fourteen ...

(2.80)
Agent Oh, what happened to you?
Jerry I had an accident.
Agent Oh, dear.
Jerry I fell off my moped during the hurricane.
Agent Did this happen while you were on holiday?
Jerry Yes. And I've come to complain.
Agent Oh, I see ... you'd better take a seat.
Jerry No, thank you. I'd prefer to stand. You said we could hire a car, but we couldn't. They only had mopeds. Old mopeds.
Agent I am sorry ...
Jerry And you told us it was twenty-five metres from the sea.
Agent Wasn't it?
Jerry Well, yes, it was. But it was twenty-five metres from the dock, not the beach. There were fishing boats right outside our room. And you said it was quiet and peaceful. Well, it was during the day, but the fishing boats arrived at five o'clock in the morning and started to unload their fish.
Agent What about the hotel facilities?
Jerry Facilities? You said the hotel had a fish restaurant ... it was a fish and chip shop. A British fish and chip shop. And the bar was full of sailors!
Agent Ah, yes. There are a lot of luxury yachts in the Caribbean.
Jerry Not that kind of sailor! There was a British naval base half a kilometre away.
Agent Oh, I see. Were the beaches OK?
Jerry The beaches? You said there were empty sandy beaches. They were ten kilometres from the hotel and they were at the bottom of a cliff. That's why they were empty.

Agent I had no idea. I haven't been there myself ...
Jerry And another thing. You told us it would be hot ...
Agent It's always hot in August.
Jerry And wet. It rained every day. And then we had the hurricane. That's when I had the accident.
Agent Oh, dear. I'm sorry you didn't enjoy it.
Jerry No, we didn't. And we want our money back!

(2.81)
Teacher Sit down, please. I'm going to ask you a few questions.
Student Fine.
Teacher How long have you been studying In English Pre-Intermediate?
Student Since January.
Teacher Has your English improved?
Student I think so.
Teacher Good, have you ever been to England?
Student No, but I've been to the States. But only once.
Teacher Right. When was that?
Student I went there two years ago. My English wasn't very good ... um ... fluent, then.
Teacher Where did you go in the States?
Student I went to California.
Teacher How long did you stay?
Student For two weeks. We travelled around. I went to Los Angeles first, then I drove to San Francisco.
Teacher Very nice. Now, let's talk about the course. Have you got a favourite lesson?
Student I liked the film scripts because I like ... acting. My class is very good and we had a lot of fun. And I liked the singing also.
Teacher Hmm. Did you do the Practice Book exercises?
Student Well, you know, sometimes. I always listen to the CD in my car. I try to speak faster.
Teacher Did you find anything difficult?
Student Some things. For example, when I listen to the recordings in class, they're often ...

Authors' acknowledgements:
In a complex series like this, which has taken several years to prepare, pilot and produce, many people are involved and have creative input. We wish to thank the many people at OUP who participated in making this book. We would like to add our further personal thanks to Karen Jamieson (Project Manager and Student's Book editing), Richard Morris (design) and Sally Cooke (Teacher's Book, 3-in-1 Practice Pack editing).

Acknowledgements
p. 48 I Want to Stay Here Words and Music by Gerry Coffin and Carole King ©1963 Screen Gems-EMI Music Inc, USA. Screen Gems-EMI Music Ltd, London WC2H 0QY. Reproduced by permission of International Music Publications Ltd (for Europe) and Screen Gems-EMI Music Ltd, London WC2H 0QY. All Rights Reserved; p. 83 Stay Words and Music by Maurice Williams © 1960, Cherio Corp, USA. Reproduced by permission of Lorna Music Co Ltd, London, WC2H 0QP; p. 139 Have You Heard the News? words by Peter Viney, music by Vince Cross; p. 165 Tower of Strength Words and music by Burt Bacharach and Bob Hilliard © Copyright 1961 by Better Half Music Co and New Hidden Valley Music Co. All rights on behalf of New Hidden Valley Music administered by Windswept Music (London) Ltd. Used by kind permission. Copyright Renewed. All Rights Reserved. International Copyright Secured.

Illustrations by:
Rupert Besley pp. 13, 29, 82, 132, 174; Kate Charlesworth pp. 100-101, 181; Jonty Clark pp. 25, 98; Paul Dickinson 123, 185; Mark Duffin pp. 131, 187; Hardlines pp 153; Kevin Jones Associates pp 62-63, 121; Tim Kahane pp. 55, 157; Andy Parker pp 171,172, 173; Nigel Paige p. 49 (br); Gavin Reece pp. 12, 23, 78, 110; John Richardson pp. 114, 165; Paul Sample pp. 17, 52, 54, 130, 175; Graham Thompson pp. 49 (bl), 74, 75, 92, 141, 194, 210, 213, 216, 219; Daniel Viney p. 33; Brian Walker p. 49 (tl); Brian Williamson p. 30

Commissioned photography by Chris King:
pp. 10, 11, 14, 15, 28, 31, 32, 33 34, 61, 80 (tr), 88, 89, 96, 97, 107, 128–129, 135, 143, 145, 149, 164, 166, 167, 169, 188

The publisher would like to thank the following for their kind permission to reproduce copyright material:
Advertising Archives p. 48; Alamy pp. 59 (l) (Kimball Hall), 95 (David Hoffman Photo Library), 99 (br) (Image 100); Alnwick Castle p. 117 (F); The Art Archive p. 176 (Bill Manns); Associated Press pp. 58 (cl), 59 (r), 85 (tl), 136 - 137 (Kevin Weinstein), 136 (br) (Elaine Thompson), 155 (D), 160 (C); Aviation Picture Library p. 200 (Steve Bates); Steve Betts p. 7; Big Pictures p. 85 (cr); Boeing p. 140; BAA Picture Library p. 70; BBC pp. 20(cr, cl,) 20 - 21, 21 (cr), 50; Quint Buchholz p. 140; Camera Press p.137 (tr); Colin Chapman p. 49 (tr); Corbis pp. 46 (ctr) (Charles Gupton Photography), (tl) (Steve Prezant), 73 (r) (Reuters/Newmedia Inc), 83 (Bettman), 102 (Keren Su), 125 (Paul A Souders), 184 (A) (Bettman), 184 (F) (Leonard de Selva); p. 178 Daily Express – Express Newspapers; p. 179 Daily Mail; p. 179 Daily Mirror; p. 179 Daily Telegraph, Telegraph Group Ltd. 2003; East Images p. 208 (Dan Brooks); Mary Evans Picture Library p. 184 (B); Getty Images pp. 43 (tc, br), 46 (tr) (Taxi), 47 (Hulton Archives), 80 (bl) (Photographers Choice), 85 (br) (Stone), 86 (t), 103 (Hulton Archive), 146-147 (A,B,C,D,E,F) (Hulton Archive), 154 (B) (Stone), 161 (D), 184 (C, D, E) (Hulton); Ronald Grant Archive p. 116 (A); Kim Knott p. 136 (tl); p. 179 The Independent; Kobal Collection pp. 21 (br) (Wetcher Barry/HBO), 109 (Columbia Tristar), 116 (D) (Lucasfilm/20h Century Fox), 117 (C) (Wallace Merie W./20th Century Fox/Paramount), (E) (Buitendijk, Japp / Dreamworks / Universal, 137 (tl) (HBO), 141 (l) (20th Century Fox); Magnum p. 104 (Martin Parr); Richard Morris pp. 26–27, 112, 155 (C), 177; Oxford University Press pp. 8 (Stockbyte), 9 (Stockbyte), 38 (Hemera), 39 (Hemera), 40 (Hemera), 43 (Hemera), 43, 45, 46 (ctl, cbl, bl, cbr) 56 (Hemera), 60 (Stockbyte), 66 (Hemera), 67 (Stockbyte), 69 (Hemera), 72 – 73 (c), 80 (br) (Hemera), 85 (Hemera), 93 (Hemera), 99 (tr) (Stockbyte), 115 (Hemera), 118 (Hemera), 133 (Hemera), 134, 139, 144 (Hemera), 162, 167, 193 (Hemera), 195 (Hemera), 196 (Hemera), 198 (t) (Hemera), 198 (b), 199 (Hemera), 202 (Hemera), 203 (Hemera), 204, 205, 208, 212, 217; Panos Pictures p. 72 (l), (r) (Eric Miller), 73 (c), 76; Paperlink 2004, p. 127 'Fish Fingers' by Daphne David; Press Association pp. 19 (bl), 58 (t) (br), 136 (bc), 182 (cr, b); Reuters p. 136 (bl) (Russell Boyce); Rex Features pp. 18(br), 21 (bl) (Xu Xiagyang), 46 (br), 58 (cr) (Sipa), 85 (cl), 116 (B), 160 (B), 161 (F); Felix Rosenstiel's Widow & Son Ltd. p. 160(A); Stay Still p. 57 (Gary Moyes); p. 179 The Sun and The Times – The Times / The Sun / NI Syndication; Sunley Estates p. 105; Teresa Thurston p. 154 (A); p. 90 United Feature Syndicate, Inc., the Peanuts cartoon, from Penguin Connexions; Peter Viney pp. 16, 18 (bl), 19 (t, br), 36 - 37, 53, 77, 80 (tl), 86 (b), 91, 99 (bl), 158, 159, 161 (E), 182 (cl); Zefa Visual Media UK Ltd p. 99 (tl)